16
2/20/01
Dear Paula
+ Barry,

Thank you for coming!
Travel well.
Love,
Lea

Places I Remember

Tales, Truths, Delights
from 100 Countries

*

Lea Lane

Illustrations by
Greg Correll

To Rand and Cary

"Sons are the anchors of a mother's life."
—*Sophocles*

To my first-born, Molly, whose life was Art

England: Impressions

In the fall - clearing old roses, gold trees
dogs walking on the heath, soccer, a model
airplane, horses passing "rotten row" every few
minutes, benches placed every so often with
touching inscriptions - "In loving memory of ___
who loved this spot"

        preoccupation with gardens - what a *sweet*
tooth - TV & movies bombarded w commercials for
"sweets" - sold in miniature boxes & fancy assortment
chocolates come by you in cinema movies. Traditions
still strong - Sunday R. Beef & yorkshire -
dinner main meal midday
    Much lower standard of living despite
will percentage of rich. "do withouts"
conversations - very conservative - small
appetites concern w "value for money" seems
to be a common trait to be concerned about
waste, cost of things
        supermarkets small, poorly stocked &
unable to cope with large(?) purchases

CONTENTS

INTRODUCTION

A FEW YEARS AGO, WHEN I WAS INTERVIEWED by *The New York Times*, I said, "There's a difference between being a tourist and a traveler. Tourists do what makes them comfortable. Travelers seek discovery."

Like many of us, I started out as a tourist and developed into a traveler. From my first tentative trip abroad in the 1960s in a polyester polka-dot dress; through my most recent foray as a seasoned, award-winning writer (in breathable cotton), I've ventured with an open mind and heart to all seven continents of our beautiful world.

The result is *Places I Remember,* over fifty years of discoveries, writings and illustrated photos from one hundred countries.

I'd call this unique book a mix of travel memoir, travel almanac, personal journal and illustrated album. Country by country, A to Z, I offer behind-the-scenes glimpses of my life as a travel writer. You'll find a whole mix of travel-related readings: personal narrative, warm memories, short takes, wise suggestions, funny stories, offbeat tangents, thoughtful musings, useful tips, bits of history, surprising anecdotes, and whimsical reflections.

In other words, this is a book for anyone who travels, or yearns to, as well as for people who are curious about our world. I left out the ho-hum and emphasized the wow, oops! and the ha-ha.

And even more, Greg Correll's illustrations of my photos, and his original graphics, have created a truly beautiful book.

Organization

Places I Remember is divided alphabetically by destinations. Sometimes I include a connective like this (*See: …*), to refer to an associated event. But each entry stands on its own, and each is unique. You can follow the alphabetical organization, or skip around.

A destination can evoke one or many memories. And although there's loads of information, this is not a guidebook of where to go and what to see. It's about *memories* of where I've been and what I've perceived through seven decades of traveling.

Sometimes I note whom I traveled with, and sometimes not. Sometimes you can't tell when I'm traveling because it doesn't much matter, and sometimes I mention dates, and it matters a lot.

You'll read about places and experiences in the time-frame I visited them, some very different from now. The tone of the pieces can be serious or absurd. And I do promise you a few laughs, as well.

Pieces may focus on simple events, such as picking up an ancient shard on a beach in Cyprus. Tales may be about an unexpected mugging in

Chefchaouen (The Blue City), Morocco

Barcelona, or a mystery in a Finnish sauna, or dining in darkness in Switzerland.

You'll meet people I remember, including a woman who cleans toilets in rural Cuba; an English bellhop with an embarrassing tic; a sitcom celeb; a Panamanian mistress; and a former prisoner who knew Mandela in South Africa.

A few names and physical details have been changed for privacy reasons, as I share frank observations, and even some romances along the way. (I was a solo traveler for much of the time. The specific aspects of my personal life *outside* of my travels—home, family, friends and such—I'll save for another book.)

Keeping Track of My Travels

My travel history behind the memories? I ventured overseas for the first time on a two-month honeymoon throughout Europe in 1965. Living in London, Bangkok and Manila in the 1970s and 1980s, I took advantage of proximity to neighboring countries, and traveled whenever possible.

I've been writing for magazines since the 1970s, and authored books and guides for many years, including *Solo Traveler*, a book about traveling on your own. Currently I'm a contributor to forbes.com.

I also travel to lead writing workshops for corporations and government offices, and appear at travel shows and conferences. I continue researching, and I prioritize pleasure trips and family trips with the attitude of "do it now or never."

It adds up. Whether working or playing, or a combination of both, I've always found a way to travel.

Because the book is formatted by place rather than chronology, and alphabetical entries in *Places I Remember* shift in time, you might want to check out my bio in the back pages.

And to help give context and figure out where I was (and which husband I'm talking about), you can refer to this basic little quickie timeline:

- *1940s-1966:* Grow up in Miami Beach, go to college in Florida
- *1964-1988:* marry, raise two sons; start travel writing; live in London, suburban New York City; divorce
- *1984-1998:* solo travel; start writing-training business; travel writing, managing editor of magazine, communications director of interactive training company; live in suburban New York, Washington, D.C., Manila, Bangkok
- *1998-2001:* marry again; travel writing; live in suburban New York; widowed
- *2001-2010:* solo travel again; travel writing; live in Miami
- *2010-present:* marry for last time; travel writing; travel when possible

The Words

I used the official, alphabetical United Nations list of the world's countries (depending on which list you choose, there are about 200 sovereign countries).

I removed all countries from the list that I had not visited (did not include where I only landed at the airport). The word "country" can be confusing, but I tried to keep it as simple as possible. For example, I chose to count England, Wales, Scotland and Northern Ireland as the United Kingdom; Abu Dhabi and Dubai are considered part of the United Arab Emirates. And although you might be surprised that some islands are considered countries, I included those that are considered so by the U.N. I still had more than a hundred countries to work from. I placed them alphabetically, then scrolled through all, letting travel-related memories seep in—sometimes a phrase or a vision developing slowly like in a darkroom. I jotted down phrases, went back several times and jotted down more.

I then selected my final list of one hundred countries, and placed them in alphabetical order.

After free-writing, I took my time and edited the entries.

The Illustrations

Places I Remember refers not only to my writing but also to my photos.

I chose from thousands of my photos to find the ones that matched the tone or experiences of the writing.

Greg Correll, CCO of small packages, inc. and a former illustrator for *The New Yorker*, interpreted, illustrated and formatted the selected photos. He also created original graphics and designed the cover and page format. He explains the fascinating process he created in the back pages of the book.

That's about it. An original book, written from my heart as well as my experiences. I really appreciate your company on this journey around the world, and hope that many of the *Places I Remember* will become unforgettable to you as well.

~ *Lea Lane*
@lealane

ANDORRA

Mugging, Gig, Reality

The tiny country of Andorra is just north of Barcelona, known for fanciful Gaudi architecture—and also for muggings. On my first day in the Spanish city, before I even got to the hotel, at noon on the street in front of the Picasso Museum, a young man yanked the purse off my shoulder, knocking me to the ground.

Normally I would have let it go, a safe response I had learned on the streets of New York City, but the purse was filled with my passport, prescription glasses, pills, keys and money. And—good jewelry. I know, I *know*, but I was traveling for the first time with an elegant man whom I was seriously dating, and I wanted to make a good impression.

I gripped the purse strap, dragged along the sidewalk by a thief far younger and stronger. My companion managed to wrestle the man to the ground and hold him down, but before we could rescue it, the purse was thrown to an accomplice on a Vespa, and I watched it disappear loudly into the traffic.

The police came and took the guy away in cuffs and I followed them to the station to report the theft and identify him in a lineup. When they questioned him, I heard his screams in the next room. Police brutality? A tape sounding like they were doing something to make me feel better? I was told he was part of a Palestinian ring.

Late in the day we waited for hours in the American consulate, along with dozens of other dazed tourists without passports, who had also been mugged. At least I had a copy of my passport in my luggage. We felt like dopes, and had missed a day of our vacation because we were careless.

I wanted to get far away from Barcelona, so the next day my companion kindly drove me up to Andorra, in the Pyrenees, between Spain and France. Mountains framed fields of wildflowers, and we followed a winding country road without quite knowing where it would lead.

We stopped at an especially dramatic viewpoint in a sloping orchard, and spread our coats on the grass beneath budding boughs and blue sky. My friend had brought a bottle of Spanish wine, local cheese, ham and grapes. We fed each other and canoodled as if we were in a slow-motion ad for Viagra.

The memory of the mugging was mitigated by that idyllic picnic in Andorra. In both cases, the man had made a wonderful impression on me, and not long after I moved to Washington, D.C., to live with and work for him, based quite a bit on those moments of heroism and romanticism.

At the time I was managing editor of a publication called "Travel Smart," and the irony of my stupidity in carrying around all those goods on the street was not lost on my readers. The Travel Channel even heard of my misfortune, and featured me on its travel news show, in a segment called "Smart Traveler Travels Dumb." That gig led to a weekly appearance about travel tips for about a year.

The relationship with the man lasted on and off for a few years, often tough and sad, and never as fine as it was at that perfect picnic in Andorra. I realized too late that—especially when you are far away, in lovely surroundings—romantic notions and dramatic gestures can produce long-term consequences sometimes even more unfortunate, and certainly more lasting, than a mugging.

ANGUILLA

Magic Carpet Ride

On my one visit to Anguilla I remember mounds of pink langoustines and heaps of crayfish. Similar to San Sebastian in Spain, another foodie haven, Anguilla diners often converse about what they're going to eat, talk about what they're eating, and then ponder the delights of the finished meal.

And in-between there's always that long, beautiful beach to relax upon before starting the delicious process again.

I was invited to Anguilla on a press trip, one of hundreds I've been lucky enough to experience since my first one. Back then I was often the youngest of a dozen writers and photographers.

The golden age for these kinds of familiarization trips dates from about the 1970s to 2001, when ever-larger jets sped us worldwide in space-available first-class seats, budgets were generous, and countries with burgeoning tourism boards welcomed us. Security concerns, crowded overhead bins and frequent-flyer complications were not as awful as they are today.

This was a time before blogging and forums made travel critics of us all. Writers were needed to describe the still exotic international scene, so select pros were hosted by governments, or by public relations agencies representing destinations, lodgings, ships, airlines, resorts, theme parks and restaurants.

Press trips, either independent or in a group, are a speed-dating version of travel, with swag. Usually on assignment from an established outlet, we're invited to review a place for a few days or a few weeks, then write and/or take photos about what we've experienced.

Most of us get along in groups, but there are often whiners who insist on upgrading rooms in every lodging and divas who refuse to eat what's offered. Stories abound about writers who came to blows over sitting in the front seat of the van, or a late arrival causing a group to miss a cruise. The most legendary squabble was when a well-known writer I know threw another's clothes into the Nile after a heated discussion about writing for the same publication.

But there are advantages. On one press trip in the 1980s I was at Kennedy Airport in New York waiting to fly to Italy, when the same carrier's plane crashed somewhere in Europe. The airline abruptly cancelled our flight because of that tragedy, but within a few minutes the public relations person handling our group got us on another flight with another carrier—and in the front of the plane.

Freelance travel writers can do very well if they have a steady gig or if they're married to a hedge funder or receive a monthly inheritance from Uncle Percy. But many of us get by with part-time jobs—writing, teaching, dog-sitting—living frugally when not on a lavish trip.

For twenty years in-between marriages, managing on one income, I augmented travel writing with varied sources of income. For about fifteen years I ran a small writing company for corporations and the government, led workshops, wrote annual reports, wrote a book on writing, that kind of thing. I also freelanced and edited copy. (I covered "O" and "P" for the Oxford Children's Encyclopedia, and know more about otters and Peter Rabbit than just about anybody.)

I rented out parts of my house, as needed, way before there was an Airbnb, and even appeared on Jeopardy! to win some money (not enough). A traveling gal's gotta do what a gal's gotta do.

Bouncing from a turret suite in a castle on the Rhine back to a mortgaged house and a month of utility bills fosters confusion and lots of dubious swag: mugs, caps, tees, backpacks and doodads, product names emblazoned somewhere. (Not to mention a drawerful of mini-toiletries swiped from posh bathrooms. I consider it "advertising.")

But seeing the world and helping others know about it makes the whole thing worth it. Rich in experience if often low in cash, my loyalty has always been to the reader.

Mutual back-scratching can sustain subject and writer for years, but the unwritten contract is to produce, and write fairly. Bloggers and vloggers and influencers come and go, but an observant, engaging writer with a good eye and an honest voice has staying power.

I realize with gratitude that although my mostly freelance life has been frenetic, for over fifty years I've managed to ride a magic carpet to much of the world, including the powdery sands of Anguilla. And what a thrilling ride it remains.

ARGENTINA

Solo's Cool, Penguins Rule

Walking gives you the world, close-up. Pilgrimages along the Camino de Santiago in northern Spain may entice the hardy to become *peregrinos*, donning that prized scallop-shell logo and walking the walk. But most of us can make do with strolling through neighborhoods, among the sounds, smells and sights of real life.

Buenos Aires is a walkers' city, filled with European architecture, tea shops, tango bars and leafy barrios. The Palermo area is trendy. San Telmo, "authentic." Barrio Norte is known for reasonable prices, central Recoleta for confectionary shops, and the famous cemetery where Eva Peron is buried, filled with crypts that ironically look quite livable in this era of tiny houses.

BA supposedly has more psychiatrists per capita than anywhere, but I assume the city has a record number of dogs, as well. I noticed many dog walkers, with maybe a half-dozen canines pulling each of them along.

Tango is, of course, central to the culture. At Café Tortoni there's dancing in the main room, but I ordered wine and enjoyed the show in the private theater. After, you can find a local *boliche* to dance and drink some more. (In most Spanish-speaking countries, a *boliche* is a cup-and-ball toy; in some, it's a bowling alley; in Argentina and Uruguay, it's a disco, club or bar. Can you imagine the mistakes that have been made by clueless tourists saying that word?)

My favorite barrio, La Boca, was originally a fishing village on the Riachuelo river. Italian settlers arrived in the late nineteenth century, and the area is still called "Piccola Italia." In 1882, after a general strike, La Boca seceded from Argentina and rebels raised the Genoese flag, which of course was immediately brought down by the president.

Dazzling colors began to appear on buildings when fishermen used leftover paint from their boats. Walking here is exhilarating, and artists are everywhere, painting the scene.

Tango dancers entwine in the streets, and one steamy Sunday afternoon in La Boca, a dancer cajoled me to tango with him as I wandered by. Although he had the moves, I was typically klutzy. But we had fun, and so did the onlookers. I like to walk alone for reasons like that.

When I was reviewing international hotels for publications, I would run in and out of hotels, checking carpets and water pressure, and after seeing maybe fifteen sites a day I would order room service and collapse into bed.

But on one trip to Argentina I felt like a star, dining on slabs of grass-fed beef at midnight with creative new friends who really had no idea who I was, but didn't seem to care. That's because I had an introduction from a world-famous South American starchitect (initials R.V.), whom I had happened to sit beside at a dinner party in New York.

He gave me phone numbers of his special friends in BA, and when I arrived there I was feted by the owner of the best hotel, socialites and artsy types who toured me around, assuming that I was the architect's gal pal.

I smiled, listened, dodged specifics and felt like the con guy who passed himself off as Sidney Poitier's son and is sheltered by strangers in *Six Degrees of Separation*.

Traveling with the boost of local connections can certainly enhance a trip, and although I never saw the architect again, I still smile every time I read about an iconic new building he is creating.

Ten years later, on the way to Antarctica, our cruise ship stopped in the Falkland Islands, a remote archipelago that's a British Territory, but claimed by Argentina as The Malvinas. Red roofs and school-bus yellow walls offer pops of color, but the landscape is mostly treeless moors, flocks of sheep, isolated farms and old lighthouses. Dozens of battered hulks in the harbor remain a legacy of lost battles with fierce South Atlantic storms.

The few thousand Falkland Islanders protect their privacy. In fact, the rumor was that locals had left land mines from the 1982 war with the United Kingdom on the sandy beach to discourage tourists. Penguins were too light to set them off, but supposedly when a cow exploded a mine, the capital lost electric power.

I did find one unexpected nod to tourism: a calendar of sheep shearers in the buff. (I liked Mr. September, but November wasn't chopped liver.) The calendar was easy to pack, so I bought a few for my single friends.

I wanted to see a colony of chin-strap penguins, so along rutted roads on a bone-crunching ride over peaty hills, I ended up at the edge of the Atlantic, staring at a dozen or so young penguins waiting for their moms to come back with dinner. I fancied them even more than Mr. September, and they and the sheep-shearer calendar men remain my most endearing memories of the otherwise drab Falklands.

Back from Antarctica, on our way to Buenos Aires, after passing through the normally rough waters of Cape Horn on calm seas, I visited Ushuaia, Argentina, where the Andes rise above "the world's southernmost city." It may be the windiest city as well, and to stay upright I grabbed onto

ropes that lined many of the paths. (On an earlier trip in Patagonia, the little plane bounced so much on a windy landing that my head was in a bag most of the time.)

Up the coast of Patagonia and a two-hour drive from the ship, I returned to Punta Tombo, a protected peninsula with the world's largest concentration of Magellanic penguins. Ten years before I had been charmed by these little creatures who hang at the beach, swim in the clear water and Charlie Chaplin-walk to their burrows. One had followed me to the van, and I wanted to stow him in my backpack.

And, sadly, whether because of the season or the warming planet, there were far fewer on this trip.

✳

The Antarctic cruise ended where it began, in Buenos Aires. I drove one day to a country *estancia* to enjoy beef again and dance with gauchos and tourists, and joined a group at a tango show that night.

I had covered over 5,000 nautical miles to and from BA, during which the ship probably gained a collective ton, and I happily contributed at least five pounds. Dozens of whales, hundreds of icebergs and thousands of penguins later I was humbled and mind-boggled.

Besides the natural wonders of South America and Antarctica, onboard I had been entertained by a whole world of talent: a Paraguayan harpist, Israeli pianist, Australian singer, British violinist, Argentine flutist and Chilean dancers. Along the way the moon fully eclipsed, and—a total surprise—I even fooled around with a crew member from Goa (fill in details as you wish; that's all you're getting).

I took this solo journey in 2008 to celebrate my recovery from lung cancer, and as I write this, many years later, I'm still celebrating life, and remembering Argentina with special fondness.

ARUBA

Pussy-Whipped and a Chihuahua

I got around in Aruba. I visited a historic lighthouse, viewed street art in San Nicolas and walked around the ruins of a nineteenth-century gold mill. Sun and fun places often offer more than beaches, and I like being active rather than lounging all day. At night I especially enjoy the pleasure of a brisk shower and then sinking into a big, comfortable, all-white bed in an air-conditioned room.

✳

Which got me thinking about beds, and of a woman I met on a cruise on the Black Sea who was especially sensitive about them, like the princess in the story who could feel a pea under her mattress. Maybe the woman was concerned about her back, or bedbugs, because she traveled with her own queen-sized air mattress, folded into a huge piece of luggage, which her husband lugged around the world.

She also carried around (or rather, *he* did) her own sheets, pillows and duvet. I guess wherever they go to sleep he takes deep breaths and blows up the mattress and places it on the bed already there, or on the floor, and then probably makes the bed for her and turns down the sheets.

I would never ask my husband to do that, and besides, as he watched the downtrodden man lugging the mattress, he told me in no uncertain terms that he never would.

✳

When I was visiting a donkey sanctuary on the far side of Aruba, I saw a week-old donkey who couldn't get on its feet, and whose mother seemed uninterested in him. Chickens were pecking around in the dust, and a turquoise lizard scurried by.

A silver-haired man in a black T-shirt, carrying a large white rat, came closer. I saw that the bundle he was carrying wasn't a rodent, but a Chihuahua. It burrowed against his chest, in the crook of his arm.

Closer still, I saw that the dog was blind. No, more than that. Her eyes were missing, scooped out of her sockets like melon balls.

I asked the man about the tiny dog. He said that he named her Lola and that she was rescued from Hurricane Katrina. He already had three Labs in his home north of Tampa, but his heart went out to this blinded little canine. His other dogs protected her, too.

When I was about ten my family drove down to Marathon in the Florida Keys, and on the way back to Miami, a stray dog that we had fed at an outdoor café followed our car onto the highway, running as fast as his heart would allow. We were so touched that even though we already had a rather spoiled cocker spaniel named Rusty, we adopted the highway dog, and named him Lucky—although he was pretty much ignored by Rusty for the rest of his life.

The man in Aruba didn't know the story of how his Chihuahua Lola lost her eyes. He didn't want to think about it. She must have been through hell, but she seemed happy now. She didn't tremble. In fact, she seemed serene. The man stroked her body, and talked softly to her.

He said that Lola compensated for blindness mainly by smell; she could even tell from across the house when his wife was cutting a piece of cake. And Lola loved cake.

The man let Lola down gently onto a porch area in the sanctuary, where you can buy drinks and snacks. She felt her way along, sniffing, but stayed near the man's soft voice.

My first dog was a Chihuahua named Mijaca. She yapped and trembled and ran in circles and hardly stayed still, and wasn't particularly likeable. When I was six, she fell over at my feet and we buried her in a shoebox under a mango tree in the backyard of the bungalow where we lived in Miami Beach.

This dog seemed different. I stroked her, and she didn't seem afraid. The man said that Lola sleeps next to him and she curls in just the right place so he doesn't roll over her. She was old, so he brings her everywhere, or doesn't go. People allow this because they consider him a "seeing-eye man," and because Lola was so little and had suffered so. Watching the man and the dog made me both sad and happy.

The man's wife, who was sipping sparkling water on the porch, looked past me, and I couldn't tell how she felt: perhaps a bit jealous of the man's devotion to Lola, perhaps not.

Even many years later—with the dog and maybe even the man and his wife gone—I still can picture the devotion of the seeing-eye man in his black tee, cradling his white Chihuahua with gouged-out eyes in the donkey sanctuary in Aruba.

AUSTRALIA

Solo In Oz, Just Plain Odd

In 2008, on assignment for a magazine, I traveled alone to this country almost as big as the States. I didn't get to the Great Barrier Reef or Alice Springs, and I skipped tropical Humpty Doo, in the Northern Territory, although I love to say its name. I did check out black opals and eat kangaroo steak (once). Here are my impressions.

Melbourne, the green, livable city, has public art, parks and arcades, and the best culinary scene in Australia. But there's a spunky side, too. St. Kilda, a nearby beachside suburb, offers frenetic nightlife and a café atmosphere, and Acland Street is the place for tea and cakes, lattes and wine, and probably pickups. Melbourne offers terrific whale spotting from a viewing platform on the Great Ocean Road. More than sixty percent of the world's whale population—humpback whales, southern right whales, blue whales and orcas—arrive in Port Phillip Bay in May from the feeding grounds of Antarctica, birthing and raising calves in Australia's warmer waters before returning to Antarctica in October.

The Yarra Valley outside Melbourne reminded me of the Napa region in northern California, but with kangaroos grazing by the vineyards. Healesville Sanctuary teems with more than two hundred native species, including koalas on branches, howling dingoes, platypuses—the creatures that look like they were created by committee—and, of course, kangaroos that hopped around me like giant rabbits with built-in baskets. And I saw something I unfortunately will never forget: Wombats depositing square poos.

Sydney seems more outgoing than Melbourne (L.A. vs. San Francisco vibe). The iconic opera house, bridge and busy harbor lined with outdoor markets took up most of my time. And the neighborhood where I dined happily on shrimp and local beer has a name I still use when I'm happy: *Woolloomooloo!*

I found more quaint names on a ninety-minute drive from Sydney to the Blue Mountains, stopping in Penrith, Leura and Katoomba. I bought a boomerang, maybe to remind me to return someday, and a classy gift for the guy who has everything: a pouch made from kangaroo scrotum.

In the mountains I kept busy riding a cable car above the Three Sisters peaks; bushwalking among waterfalls and canyons; and looking for lyrebirds, cockatoos and kookaburras in a eucalyptus-forested valley. I did not spot any of them, but I liked trying.

And to end my Australian sojourn I dined and overnighted at a nineteenth-century lodging on a clifftop. All quite happily alone.

I collect superlatives, odd facts and fun names as I travel, even though they're not altogether provable. And this land down under offers a bunch:

- Australia is the world's sixth-largest country; the Kimberley region in Western Australia alone is three times the size of England. The North West territory has the spectacular (and fabulously named) Bungle Bungle Range in World Heritage-listed Purnululu National Park.

- Also in the area, the world's only *horizontal* waterfalls, "one of the greatest wonders of the natural world," according to naturalist David Attenborough. The very high tide shifts through a gap in the ridges of the McLarty Range, building up on one side of the narrow cliff passage and pushing through to create the appearance of a waterfall. You can ride through them on a boat or view them from a seaplane.

- At Australia's Coral Coast you can swim with the world's largest fish, the whale shark, and explore Ningaloo Reef—the world's largest fringing reef. And Australia's Golden Outback, the Gold Rush country of the 1890s, offers the largest collection of wildflowers on earth.

- Australia's largest property is the same size as Belgium. Fraser Island is the world's largest sand island, and you can drive a golf cart more than 850 miles on the world's longest golf course. (Assuming you would not walk!)

- Australia is home to 21 of the world's 25 most venomous snakes.

- Uluru, also known as Ayers Rock, in the Australian Outback, is the largest monolith in the world, taller than the Eiffel Tower.

- The Great Barrier Reef is the planet's largest living structure, the size of seventy million football fields. The reef even has its own post office box. It is also dying. (*See: Tanzania*)

- It would take around thirty years to visit one new Aussie beach every day—there are about eleven thousand.

- Aussies drink about 680 bottles of beer a year per adult. When they crave a bottle they sometimes say, "I'm dry as a dead dingo's donga."

- Animal trivia? A million camels roam wild in Australia's deserts—the largest number of purebred camels in the world. Australia actually exports them to the Middle East.

- Australians are the only people in the world who actually eat their national emblem, choosing from among some sixty types of kangaroos. The meat is considered a leaner, healthier alternative to beef.

- Wordplay: Australia's capital city, Canberra, means "woman's cleavage" in Aborigine, so named because the city is cradled between two mountains. (Think Wyoming's Grand Tetons.)

- And perhaps my favorite odd fact, which makes sense when you think about it: The first police force in Australia was made up of the most well-behaved convicts.

AUSTRIA

Surprising Little Castle, and The Lost Eyeball

In 1965, when I was twenty-two years old and living a somewhat charmed life as a graduate student married to another grad student with a trust fund, we had booked special hotels throughout a two-month European honeymoon. I had never been overseas, and what a grand way to begin. I remember poring through brochures for months ahead of the trip, looking at pictures of old lodges and timbered buildings, amazed at even the foreign smell of the paper.

In Austria we stayed in a small castle, Schloss Fuschl, nestled on a peninsula in the woods outside of Salzburg. I remember rowing on the Fuschlsee, a woodland lake, and marveling at the setting.

The building dates from 1450, when the prince-archbishops of Salzburg first used it as a hunting lodge. In 1816 it passed to the Austrian state and fell into disrepair, but was revived as a hotel in the 1950s, becoming a glamorous venue. When we arrived, there were dreamy amenities, from Old Master paintings to a bowling alley.

And all that history. I was thrilled—a Miami girl staying in a castle. I imagined the earlier days of banquets laden with schnitzels and sparkling wines, lawn games and moonlight romps in those woods.

I didn't realize until recently that in the 1930s the lodging was owned by Gustav Edler von Remiz, who was imprisoned by the Nazis in Dachau, where he died. His property was confiscated, and the building became the summer residence of Joachim von Ribbentrop, a Nazi foreign minister, who used it for diplomatic receptions for Germany's allies.

So that idyllic lake and that bowling alley—and maybe even the mattress where I had laid my fantasy-besotted head—had been crawling with Nazis just twenty years before.

Not. Dreamy.

The strangest memory of Austria is a trip I *didn't* take there, about ten years after the schloss honeymoon.

We (hubby, two sons, nanny and I) were living in the London area in a Hampstead Garden Suburb house (*See: Holy See*) on a dead-end lane called Wild Hatch, just off Hampstead Heath. It was next to the Golders Green Crematorium, which was quiet, like a cemetery, but with a lovely, well-fertilized garden and a tasteful smokestack (of course). Our neighbors included the president of British Airways, who used to mow his front lawn—in a suit. Once I backed our car out of the driveway and ran over his rose bushes.

"So sorry those bushes were in your way," he said. That kind of Brit, and that kind of neighborhood.

Our nanny was a big girl in her early twenties, from near the White Cliffs of Dover in southwest England. She swooned over Elvis Presley—literally. When I gifted her with a poster of the singer, she promptly fell to the floor.

Hubby and I had planned a skiing getaway to the Austrian Alps and had set up all kinds of activities while nanny would be taking care of the boys. She was an integral part of the trip.

The morning before we were to leave, nanny realized that she had left her passport at her home with her mother. This was in the days when you needed passports to go from country to country in Europe.

Our trip was in jeopardy.

"We can pick the passport up at your home by messenger," I said.

Nanny called her mother, and came back to us, distraught.

"Me mum can't find her eyeball."

"What?"

"She doesn't know where the passport is and her eyeball fell out and rolled somewhere and she has to find it."

I had no idea what she was talking about, but it didn't sound good.

Her mother eventually found her prosthetic eyeball, and the passport, but too late for us. We didn't get to Austria, and we didn't tell anyone why.

BAHAMAS

Rueful Renewal

My very first press trip was to the Bahamas at a retreat with a touchy-feely vibe of the 1970s. I was a contributor to an upscale regional magazine and living in the New York suburbs, in my thirties, married with two small sons.

About twenty years later, now divorced, I was invited on a "Love Boat" cruise, a Valentine press excursion to the Bahamas, where just about everyone on-board was renewing marriage vows. My memories are a time-capsule of people and customs before the new millennium.

Our small group of journalists and celebs included Gavin McCloud, who since leaving the show appeared on Princess cruise ships in the Captain Stubing persona from *The Love Boat*. He had grown up in Westchester County, New York, near where I was then living. Gavin was friendly and open and seemed to love cruising the world, meeting and greeting people who called him "Captain" and rushed up to hug him.

I interviewed him for the local Westchester papers and he told many tales of his life, including when he played Murray on *The Mary Tyler Moore Show*. Among his remembrances was that Ted Knight, the actor who played Ted Baxter, was especially nice, and that Mary Tyler Moore, despite her fame and fortune, was often depressed.

Another in the invited group was Rue McClanahan, who had played Blanche, the flirty southern gal on *The Golden Girls*. In real life she was sweet and soft-spoken, and at the time was between marriages. She confided that she was flattered when a man on-board had given her a teddy bear. I had to remind her that if he was on this cruise he was not only married, but getting *remarried*.

Rue reminded me of Blanche in several ways: lots of giggles, ultra-feminine, full of life. She talked of working with Bea Arthur, both on *The Golden Girls* and on *Maude*, where Rue portrayed Vivian, Maude's best friend. She and Betty White, who socialized offset, were not friends with Bea, who I gather was demanding and eccentric. And she laughed that the actress who played

Sophia, Estelle Getty, was younger than Bea, who played her daughter.

We guests of the ship hung out together for the long weekend, drinking margaritas and watching Insta-worthy Caribbean sunsets slowly turn into star-filled nights. But my strongest remembrance is standing on an upper deck watching hundreds of people dressed in red, renewing vows along with "Captain Stubing" and a minister. We commented on the couples standing below us, and joked that some of them didn't look so happy.

Rue seemed especially interested in finding love again, and wistful about all the remarriages we were witnessing. After that cruise I followed her later career as she appeared on Broadway and in supporting roles on television. She never stopped working, despite illnesses and losses. And years after the cruise I read that she had found love again before she died.

I found love too, and would marry again—twice. I do wonder how many of those remarried folks on the cruise stayed together. Perhaps not the guy with the teddy bear.

BELGIUM

Timing and Last Call

In Belgium in the mid-1960s, churches and museums were filled with mystical art and few tourists. I savored new tastes: salty mussels in white wine; thin, crisp frites dipped in mayonnaise; deep, dark chocolate; and the revelation of frothy fruit beers in an era when Bud and Pabst were the norm.

In fairy-tale Bruges, swans floated by as I wandered empty paths along narrow canals. Antwerp showed off the most beautiful train station I had ever seen, and the Grand Place in Brussels, the most magnificent town center in Europe. (And around a corner, the famed statue of the little boy that pees. Cheesy, yes. But cute.) I lingered at all of these places, and felt a part of the scene.

※

I returned to Belgium about forty years after that first visit, but the ancient towns dotting the countryside—Bruges, Ghent, Mechelen—were now well-known to travelers, so canals were filled with crowded tourist boats and visitors flocked like ducklings behind sign-holding guides. Shops were filled with touristy trinkets. You couldn't get a seat in a good restaurant, and lines snaked behind the food trucks selling paper cones of frites and mayo.

We got up as early as possible to beat the tourists, but the country didn't seem the same as the first time around. The magic was missing.

But then my guidebook publisher emailed me that they were updating their Belgium book, and could I possibly get to Belgium to cover the chapters on Bruges and Ghent?

I was right there already! I rushed into writer mode, now on a sudden mission, and forgot disappointments about the crowds. I discovered more deeply the haunting remains of two world wars that shredded the countryside, astounding Art Nouveau buildings and a modern dance troupe moving sharply in blue light. I rediscovered Flemish artists from Bruegel to James Elson, and Flemish artwork of religion and myth filling churches and museums. I found places and appreciated things beyond the ordinary, looking deeper and harder.

You don't need to write a guidebook to focus when you travel. Find the unexpected. Get up early and stay late. Look beyond the crowds. Make it work.

※

In October 1914, Allied and German forces began the first of what would be three battles in Flanders, on the north coast of Belgium, during the First World War. The area between the positions established by both sides—from Ypres on the British side to Menin and Roulers on the German side—became known as the Ypres Salient, a region of many of the war's most brutal struggles.

The Second Battle of Ypres was the first mass use by Germany of poison gas on the Western Front, and the casualties suffered at Ypres made the city a center for post-war remembrance for all sides—British, Commonwealth, German and Belgian.

Ypres was rebuilt to resemble its pre-war state, and its war museum in the rebuilt medieval Cloth Hall is exceptional. But what I most wanted to experience was the centerpiece of British and Commonwealth commemoration, at the Menin Gate. Here are listed the names of 54,896 soldiers who have no known grave. Each evening a bagpiper and buglers sound "The Last Post" and lead attendees in a minute of silence for the fallen.

Of course, it was a moving experience. But what I didn't expect was to be moved as well by Kathe Kollwitz's famous 1931 sculpture, "The Grieving Parents," on the German front, inspired by the loss of her youngest son at First Ypres. Visiting these hallowed battlefields and cemeteries, some covered in poppies the color of blood, you become keenly aware of the loss of a generation of young men on both sides, who died in a senseless war that sadly did not end all wars.

BELIZE

Parade of Lobsters, a Shaman, and Erma Bombeck

Ah, yes. Fresh breezes, shuffling barefoot along the sand streets of Amber Gris Key, the delight of speaking English in Central America. A few of the many charms of Belize.

I remember night-snorkeling near the Caribbean's Blue Hole, watching lobsters parade through the water single-file in the spotlights, claws waving above their heads as if they were beauty queens in a pageant. I realized then that crustaceans aren't just delicious. They can be *celebratory*.

I traveled to Belize in the early 1990s with a press group, staying first by the beach and then inland at a thatched, luxe jungle lodge owned by film director Francis Ford Coppola, where the focus was on restoring local herbs.

We spent an afternoon guided by a grizzled shaman, walking along an even more ancient trail. He pointed out medicinal plants used for centuries that may well die out if younger people fail to learn about, protect and nurture their healing properties.

Many indispensable medicines can be traced back to the earth's wild bark, leaves, flowers, berries, herbs or roots, including the cancer drug taxol, the malaria drug artemisinin, and the opiate morphine. Even aspirin was first made from willow tree bark, and Hippocrates supposedly prescribed it for pain, either chewing it or in tea.

It's easy to dismiss an old shaman. But I hope scientists have checked out that trail.

That evening in a candlelit hut in the jungle I was massaged with fragrant oils produced from the greenery and herbs we had seen earlier in the day.

One of the perks of traveling the world for over fifty years has been experiencing spa treatments based on local products. My body has been covered with, among other things, mushrooms, olive oil, seaweed, honey, dirt, hot rocks, crystals, jasmine, chocolate, gold leaf, sea water, oatmeal, mud, maple syrup, acorns, sea salt and pink salt, pineapple and whale sperm. And that's only a partial list.

I've been rubbed, massaged, abraded, twisted, pummeled, saunaed (*See: Finland*), loofahed, hosed, pinched, soaked, creamed, bathed, steamed,

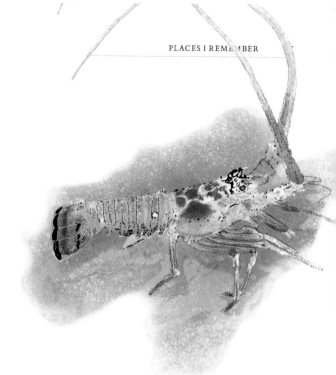

plucked, vibrated, waxed, doused, tweezed, lasered, peeled, buffed, bronzed, brined, tanned and kneaded.

In Mexico I luxuriated in a midnight "moon massage" by the Caribbean. In a wellness clinic in Chile the cubicle smelled of antiseptic as I was stretched like taffy. In Japan, a woman or man (never figured out which and didn't much care) stepped all over my back. In Baden Baden, Germany, I soaked (soaked?) in thermal springs.

And don't think I'm not patriotic. At the Homestead in Virginia I was hosed as if I were a four-alarm fire, and then I dog-paddled in a paper bathing suit in the same enclosed pool where Jefferson once swam—I hope not in a paper Speedo. And in Berkeley Springs, West Virginia, where Washington himself presumably soaked between battles, presiding over an infant country and tooth-sanding, I stepped into a steam box that looked like a freezer with only my head sticking out, and emerged looking like a tomato with a white stem.

You get the point.

✳

One of the press trip participants on the Belize trip was Erma Bombeck, a brilliant humor writer, who had written a travel book. I was a huge fan, and was surprised that she was quiet, even shy.

Erma did share lots of travel wisdom from her writings. Some of my favorites: "Did you ever notice that the first piece of luggage off the carousel never belongs to anyone." And, "When you look like your passport photo, it's time to go home." And, "Once you see drivers in Indonesia, you see why religion plays such a part in their lives."

And then there was, "I have paid as much as $300 a night to throw up into a sink shaped like a seashell." That one hits home now. Erma had some health problems and unfortunately, died not that long after the trip from complications of a kidney transplant. And despite the herbal cures along his path, even the shaman is now gone unless, because of his natural medicine, he lived to 110.

I do wonder if his traditions have been passed on or have been forgotten, and if the herbal trail remains or is covered over by the jungle. Or maybe the area has been churned into an all-inclusive resort or a condo complex with a spa and nicely packaged wellness products—oblivious of ancient treatments forever lost in the earth beneath.

BERMUDA

Pretty in Pink, and Every Man for Himself

Not far off the coast of North Carolina, this British Island territory is too cool to be tropical and too uncool to be a party destination. Think golf, tennis, boating, croquet—*veddy* English, in keeping with its history.

Although there's a fortress, Bermuda calls to mind colors rather than wars. Polite people with an overlay of English manners and accents wear green plaid shorts. Pink hotels with manicured lawns are hedged with ruby-red hibiscus and purple bougainvillea, and pastel houses are punctuated by white terraced roofs built to collect rainwater in underground tanks. The pretty palette dates back to the seventeenth century.

But beyond the cerulean blue ocean, it's not all rainbows. There's the Bermuda Triangle, also known as the Devil's Triangle or Hurricane Alley. Aircraft and ships are said to have disappeared into its loosely defined region. In fact, it's an illusion, no more dangerous than a Bermuda onion.

I've been to the island a half-dozen times, and lazed on Elbow Beach and Horseshoe Bay, with their blush-tinted sand and breezy scent of surrounding cedar. I've shopped in Hamilton for jewelry on Front Street and visited the lighthouse and the huge Royal Navy Dockyard.

The peaceful Bermuda landscape reminds me of the southwest coast of England, from where the island nation originated. There are lots of great old houses and churches to explore. Relaxing, yes? But I've met more than a few people who suffered broken limbs from renting and riding motorcycles on the narrow roads. I guess, like in New Zealand, there's an urge to do something a bit risky within all this pleasurable, peaceful comfort. That's the way of life.

※

Bermuda is a frequent stop on ships crossing the Atlantic from Europe. On these longer cruises I especially enjoy talking with international crew members, and often request dining with the entertainers. (*See: Argentina.*) I've remained social-media friends with several of them in the last few years, including English magician-comedian Danny Buckler, and a charming young Irish-Italian-American singing duo, Joe and Liv. And I've hung out with entertainers Linda Lavin and Bil-ly Stritch and political mavens Charlie Cook and James Carville. (*See: Bahamas.*)

When you're all floating in a boat, especially in rough waters, you bond a bit with fellow passengers of all types. However, with politics becoming tribal, dining with fellow shipmates has become more complicated than when I used to request to the maître d' as I entered the dining room, "Please seat me with someone interesting." Now, it's more like, "Please seat me with someone I won't wind up throwing my rolls at."

Anyway, on an Atlantic crossing from Barcelona, headed for a stop in Bermuda, my husband Bill and I were having dinner in the ship's main dining room, seated with a single woman and the singer who had entertained us the evening before—an old pro with a Sinatra vibe, who had cruised hundreds of times.

Our table of four was maintaining a pleasant shipboard conversation, mostly sans politics, religion or aches and pains, when suddenly the ship started to tilt. I forgot if it was leaning toward starboard or port, but we knew we were no longer moving through the water the way we had been before. This was confirmed as drawers opened and silverware fell out at serving stations, and dishes and glasses on the table clattered to the floor.

I got especially nervous when the captain, who had been dining at a nearby table, ran out of the room, his napkin still under his chin.

What had happened? There were no icebergs in the vicinity. The waters were calm. But after about a minute of tipping further, we realized the ship was not righting itself, and I thought of actress Shelley Winters in *The Poseidon Adventure,* floating around in an upside-down vessel.

I asked the old-pro singer sitting next to me, "This isn't that unusual, right?"

And he answered, "No, tipping over in the middle of the ocean is *highly* unusual."

At which time I wanted to grab my husband's hand, but the woman on his other side had already gotten there. Her red nails dug into Bill's arm and her head was on his shoulder, eyes gazing at him in the way mine should have been.

"Great," I thought. "Not only am I going down with the ship, I'm doing it on my own!"

We remained at an angle for quite a while in the middle of the North Atlantic. Eventually, now that the captain was out of the dining room and on the bridge, he accomplished some kind of magical maneuver and managed to get us back on course to Bermuda.

Explanations varied, but the problem seemed to have had something to do with a gust of wind, a top-heavy ship and a quick turn while the captain was otherwise engaged with the guests.

But back to our table. Even though it wasn't about her politics, I did want to throw a *buttered* roll at the lady next to my husband.

BOSNIA AND HERZEGOVINA

Dark Hope

Princess Grace of Monaco had just died in France that fall day in 1982 when I arrived in Sarajevo. And then an attendant in a public toilet at the airport swiped me on the shins with a filthy broom when I had no money to tip her. A terrible beginning.

I placed my feet on indented footsteps set in the sidewalk where the assassin shot Archduke Franz Ferdinand in 1914—an event that sparked World War I. Little did I realize that less than ten years after I stood there, another awful war would explode around that very spot.

With planning underway for the 1984 Olympics, the mood in Bosnia was soaring. The region was in a still-intact Soviet Yugoslavia of many cultures, and there seemed no awareness of the upcoming violent conflict that would be considered the worst in Europe since World War II.

Our press group toured Olympic sites, and in the soccer stadium where the opening ceremony would take place and medals would be awarded two years later, photos show me smiling in a striped shirt. (When we look back on travel photos, we so often see that we looked better than we thought—and of course, younger, and blankly unaware of the future.)

I could not know on that sunny day in the stadium that from 1992 to 1996, the venue would become the center of the conflict, surrounded by military factions. Executions would take place on podiums that had celebrated the world's best athletes, and the stadium would become a graveyard for some of the ten thousand people who would die in the Sarajevo siege.

I stood at the just-finished bobsled run and climbed to the top of the ski jump in the hills above the city and the Miljacka River, staring shakily at panoramic views beyond the steep drop. I could not imagine that there would be devastating Serbian artillery in those very hills where Olympic athletes were soon to compete in good fellowship. And that after the war, the Olympic sites would be left to rot, with ski slopes and the bobsled track turning into canvases for local graffiti artists.

* * *

The nearby city of Mostar developed in the fifteenth and sixteenth centuries on the Ottoman frontier, spanning a deep valley of the Neretva River, connecting Christian and Muslim communities.

In 1982 I saw many people crossing from community to community at Stari Most, the historic old bridge. Many of the city's families had intermarried over the years. Boys were diving off the bridge into the river for money, and the scene was harmonious.

But most of Mostar, including the famed bridge, was destroyed in the 1990s conflict.

The arc of history lurches forward, backward, and hopefully, forward again. A country where "everyone gets along" can deteriorate fast—and much of the time—heal again.

The bridge and many of the edifices in Mostar have been restored by UNESCO, and in Sarajevo, the surrounding woods have returned most of the area to nature.

Time heals. But history warns.

BOTSWANA

Hippy, Hippo, Hooray

Meghan and Harry fell in love in Botswana, but well before that I had wanted to visit the unpronounceable, unforgettable Makgadikgadi, the country's huge super-lake that formed millions of years ago and dried up thousands of years ago as the earth's crust shifted. Those ancient lake shores were the setting for the transition from ape to man.

Botswana also offers unique African species including aardvarks, gemsbucks, springbucks and elusive brown hyenas. And what could be more enchanting for animal lovers than to walk the Kalahari among habituated yet wild meerkats, popping in and out of their holes like whack-a-moles?

I never got to Botswana's Kalahari or Makgadikgadi, and came no closer to a meerkat than to Bigfoot. Instead, my husband and I did what many travelers do with time and money constraints: tacked on a day trip, a last-minute river safari in Botswana, only a few miles from Zimbabwe, where we were staying overnight to see Victoria Falls. (*See: Zimbabwe.*)

The Okavango Delta is a vast inland river delta in northern Botswana, and when its sprawling grassy plains flood seasonally, they become a lush animal habitat. Even in our one-day quickie we observed lots of elephants, giraffes and antelopes near the water.

The stars were the hippos. They surrounded our little open boat, raising pink-sunburned radio-faces in menacing scowls and big-toothed yawns, then submerging into big blobby swells. It felt like a Disney ride.

✳

I remember other hippos encountered in my travels: hundreds crowded in fetid water in a river in the Ngorongoro Crater of Tanzania. And in Malawi, grunting, growling hippos chomping on foliage only a few feet away from our tents as we slept.

Our group at that camp was warned not to walk alone at night without an armed guard. When a hippo gets hyper, there is no more dangerous animal.

I follow instructions in distant places, especially when I'm alone. So even though the guard who was supposed to accompany me to dinner was already a half-hour late, I waited as instructed in my tent, growls emerging not from wild animals in the distance but from my stomach.

It was getting dark, and the armed guard had not come to fetch me. When I peeked out, I couldn't see anyone except a woman gardening in the distance. All was quiet and I decided that since the *boma*, the open area where dinner is served, was only two minutes away, I could walk myself this one time.

So, I took a chance, following my hungry gut rather than my cautionary head, and ventured out briskly. I came closer to the heavy-set woman in the distance, who was still bent over. Then I stopped suddenly, realizing that a woman wasn't leaning over to garden. It was a hippo, *eating* the garden. A hippo, not a hippy woman.

I ran like a cartoon character, faster than I probably had before or certainly have since, into the closest tent, where two other women huddled who also had not been accompanied to dinner, and who had also seen the gardening hippo.

Our absence was eventually noticed, and a guard finally came to escort us to a very late meal. And we were accompanied from then on, thank you very much.

BRAZIL

My Man in Rio Was a Gem

Hong Kong, San Francisco and Sydney are often mentioned as cities with the most beautiful settings, but I'd vote for Rio de Janeiro. Curving Copacabana and Ipanema beaches are edged with swirling mosaic sidewalks. Sugar Loaf Mountain soars above the harbor and the Christ the Redeemer statue blesses the city below.

There is ugliness, though, in Rio's *favelas*, slums that from afar cover the city's mountains like snow. Up close they reveal the stench of poverty, neglect and crime, remnants of a tragic past.

But slavery has left fascinating traditions. One night in a hot room with participants dressed in white, I attended a *Macumba* black-magic ceremony. A squawking chicken lost its head to a blade that flashed silver, then crimson. Visitors were told to be silent, and since there were knives brandished, I remained totally tight-lipped. I could smell the blood for hours after.

The highlight of tourist shows and performances along the beach, the martial art/dance called *Capoeira* was born out of extremes as well, devised by Brazilian slaves as a way to train for rebellion. And there's the samba, also brought from Africa—more trance than dance. In a local club I swayed for hours to rhythmic, steady drumbeats. You jump in and never stop, as partners of all kinds come and go.

Caipirinha, Brazil's potent tropical cocktail made from sugarcane liquor, fresh lime juice, sugar and ice, helps stoke the trancing/dancing. At traditional Sunday lunch the next day, I drank the green drink and ate a combo of meats, including tongue, sausage, and "don't ask," with sides of rice, beans, collard greens, oranges and hot pepper sauce. A world-class wake-me-up and let-me-take-a-nap-after meal.

After that repast, I did stumble into the sun and then to bed, as many do, emerging back to the beachfront when the heat within and without subsided. Back then, in the early 1980s, I noticed thong bathing suits for the first time, on young and old, in this land of the Brazilian bikini wax, endless beachfront, and endless bodies.

Even the most impoverished *cariocas*—what the locals call themselves—find frenzied joy in two things: soccer and Carnival. Crowds of maybe a hundred thousand standing soccer fans at the Rio stadium create vibrations and roars that never seem to end. Long-retired soccer star Pele remains more a god to Brazilians than the god of fire he was named for.

I've experienced the world's second biggest celebration in Barranquilla (*See: Colombia*), but Rio's tops them all, with two million people a day on the streets. Just about everybody participates in some way throughout the year, and I visited a club preparing sequined, feathery, over-the-top costumes.

On that trip I was at the worldwide headquarters of H Stern, the flagship jewelry store of many around the world, admiring the twinkling, colored gems mined from nearby Ouro Preto, a colonial town I had just visited. I hung back when my press group left, talking to the salespeople and hoping perhaps to find an affordable little stone among the rainbow prisms.

I felt a tap on my shoulder from a woman in black. "Excuse me, but Hans Stern would like to talk to you."

"Hans ... You mean ... *H* Stern?" I thought of all the stores with that name. There actually was an H!

I was escorted through several gates and elevators to the top of the building, with a view of the forested mountains dropping to the water and the wide beach below. And there behind a desk in an office lined with books was a small, sixtyish, bald man with a big grin, looking more like a professor than a mogul.

Hans Stern, a German Jew, immigrated to Rio at the outbreak of World War II, when he was seventeen years old. And when he found out earlier that I was an American writer, he decided he just wanted to gab.

We spoke of history and politics and America—anything, it seemed, but jewelry. And he must have liked our conversation, because when I got up to go, he handed me a heavy gold charm of a closed fist.

"This is a *figa*, a good-luck symbol that came to Brazil with the seventeenth-century slave trade," he said. "To bring luck, a figa must always be a gift."

As I stepped into the taxi he had called for me, Rio itself had become jewel-toned, with sky and sea the color of topaz, tourmaline and amethyst. When I returned to the hotel it was dark, and my fellow travelers were worried that I had been kidnapped, mugged, raped and murdered, in no particular order.

I told them it was the opposite. I had been gifted with good will. And, I hesitated, "jewelry."

The other writers were understandably jealous, but as one put it, "We didn't get a gift, but at least now we know what 'H' stands for. I thought it was *Howard* Stern!"

BULGARIA

Righteous Among the Nations

I knew little about Bulgaria, a country formerly part of the Soviet Union, except for the thick, tangy yogurt that I ate whenever I saw it specified on a menu, and the boisterous charms of a curly-haired Bulgarian I had dated in New York a couple of times in the 1990s.

To find out a bit more, at the end of a Danube river cruise that started a couple of weeks before in Germany, my friend and I added a week of touring in Bulgaria. We lucked out with a dark-eyed driver who spoke English. He guided us to Black Sea beaches, Thracian gold displays, rolling vineyards and inexpensive village houses, some of them second homes for Brits. Grander architecture was often gingerbread Victorian with a Bulgarian twist.

We explored ancient ruins, frescoed monasteries and gargantuan Soviet sculptures carved into walls and mountainsides. Fresh food, big red wines and zippy folk dancing shows rounded out our experience. We were impressed.

But, according to our guide, there was also overwhelming post-Soviet graft. And although so much was wonderful in his country, there were few direct flights from major cities, so tourism remained flat. He confessed he was so sick of the corruption that he wished he could live somewhere else, maybe Dubai.

My major shopping memory in Sofia, the capital city, is a flea market with tables covered with inexpensive Nazi memorabilia: cartoons, insignia, photos. I was tempted to buy them all—collectors would pay me handsomely—but the idea was loathsome.

In contrast, I discovered a beautiful, intact synagogue, and learned something that few people knew about Bulgaria. In 1942, when the country had consented to the German request for 48,000 Bulgarian Jews from the occupied territories of Macedonia and Thrace—not one of them was deported or murdered by the Nazis.

Credited with saving them from deportation were Dimitar Peshev, deputy speaker of parliament; opposition politicians; the Bulgarian Church; Tsar Boris; and ordinary citizens. This was kept secret by the Soviet Union, because the regime could not stand giving credit to the former authorities, the church or the king, all considered enemies of Communism.

On January 10, 1973, Bulgaria was officially thanked by the government of Israel for its defiance of Nazi Germany. And Peshev was awarded the title of Righteous Among the Nations by Yad Vashem, Israel's memorial to Holocaust victims, for his unwavering struggle against the plans to deport Jews to death camps.

The synagogue in Sofia still stands. And good Bulgarians helped keep it standing.

BURMA (MYANMAR)

On The Road To Mandalay

Southeast Asia tourism arrived decades ago to Thailand, Malaysia, Vietnam and Cambodia. But like Cuba, Myanmar, formerly known as Burma, remains a throwback to an earlier time amid its more modernized neighbors.

Myanmar consists of more than one hundred ethnic groups, and borders India, Bangladesh, China, Laos and Thailand. Right now, the focus is on the country's humanitarian violations against the Rohingya, the Muslim community that is being erased in this primarily Buddhist country.

When I traveled there in 2015, this atrocity was not much in the news and there was hope that a new regime would improve the situation. (So far that hope seems lost, but world opinion may still prevail.)

Myanmar seems a Sleeping Beauty aroused from decades of slumber, and I was grateful for the chance to experience the region before it developed high-speed trains, fast-food chains, wired cities and trendy clubs like the rest of the region.

Bill and I flew into the capital, Yangon—formerly Rangoon—and walked to Scott Market, amid street booksellers and past decrepit, once grand buildings. Late in the day in a mango-hued sunset we looked up to the golden glow of the

towering sixth-century Shwedagon Pagoda, filled with hundreds of Buddhist relics.

Paved roads are still few, and the muddy Irrawaddy River was our means of transport through the country, as it has been for Burmese villagers over millennia. By day we disembarked near dusty paths, as women washed clothes in the river, and children played along the shore. At night the boat plied by a moving panorama of moonlit pagodas against starry skies.

Over two thousand Buddhist temples in varied states of disrepair, most dating to around 1100 A.D., rise like alien creations in Bagan, varying in size and design but creating a magnificent pattern for miles. There's an archeological museum, but the entire area is an outdoor museum set in fields—and I explored dozens of crumbling temples set amid wildflowers and vines.

Rising by hot-air balloon into the hazy sunrise, overlooking thousands of temples, is magical; but I remember a balloon ride over Vermont fields, and a rough landing in a tumbled basket, so I decided to enjoy the surreal scene of balloons and temples from a down-to-earth seat in a pony cart. And to make up for my timidity, at sunset I climbed three levels up one of the tallest pagodas, high enough to see temple tops for miles across the plains.

Near Bagan, we came upon a festivity for novice monks, a kind of Myanmar group bar mitzvah. We joined a parade in which villagers dressed in elab orate costumes, and horses, cows and tractors were decorated in crepe. Parents took photos of the young men in their finery, as proud parents do all over the world.

Rudyard Kipling, the nineteenth-century poet, wrote lines I learned in high school, put to a song: "On the road to Mandalay, Where the flyin' fishes play, An' the dawn comes up like thunder over China 'cross the Bay."

I never thought I'd get to such a poetic place, but there I was as red dawns came up over wood-carved temples, filled with Buddhas and smelling of earth. My diciest venture was maneuvering gingerly across a rickety wooden bridge with gaps big enough to fall through. I had no intention of ending it all among the flying fishes.

At Inle Lake we talked with a lady who had worn heavy rings around her throat for years so that her shoulders dropped and her neck stretched as long as a snake. She sat with her 15-year-old daughter, whose neck was also stretching. I was both fascinated and appalled. And sad.

In stilt houses above the lake, craftspeople created delicate paper parasols filled with crushed flowers, and we boated along canals out to the lake to watch fishermen balance on one leg, guiding an oar with their other foot to stir the water, as they have throughout the centuries.

What will happen in magical Myanmar? Hatred of "others" is a moral outrage, not a path to success. If I had known then what I know now, I would not have been comfortable traveling there. And yet, in my ignorance, I was lucky to have experienced a step back in time.

CAMBODIA

To Go or Not to Go, That Is the Question

Many times I travel far to a place I probably will not return to, and while there, miss things I may not get the chance to see again.

I can think of the West Islands on the edge of Iceland. Having driven the Ring Road most of the way, I debated and decided to wait for another time to head that way. I came close to Albania when I was writing a guidebook about the Greek

Islands; Corfu is just off the Albanian coast, but I decided no.

Along the Skeleton Coast of Namibia, huge white sand dunes fringe the rough Atlantic and deserted beaches are strewn with shipwrecks. Although I was maybe an hour away by car on my one trip to Namibia, I had other obligations and missed my chance to drive the coast.

I'm hoping to return to all those places, but opportunities diminish as years pass.

The most cost-effective, time-effective plan is to carefully check out the special sites and sights of an entire region before you leave. Build in time for extending your trip to special places while you're in the vicinity.

And this story shows you why.

In Vietnam in October 2006, the scenery and food were exceptional. The country was thriving. I was surprised to find that the Vietnamese did not seem bitter about Americans decimating huge swaths of their country and their people only a few decades before.

But I wasn't feeling well. My heart was racing, I felt off-balance, short of breath. And while I felt somewhat secure being in a group, I still wondered what was wrong.

The headlines were all about the actress Farrah Fawcett having cancer. I thought of her amazing hair and wondered if she would lose it. It bothered me in the middle of the night that one so seemingly vibrant was really sick, and reminded me that I was feeling off.

Without telling the group, I taxied to a 24-hour clinic on a Hanoi side street, and found a doctor who spoke a bit of English. He checked my vital signs but probably had little idea what I was talking about, and figured that I was a privileged hypochondriac. He suggested I see a doctor when I returned to the States.

Although nothing seemed dire, I suddenly got the feeling that I might never be in Southeast Asia again. And that created an ironic situation: I was on my own, halfway around the world, not feeling well. Should I leave the trip early and come home? Or, counterintuitively, should I extend my trip and travel by myself, last minute, to Cambodia?

The latter made strange sense the more I thought about it. I had always wanted to see the ruins at Angkor Wat, and I felt that if I didn't see them right then, no matter the cost and the change of plans, I might never see them.

I became determined to get to Cambodia for three days, and found a travel agent in Hue, paid for a last-minute flight from Vietnam and changed my ticket to the States.

When my group flew back home from Vietnam, I flew from Ho Chi Minh City to the pretty little airport in Siem Reep, Cambodia, and was met by my guide, Leap, who drove me to my Art Deco hotel, a throwback to the French occupation there in the 1930s. I noted the growing condo developments for rich South Korean vacationers, and the huge, almost-finished museum, which today houses many of the fragments of ancient Cambodian dynasties.

The Angkor Wat ruins were as spectacular as I had hoped, with thick vines growing over and into ancient temples, one after another. I remained tired from my mystery malady, but I felt safe with Leap next to me, helping me walk over tumbled stones, His name he assured me, meant "good luck."

Leap was a child during the time of the Killing Fields in the 1980s, when his parents, professionals in Phnom Penh, were driven out of that city with millions of others and worked to death in the countryside. Yet, like the Vietnamese who did not seem to harbor anger at Americans, he did not seem bitter that the Khmer Rouge had devastated his family and his country.

"There is no way to know who among us now were the captors or the captives," he told me. "We don't ask. We just live. That is the Buddhist way."

Perhaps I had embodied that attitude in my own small way by traveling on my own despite my fears, to explore the magnificent ruins of an ancient culture.

When I returned home I had a complete physical, and sure enough I was ill. Although I had never smoked, I was diagnosed with lung cancer.

Unlike Farrah Fawcett, I was lucky. My cancer was found early. The trip had been a risk, but in the end, a gift to myself. And I still remember Leap's name and his haunting message as much as I remember the magnificent ruins in that last-minute detour to Cambodia. You never know what life may bring. "Just live."

CANADA

No Blame, Some Shame

The satirical song goes "Blame Canada" but I can only blame myself if and when I overdo it. Many of these eight remembrances, and especially the last, exemplify just that. The others are just sweet memories.

⁂

Historic events happen while we travel, and we often remember just where we were at the time. O.J. Simpson's flight in his white van interrupted me in the middle of reviewing hotels across Canada for a travel guide. I holed up in my room in a boutique hotel in Quebec City, eyes glued to the TV, gorging on poutine, a Canadian concoction of fries and cheese curds covered in gravy. By the time the car chase was over, my head was in the porcelain throne and I could care less.

⁂

Years later I had my own nerve-wracking car ride. Driving solo from Lake Louise to Jasper, past long-retreated glaciers, I got lost amid a herd of bachelor elk, staring me down on the side of the road at twilight. I fought a creased, uncooperative map to get my bearings, unaware that someday GPS would be invented. That night I ate elk steak and felt strangely satisfied.

⁂

Sea kayaking in the Bay of Fundy, my friend Valerie and I paddled frantically against a rapidly

rising tide. The strong, much younger group far ahead seemed to have forgotten about us. Someone finally noticed we were missing and led us back to shore, but meanwhile Val and I bonded and became lifetime buddies. (Nothing like floundering against the highest tide in the world to bring people together.)

※

In New Brunswick, Valerie and I participated in the noisiest festival anywhere—the raucous commemoration of 1755, when the Brits attempted to remove approximately ten thousand Acadians from British North America. Many fled to Louisiana and became known as Cajuns, but the few who escaped deportation stayed in Caraquet, the unofficial capital of Acadia.

Dressed in the colors of the Acadian flag—red, white, blue and yellow—we joined an informal parade milling up and down the main street for an hour, creating noise with drums, horns and noisemakers from pots and pans to shouts. Best venting ever.

※

My idea of a tattoo has nothing to do with ink ever since I attended the Tattoo in Halifax, Nova Scotia, with hundreds of bagpipes and drum corps. Robed figures crossed the stage, Star Wars characters accompanied military bands, cars were disassembled, light shows dazzled, Canadian military and units from other countries strutted their stuff. The show is unique to Canada and the Maritimes, and changes every year. You never know what to expect.

The Rocky Mountaineer, the glass-domed train that travels from Vancouver up through the Canadian Rockies, offers daytime scenery, lunch in the dining car or at your seat, and overnights in Canadian towns. The most exercise we got on the rails was when one man yelled, "Bear ahead!" and everyone grabbed their cameras and ran to the windows where he was pointing. I soon caught on to this "little boy who cried wolf" syndrome, and, of course, when a bear and her cubs finally appeared, I snoozed right through his shouts.

My first travel memory of Canada was over fifty years ago at Expo 67, the World's Fair in Montreal, set on islands in the St. Lawrence River. My most recent adventure, in 2019, was a road trip with my friend Margie from New York, who learned to play the harmonica at seventy. Five years later she was playing gigs for fun, and I was invited to be her companion/roadie/groupie on what we called her "first international road tour."

Changing leaves tumbled down in the maritime breeze as we giggled our way through Halifax, Digby and St. John on Canada's eastern coast, tearing into two-pound lobsters and sharing the ups and downs of living long and large. We were Thelma and Louise years down the road with butter on our fingers, and a happier ending.

Another "Louise" is a turquoise, glacier-fed lake ringed by the Canadian Rockies and overlooked by a stately chateau-hotel. Because I wanted to enjoy the view from above, I decided to ride a horse along the ribbon of trails winding up to the Tea House near the top of the trail.

I hadn't been on a horse in years and I had never ridden along a precipice, but was assured that an 87-year-old lady had taken the same horseback excursion a few days before and had a terrific time.

My bony steed, Nelson, seemed weary when I patted his head, and as he walked from the stable, seemed unsure-footed even on the flats. I wondered if the white on his head meant he was almost ready for the retirement pasture, and I worried that maybe besides being thin, he was depressed, or maybe even demented. I reassured myself that at least he walked slowly, and that a guide would accompany me.

As we plodded along the rising trail, I didn't want to look down, which was the whole point of the excursion, so my view for most of the way was the backside of the guide's horse or the void behind my shut eyes.

Gravel kept falling down the cliff into the lake and Nelson wanted to stop a quarter of the way through, and I don't blame him one bit. Yet there was no room to turn, so he had to keep moving forward, and so did I, atop him.

We walked along that mountain edge for five hours total, with a brief halfway stop for tea and nowhere to go but down, which turned out to be worse than going up. I often had to lean way back to keep from sliding off Nelson and plunging into Lake Louise. Many times my elderly steed suddenly halted, and sometimes he stumbled, throwing me forward and sideways in the saddle, with my butt cheeks squeezed tighter than my closed eyes.

It reminded me of when I was on a bad camel in the Sahara. Trust me, you don't want to find out too late that your camel is itchy or has indigestion. It's a long way down. On that ride I just closed my eyes and went with the movement and made it through, something most of us have done many times, if you know what I mean.

I tried to do the same with Nelson, but I became sore and nauseous. By the end of the ride, when he actually galloped to the stable to end the ordeal for both of us, even though I was bobbing up and down like a rag doll, I felt relieved that he was rushing back. And just before we got to his stall, I *let myself fall off* to the dusty ground before he even stopped, as if I had opened a door and thrown myself out of a slow-moving car to get away from an abuser.

Lesson of the ride from hell: Don't be shamed into doing something you don't want to do. Even if an 87-year-old woman has just kicked ass at it.

CHILE

Easter Island and The Christians of Pitcairn

The first time I visited Chile, the skinny, mountainous country on the western side of South America, it was all business, reviewing hotels for a guidebook, as I did often in my forties and fifties, traveling on my own throughout many countries.

Hopping in and out of hundreds of guest rooms throughout Chile, I'd check carpets and bathrooms and general room conditions—what I called "hack work." Before entering a guest room,

I'd yell "Room check," but once I surprised a naked man, who actually seemed pleased to see me; and another time, came upon a naked couple in bed, too busy to hear me.

I tried to add one fun, exploration day for every couple of work days, so I would spend a few weeks at a time traveling, but I often was so tired from checking out maybe fifteen hotels a day, I would spend off-days chilling by a plaza, watching people.

My favorite lodging in Chile was outside of Santiago, an elegant horse ranch that was the birthplace of a former governor. Aristocrats—descendants of Spanish conquistadors, no doubt—lived there for centuries, and I was escorted around the vintage premises and didn't have to yell "Room check."

My driver, an art and history buff, was excited that I was able to see the property and sat outside in the car as I viewed the stunning rooms and antiques. After reviewing the place, I asked the owner politely if he could come in to see the historic room where the Chilean governor had been born.

The owner gave me the side-eye and a strong "No." I guess he figured that the driver would never be able to stay in a place like this, so it wasn't worth the effort to be kind. No matter how many times I observe class-consciousness throughout the world, I'm still shocked and saddened.

Suggestion: Don't give a snobby impression to a hotel reviewer who will be writing about your establishment, or it might haunt you for years. I report what I observe, and not just about the furnishings.

※

On my way back from an 18-day trip to Antarctica, after unexpectedly calm waters to

Cape Horn, we cruised alongside hundreds of glaciers at the bottom of South America, and sailed among the islands of the Beagle Channel, a strait in Tierra del Fuego, between Argentina and Chile.

Along the way we passed nesting birds, a shipwreck and a lighthouse on a rocky island. Charles Darwin, who sailed here on board the HMS Beagle, probably observed the same local fauna. I closely viewed sea lions, sea elephants, penguins and look-alike black-and-white cormorants. (They can fly; penguins can't.)

At Isla de Los Lobos, a colony of sea lions lolled in front of picture-perfect snow-capped mountains. Further east, Martillo Island was a rookery of Magellanic and Gentoo penguins. But I saw mostly cormorants, which reminded me of the many penguins we had seen in Antarctica, just not as cute. Count me on Team Penguin, perhaps my favorite bird of all, along with adorable, clown-faced puffins, although I admit I tasted puffin—once, a small bite. For research. I'm sorry. *(See: Iceland.)*

In 2016, my husband Bill and I spent a few days in the Chilean capital of Santiago before cruising to the South Pacific. In nearby Valparaiso, where the cruise began, I took photos of the colorful street art on the walls and stairs up and down the hills.

We paid homage to the house of poet Pablo Neruda, one of the most romantic or sappy poets ever, depending on whether you're in love or breaking up. (At that moment, with Bill, Neruda's poetry seemed truly romantic.)

In Vina del Mar, just outside Valparaiso, before embarking on the cruise, our guide recommended lunch in a casual-looking restaurant overlooking the beach. The seafood tasted fresh, but ignoring the exchange rate, we got snookered into paying over $100 for a "special seafood sauce." The cost was bad enough, but the first evening onboard the ship I had the worst case of food poisoning I can remember. Special sauce, indeed.

Luckily, I had about a month to recuperate, stopping at remote South Pacific islands and ending in Tahiti and Moorea. On Robinson Crusoe Island, we looked for hummingbirds and fur seals among the cliffs, and at the fishing village of San Juan Bautista, discovered a small cemetery near a cavern where political prisoners were once held, now called the Cave of the Patriots. I've found over the years that rebels in many countries, including the United States, wind up being considered the heroes of history.

At isolated Fakarava atoll we enjoyed a splashy interlude where we swam and snorkeled. At idyllic Bora Bora I bought one black pearl, which cost as much as a whole string of white ones. We also stroked a group of stingrays in shallow water and lunched at a table right in the Pacific, eating the same fish that were nibbling at our feet.

The highlight of the voyage was Easter Island, a Chilean territory over two thousand miles away from the mainland. Natives call it Rapa Nui.

About a thousand years ago, Polynesians came and constructed more than a thousand moai statues, many of which were raised miles from their quarries, using methods that still puzzle scientists. The stoic heads and bodies were created out of volcanic rocks during the thirteenth through sixteenth centuries. Many stand on pedestals, and some wear hats, looking a bit silly, as if they were dressing up for tourists.

As the population grew, the vast quarry was deserted, with dozens of moai left unfinished and abandoned. By the 1870s, the island population was just over a hundred people, down from thousands at its peak. Wild horses still graze throughout the island, a remnant of that time. What caused the collapse? Theories include resource depletion, disease, civil war and rats that destroyed the forest.

Tourism has given hope. In 2017, Easter Island—with 6,000 residents—attracted more than 100,000 visitors. Hotels, restaurants and tour businesses take in more than $70 million every year.

But climate change threatens low-lying areas of all the Pacific. The United Nations warns that the moai and many of these unique remains, including the platforms called ahu, may be erased by 2100, with sea levels rising five to six feet. Waves on Ovahe Beach have already carried off almost all the sand, leaving jagged volcanic stone and damaged, unmarked burial sites.

The volcanic crater at Orongo was the center of the civilization's activity around 1600, before European contact. Islanders gathered annually to watch young men race through open water to a nearby island to fetch bird eggs, and the winner determined which clan would rule the following year.

The stories of those races are told in a half-dozen large petroglyphs carved in stone, perched over the edge of the caldera, vulnerable to storms and gravity.

So yes, a trip to Easter Island is a rewarding adventure. But ASAP, I'm sorry to say. The demise of Easter Island if it comes again, will not be a mystery.

✳

Another vulnerable land mass on this cruise from Chile to Tahiti was Pitcairn Island, a mile-long, uninviting lump of rock in the middle of the South Pacific, and probably the smallest, most remote inhabited place in the world.

We cruisers were going to meet the islanders, but before we did, we learned of the strange history (and bear with it because it is a bit weird). Fletcher Christian and the mutineers immortalized the island in 1790 after the famous Mutiny on the Bounty, when crew members refused to leave Tahiti to go back to England with Captain Bligh. Christian and the crew eventually stumbled upon uncharted Pitcairn, settled in, and destroyed the Bounty to erase the mutiny.

The nine mutineers brought a few Tahitian women and men along with them, and claimed most of the women for themselves. But within a few years all but one of the mutineers were killed, including Fletcher Christian himself, clubbed to death by Tahitians. His son, Thursday October Christian (whom I gather was born on his name, like a celebrity rapper's kid), survived. He is the ancestor of almost everybody called Christian on the island today, a mix of British sailors and Tahitian natives.

In 1808, an American seal-hunting ship discovered Pitcairn and found a man named Alexander Smith (also known as John Adams), who claimed to be the last surviving member of the original crew of mutineers on the Bounty. After that discovery, Pitcairn became a part of the British empire in the early nineteenth century, and remains so to this day.

The island's population never grew to more than a couple of hundred people, peaking in the early twentieth century. Nearly all of the residents of the island to this day, now numbering only in the forties, are descendants of the mutineers.

(An interesting contemporary note: A 225-year-long feud between Captain Bligh and

Fletcher Christian came to an end recently when Maurice Bligh, in his seventies, the great-great-great-grandson of the famous captain, and Jacqui Christian, in her forties, the great-great-great-great granddaughter of the lead mutineer, greeted each other in Tahiti. In a gesture of goodwill, Christian brought the Bible that her mutineer relative stole from the Bounty's captain. Bligh, in an act of friendship, returned the Bible to the Pitcairn resident, whom we cruisers got to meet.)

Because of ocean swells we couldn't dock on Pitcairn, so practically the entire population took to their boats and came aboard our ship. The islanders sold their merch, ate a hearty lunch and bickered like Kardashians. After all, life on Pitcairn is not exactly stimulating: Visits from an infrequent mail boat and an occasional cruise ship are the highlights of their year.

Our group of pampered cruisers wondered whether these folks would try to stay on the ship and wind up like their infamous ancestors, on Tahiti, where our ship was headed.

We had also heard whispers about the Pitcairn sex scandal of a few years back, involving the mayor, six other men and underage girls, truly un-Christian deeds by the Christians. Pitcairn, in fact, has the distinction of having the most sex offenders per capita of any place on Earth. A superlative that no one mentioned at our get-together.

When the Pitcairn Islanders sped back to their rock, we stood on the deck, some of us now wearing our "I Love Pitcairn Island" T-shirts, with a sense of relief and not a single mutinous thought.

We were happy as hell to be staying onboard and heading on our way to Tahiti.

CHINA

Moving Fast

In 1984 I ferried solo from Hong Kong via Macau for a day trip to the Canton region of China, to get a peek at the toe of the emerging giant. My first shock was seeing students sitting by themselves in a classroom, reading quietly. That generation of children is currently running the country, and their studying has paid off.

I lunched at the one modern hotel in the region, a Holiday Inn with a tiny gift shop selling chopsticks, fans and trinkets that were…made in China. The toilets were the only Western ones around, and had memorably sticky, black-lacquered seats.

Two-lane main roads were clogged with pedestrians and bicyclists wearing drab green pajama-like outfits and Mao caps; land was tilled with oxen and primitive tools; and farmers with cone hats, trailed by ducks, bent along the rice paddies in clichéd China scenes.

At a rural market, goods were scattered on the ground as if in a yard sale in a poor neighborhood—a few eggs, a chipped plate, a rusted birdcage. A stooped man with a droopy Salvador Dali mustache stood so close I could feel his breath and he stared in my eyes as if I were for sale. (No offer made, and I did feel a bit rejected.)

Workers swarmed in the distance, seeming to break the mountainsides down with hammers and chisels. I thought of the Egyptian pyramids, and realized the incredible potential of this patient and mighty Chinese workforce, but I could not possibly conceive of the changes to come in the following century. China's past was evident; the future, uncertain, poised at a beginning.

*

About ten years later, in the early 1990s, I was scheduled to write the first guidebook on China for a major publisher and the first section on Chinese hotels for the major travel trade publication.

Since I had the clout and China was just starting its tourism industry, I asked the media relations person in New York, "Can you help me out?"

The Chinese rep immediately answered: "No." And then, an unexpected "You … very pushy!" This was before China understood the power of public relations. Today it has one of the most well-funded, active tourism offices in the world.

*

I traveled again to China in 2006, when a cardiologist invited me to Shanghai. I had known him only a few months, but as he was lecturing at a conference and would be in the public eye, I felt ready to accompany him.

We were supposed to meet in L.A. and fly to Shanghai together, but my connecting flight was late, and I arrived solo in China for the second time. The changes were startling. The air smelled like fuel and was thick with pollution. I boarded a magnetic levitation train from the airport into the city center, tilting along at over 400 kilometers an hour. So much for the slow-paced transport of 1984.

The skyline was crammed with skyscrapers, flashing colors at night. The Rolling Stones were making their first appearance in Shanghai, and their faces were plastered on buses and billboards. Restaurants buzzed with diners and the streets were crammed with people enjoying soup dumplings and other local foods, but they were now dressed mostly in western style.

My huge hotel stood across the river from the lights of the Bund, the famed Art Deco boulevard of former colonial embassies. The next day I walked along the riverfront, where a pre-teen boy was standing on a box, drawing a crowd, his cap filled with coins on the ground in front of him.

He was choking himself with a metal bar.

The boy's face flushed red as he wound the bar tighter and tighter around his thin neck. When he seemed about to pass out, he gasped and let the bar go, and people clapped.

I walked away shocked, but on the next street another boy, a competitor, was doing the same thing. The passersby spooned gelato and talked on their cellphones as they watched this boy, as well, come close to choking.

I saw the future: entrepreneurial kids, the speed of progress, the work ethic, the lack of regulations—China was impressive, and scary.

*

My companion and I had some problems. I was interested in traveling around, he was focused on the study of aortas. He also turned out to be arrogant and stubborn, which shouldn't have surprised me, but I wasn't going to let that stop me from enjoying my trip.

On his off-hours I coerced him to museums and old neighborhoods and the Shanghai version of Cirque de Soleil—beautiful but far more dangerous, with a finale of six motorcycles roaring around in a spinning steel wheel. Death was a possibility, with one mistake.

In tranquil Hangzhou, trees were budding pink and white and families strolled and picnicked along the shore of West Lake. In the canal city of Suzhou, where the architect I.M. Pei was born, we walked among intricate gardens, pagodas, temples and lakes and by elegant stone bridges. At night in one garden, different pavilions showcased Chinese music, art and drama.

Doc didn't want to go to Tongli, a preserved ancient city near Suzhou, so one day I grabbed a business card and cabbed from the hotel alone. Traffic was congested, and the air thick and gray; along the way endless, huge manufacturing complexes and new housing blocks were filling the farming fields.

I meandered and rickshawed among old shops, canals and wooden bridges in a classic scene appropriate for a Chinese scroll. At Tongli's famed sex museum, fertility idols were a forest of appendages.

Few Westerners were around. No English was spoken. I was happy, immersed in the crowds. My best times on my China trips, as in so many countries, have been on my own when I fold into the culture.

The country has evolved faster than anywhere I have ever been. In the forty years between my first and last visit—with a tour group in 2016—China had moved from primitive to futuristic; from bicycles to maglev trains and fifty-lane highways; from polluted air to solar heating and Green cities, and now more frequent blue-sky days.

If I return, I know that the remnants of thousands of years, like the Great Wall and the Summer Palace in Beijing will remain, but hybrid politics, pragmatic rules and innovative changes will continue, for better or worse. This, I believe, is China's century.

COLOMBIA

I'm Covered in Flour!

My travel-writer friend Lorry, a New Orleans resident and a Mardi Gras maven, wanted to compare her beloved Louisiana version of Carnival to the South American Carnaval.

We chose the second-largest blowout in the world, in Barranquilla, Colombia, on South America's Caribbean coast. Their Carnaval has been carrying on since the nineteenth century, and received a UNESCO Heritage Award as a "magnificent example of folkloric expression."

Entranced by colonial Cartagena a couple of years before, I felt comfortable in Colombia, despite its perceived and real problems with drugs and crime. The country had just paid big money for an unfortunate marketing slogan: "The only risk is that you'll never want to leave."

"Risk" is not a good word when your perception at that time was danger. (Better would have been "Wake Up and Smell the Coffee!" I offered that one up for free in a few seconds.)

Jotting down or recording impressions is a good way, along with photos, to secure travel memories, and I kept my original notes—many of them raw.

When you write or record notes, don't worry about grammar, spelling and word choice. Just try to be as specific as possible, and put down your impressions as soon as you can, preferably in the moment. Here are my real-time notes as an example; I left them pretty much as-is so you can get the idea of journaling.

Friday

First impression of Barranquilla: speeding drivers, art-deco architecture in pastel hues, blue neon lighting, plastic surgery clinics. Buildings festooned with festival flowers, animals. Breezy, balmy.

The "Romantic Museum," recommended by locals. King Momo, a big-shot local chosen yearly for the parade. A dozen Carnaval-Queen gowns (any kind of queen would dig their razzle-dazzle). Enjoyed a miniature construction of this commercial port city, a melting pot of cultures and religions. History, antiques.

Residents over the years: Nobel-Prize-winning writer Gabriel Garcia Marquez, (wrote *One Hundred Years of Solitude* near here). Shakira, who earned a statue for giving back to her hometown, not just shaking her hips.

And Nina Garcia, an editor at *Elle Magazine* and one of the judges of my beloved *Project Runway*. A Barranquilla homie.

Window-shop in a generic-looking mall. The dollar is okay here. Lorry buys a cute halter top, I purchase some coffee.

Also poke around a nearby handicraft area: woven bags, glittery carnaval tees, lots of miniatures of Marimonda, the elephant emblem of this celebration—representing truth, wisdom and anything else you want.

Step into the contemporary cathedral across the street, built in 1982. Vast stained-glass windows rise to cavernous ceilings, huge interpretive sculpture of Christ, impressive mosaics. Lunch at La Cueva, our one really special

meal (the rest, empanadas, sausages, sandwiches on the go). This has been the Barranquilla meeting place for "hunters and intellectuals" for 60 years. Art, elephant footprints, lore of 1950s artists and writers and drunks. Cool. Weird. Welcoming.

Music called "cumbia" continues as day turns into night, around barrio corners, from crowded, colorful bus- es—drum, re- corder and a cheese-grater thingy that sounds like maracas when scraped. We latch on to connected locals and poke into a party where "Angie" the gracious Carnaval Queen shows up, along with the regional governor. They make the rounds of dozens of these gigs.

Sup on coconut water, empanadas, not much else. Go to bed hungry but eager for tomorrow's main parade.

Saturday

Many carnaval events over several weeks, up until the Tuesday before Ash Wednesday, but today's "Battle of the Flowers" is considered the highlight.

Arrive around one. Family crowds, good vibe. Young people handing out toilet paper for porta-potties, and condoms (for later?), with ads on the packaging. Also, Bible pamphlets from fundamentalist churches. Most of them dumped in the gutters. Viewers stand for hours in the sun, smiling, chatting. Some beer, lots of water.

The scope: five-six hours, several miles, thousands of participants. Vivid colors, smiles, music that vibrates through your body, dancing, floats. Fast pace. No lags. Fire-eaters, jugglers on stilts, beautiful women swiveling in provocative get-ups, near-nudity. Gorilla suits, masks, feathers, floating balloon animals, transvestites playing to the crowd, sequins flashing in the sun, big skirts, headdresses, movement.

Most unusual participants: small men covered in mud, eating mud.

A red carnation, thrown by a gorgeous girl on a float, hits me in the head. Battle of the flowers?

On and on. Street vignettes poke fun at evil and powerful. Not PC—Middle Easterners, Castro, Osama, Bush as a devil with a penis gun (no boos though). Cesar Chavez (not a fave here) and a Latin version of Hitler, with a placard advertising an optician. (I swear I hear people say, "Hi Hitler!" instead of "Heil Hitler.") No comment.

Eventually get doused in puma, a flour mixture. A mess! Also pose for a camera which turns out to be a water pistol. Afraid I'll turn into a doughboy! But I feel safe and exhilarated and stay till the end. A spectacular parade.

Sunday

Didn't sleep much last night as street music goes on until 4 am. Sounds as if outside my window, but no one there. Early breakfast of empanadas, steak with onions, watermelon and coffee in the hotel patio, by a fountain. Beats my usual wheat toast and tea.

At the airport, get frisked twice, put through two machines and my goods get sniffed carefully, including sealed coffee. The lady ahead of me carrying on a five-foot feather headdress, much admired, and also sniffed. Funny.

So those are the notes.

Lorry said she'd never seen anything like the parade. According to her, Mardi Gras in New Orleans celebrates decadence, and this was a much larger, more joyful celebration of local culture.

Now good travel buddies, we planned to visit a great carnival every four years: Venice, Trinidad, Rio, of course. That would have gotten us to 2020.

Lorry died unexpectedly a couple of years after Barranquilla, only in her forties. I never went to another Pre-Lenten celebration, and I think of her every February, when they begin again.

COSTA RICA

Water, Water Everywhere

*P*ura Vida—"the good life"—is the phrase associated with Costa Rica. I remember deserted beaches framed by volcanic mountains, monkeys swinging in orchid-draped trees along lava-encrusted trails, and waterfalls big and small, gushing and trickling. But, most of all, I see a river winding through banana plantations.

I was on a five-day press trip, and we had come to the river from San Jose, the country's compact capital with its pretty concert hall. We chugged along on a train that wrapped in and out of forests where low-level clouds hung through sweet cedar and hanging moss.

I had rafted a few times before—in Colorado and West Virginia in rapids up to Level 4 out of 5. But these Costa Rican river rapids were mostly Level 2 and 3, so I anticipated a relaxing afternoon, with a picnic and champagne at the end.

Our group divided into three rafts of six, each led by a guide. Ours, Miguel, had recently piloted a well-known American congressman on this river, so I figured he was used to foibles and attitudes, and could lead us on a good ride.

One of our group, Jane, had never rafted before. In fact, she couldn't swim. "This better be worth it," she said, gripping her lifejacket as she settled into the raft.

We paddled in sync, instructed by Miguel. The day was languid, and the rhythm of our oars felt soothing. Toucans and macaws flew by. The air was clean and hot.

A few minutes along we were jolted by the first rapids, but even Jane felt exhilarated after we passed them, and returned to calm water.

This went on for a few minutes: moving slowly ahead and then rolling a bit in frothy rapids, sliding around smooth rocks.

And then I turned back toward the roar of rushing water. Whoa! I could feel water rising in huge waves under the raft, and we started losing our direction, spinning around. Was it a dam opening? A flash flood? A tsunami?

"Do what I say," Miguel shouted. "Or we'll drown?" asked a fellow paddler. Miguel said nothing, which I figured was an answer.

"Stroke left." I dug deep. "Stroke right." The other side dug. "Backpaddle!" And around we went, fighting the watery swirls to move ahead, stay afloat. Our oars flashed and scooped, flashed and scooped.

Suddenly in the raft ahead three people popped into the rushing water around hidden rocks. We maneuvered over and tried to fish them out, but they were going under again. Miguel had told us to point our toes downriver if we fell out of the raft, but the volume of water made it impossible to point anywhere. They were spinning.

It took several minutes to haul one of the victims into our raft. The term "drowned rat" came to mind. She didn't look us in the eyes, and crumpled up, dripping and shivering.

The other raft eventually rescued the other two dislodged writers and we managed to paddle to shore.

We never found out what caused the water to rise so fast—a first according to Miguel. When the van picked us up, I gifted Miguel with all my Beatles tapes, and he played them all the way back to San Jose. We sang "Yellow Submarine" with special verve.

And Jane, the reluctant newbie in our raft, said it all: "If that's rafting on Level 2 water, I'm never coming near a river with a Level 5!"

CROATIA

Victor/Victoria/Lea

When I stepped onto the gangplank of the Westerdaam about twenty summers ago, chartering a cruise was one of the few ways the LGBTQ community could let it all hang out.

I was invited along on this all-gay cruise, for what reason I am still not sure, but the itinerary included ports in Italy, Croatia, Greece and Malta, an offer I couldn't refuse whatever my sexual orientation.

As I boarded the ship, I was expecting the normal polite nod from the formally dressed cruise director. But a man in a sleeveless tee and flowered shorts air-kissed me on each cheek and announced, "Hi there, *gorrrr-geous!*"

This was going to be fun.

We embarked from Rome with about two thousand gay men, a sprinkling of lesbians and two straight passengers: my friend Lois and me. Of course, everybody assumed we were a couple. Not that there's anything wrong with that, as Seinfeld would say.

So rather than trying to explain hundreds of times that we were straight travel companions, Lois and I went along with it.

It was confusing: I had suddenly become a closeted straight, judged sexually (and wrongly) as gay, by men who were often closeted and/or judged wrongly themselves, as straight, outside of this ship.

At the safety drill, the boxy life jackets were deemed "so '80s" and too orange. And the cheeky questions! Who would go first into the lifeboats, tops or bottoms? Could we bring at least a few products with us? And could one bear be placed in each lifeboat to do the rowing? (You probably know that "bears" are big, hairy gays; tops and bottoms you can figure.)

When the ship docked in Dubrovnik and other destinations and we swarmed into the sunny ports, I noticed cruisers from nearby ships staring at our thousands of openly affectionate males. And the pointed fingers often came from pretty weird-looking folks. (Remember, this was a time of different attitudes. What a difference a few decades make.)

Onboard entertainment included a D-list comedian named "Ant," who bitched constantly. But the hit of the cruise was a singer/comedienne from Chicago named Amy, who reminded me of Bette Midler in her early bathhouse days in the East Village. Amy could sing a beautiful "Imagine," but her most requested song was "Pussy, Just a Friendly Little Cat."

Theme parties on deck started late and ended early in the morning. Leather Night was filled with the smell of rawhide and Paco Rabanne, and the sound of cracking whips. Every appendage—and then some—appeared strapped and bound.

At Gods and Goddesses Night, my diffident English tablemates emerged after dinner as barefoot deities, wearing only thongs and fig leaves, with wreathes atop. I complimented them on their butts, and they, true gentlemen, were genuinely flattered and politely returned the compliment, though my derriere remained (mostly) covered throughout the cruise.

The true Victor/Victoria moment was the masked ball. Some guys had purchased masks in Venice, some brought handmade ones from home. Identities were now even more confusing. I knew that Lois—tall, short-haired and wearing a black pantsuit—was really a straight woman, but even I started to perceive her as a lesbian disguised as a masked man.

I danced with her, in the spotlight by the pool, masked in a pink feathery thing, embracing the inadvertent confusion, and for the moment not sure of who she or I, or anyone else, was. And I didn't care at all. I felt free and me.

It was one of those perfect moments, when sea and sky merged and the earth tilted just a bit, mostly to the left.

My gender-bender cruise was the happiest I ever experienced.

Nothing could be better than being a straight woman at sea among thousands of gay men. Age is irrelevant if you have some wit and a good haircut. And looks don't count as long as you don't wear polyester.

CUBA

Ribbons of Rice and An Unforgettable Woman

My motto is "keep moving." With nature and politics in flux, you take a chance by waiting to travel where you really want to go. Over the past fifty years I missed visiting many special places, including the now war-torn antiquities of Iraq and Syria; the Khyber Pass in Afghanistan; the Yangtze River *before* the Three Gorges Dam; Iran—all by putting them off too long.

Despite new government regulations, Cuba is still worth seeking out and visiting now. This isolated post-Communist island country with a throbbing heart may be only a 45-minute flight from Miami, but for Americans it's hard to find a more politically different destination anywhere in the world. Impressions that linger from my trip in 2015:

■ During "The Special Period" in the early 1990s with the U.S. embargo and the break from the former Soviet Union, Cubans came close to starving. The limited, homegrown diet still reflects that situation. Dinners are a varia-

tion of vegetable soup, beans, rice, chicken and pork, seafood. Flan or fruit for dessert. Good local beer, rum drinks and strong coffee help wash down smallish portions. Cuisine is not the strong point of a Cuba trip.

■ Ribbons of rice take up half the space of many country roads, alternating so cars have to line up one at a time and drive on the other side when the rice changes sides. Cubans have become self-sufficient organic gardeners since the early 1990s, when food was scarce, and now there is not enough space to dry it.

■ The main reason colorful, restored old cars are everywhere is that no new ones arrived after the embargo. They are the most obvious retro items. When I visited there were no ATMs, a complex currency without credit cards, minimal air-con, and horse carts driven on the main roads next to huge trucks. Not a Marriott or Hilton in sight, no Big Macs or KFCs, no Ikeas or Starbucks. Mostly government-run businesses with emerging *particulars* (privately run rooms) and *paladars* (privately run restaurants). Life focuses on music and the arts, and the pace of a previous century.

■ People are curious and friendly. English is a second language for many. Children smile easily. Cubans seem able to differentiate between people and governments.

■ Guns are outlawed, muggings are practically nonexistent—even pickpocketing is rare. That may change when goods once again start to flow and Cuba becomes more privatized, and Cubans become more material-minded.

■ Tipping isn't the current custom. "Gifts" such as shampoo, pens, toothpaste, small toys and such are still in short supply in this long-struggling economy.

- Because wireless is spotty, you'll wean yourself away from devices while you're there. It feels good, and maybe life without constant connection will stick a bit when you return.

- The architecture is more European than Caribbean, even in its dirty, crumbling state. The buildings that are repainted and restored seem somehow less authentic.

- Ernest Hemingway's former home north of Havana brings him to life: hunting trophies, his typewriter, pencil lines on the walls where he marked his weight next to a doctor's scale, leather boots and WWII correspondent uniforms, pets' tombstones, the pool where he used to swim afternoon laps. And his wood-trimmed fishing boat.

- History as interpreted at the Guantanamo museum about the Bay of Pigs is backwards from the way Americans see it: The United States is the villain, Cuba is the hero. It comes as no surprise, but is still an odd reality. You find that around the world, and it changes the way you look at things. History is subjective.

✳

A lean, middle-aged woman stands at a rest stop in the Cuban countryside. We tourists queue to use the basic restroom, and as we finish doing our business the woman takes a bucket of water drawn from a spigot, goes into the vacated stall, flushes the water down the toilet and cleans up the area.

In between cleanings she speaks in rapid Spanish to those of us waiting in line. She smiles sometimes, and we catch phrases and recognize that she is proud that her daughter is a doctor, and her son, a professor.

The woman does this all day, most days: cleaning the toilet, mingling with tourists and pocketing a few tips to augment the $20 or so she receives a month.

She is formidable and intelligent, making the most of her situation, with dignity. And she is unforgettable.

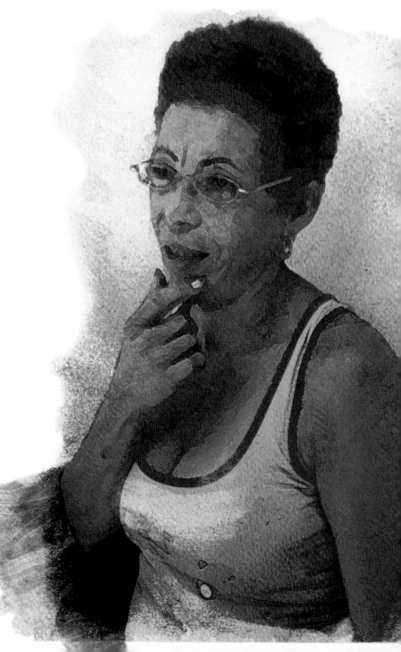

CURAÇAO

Rebbitzin of a Snoa

Ninety miles north of Venezuela, Curaçao is an island with dozens of cove beaches and offshore coral reefs rich with marine life. On one dive in murky water stirred up by a rainstorm, I lost sight of my diving buddy for a minute or so. I realized then that I was too nervous to depend on my instincts, and decided to stick with snorkeling.

But I remember the island for a very different reason, as well.

The capital, Willemstad, is known for its iconic Queen Emma Bridge and brightly colored Dutch Colonial architecture. But one of its less-known treasures is the seventeenth-century Mikve Israel-Emanuel, the oldest surviving synagogue in the Americas. The Jewish community dates from the 1650s, when Sephardic Jews from Spain and Portugal arrived, and later, Jews from the Netherlands and Brazil.

Locals call Mikve Israel-Emanuel a *snoa*, short for *esnoga*, the old Portuguese and Ladino word for synagogue. When I first heard that word, I thought it sounded silly.

The vaulted ceilings in the Curaçao snoa are similar to those in the grand Portuguese synagogue in Amsterdam, built when Judaism flourished in the Netherlands. The sand floors remind congregants of how their ancestors had to cover the floors of their prayer houses so that their footsteps would be muffled during the time of the Inquisition.

The building resonates with pathos and history, but being a Jew who rarely went to services or prayed, try as I might, when I visited that ancient building I could not feel the spirituality within. I considered myself a modern, secular woman who embraced all religions and atheism as well. Nature was what called to me in a spiritual way. The redwood forests were my cathedral of choice. You get the gist.

Soon after, much to my surprise, I married a rabbi.

Yes, this long-divorced, non-observant lady became the rabbi's wife at a temple in New York, and soon attended Sabbath services every Friday night.

And sometimes, just for fun, I'd introduce myself as a "the rebbitzin of a *snoa*," and people would not know what I was talking about, and giggle. And I'd tell about my visit to Curaçao, and standing in Mikve Israel-Emanuel, a place I will always recall for an unusual reason indeed.

CYPRUS

Ancient Shards

Cyprus is a "golden-green leaf thrown into the sea" and a land of "wild weather and volcanoes," in the words of the Greek Cypriot poet Leonidas Malenis. Settled for more than ten millennia, the island stands at a crossroads between Europe and Asia. Generations of conquerors, pilgrims, and travelers have influenced its main cities—the capital of Nicosia, Limassol, Famagusta and Paphos.

In 1971, I was in my twenties, and my husband and I were cruising on a Turkish ship from Israel to Turkey, via Cyprus. The itinerary was so fascinating we didn't mind that we were traveling in third-class. *(See: Israel.)*

We walked along a beach with soft waves lapping the shoreline for miles into the hazy pink distance of a Cyprus morning. The wonder of it—a coastline this serene with no buildings in sight, as far as I could see.

I thought of Miami Beach, where I had grown up, lined with hotels, the beaches mostly cut off from public access. Perhaps someday this stretch of Cyprus sand might be crowded with buildings and tourists. But at this moment the beauty was all ours.

I stood there so long ago, probably in the polka-dotted wash-and-wear dress that has shown up in so many photos of my earliest trips. We were walking in the scrub beyond the empty beach, and suddenly I felt something hard under my foot.

I looked down and then picked up a shard of pottery.

"Watch your step," the guide said. "Sharp things like that are right under the sand."

I held the shard up. "What *is* this?"

"Something very old." And he turned and led us on along a path.

"Very old." It was probably the oldest man-made thing I had ever held in my hands. I turned it around. Maybe thousands of years old. Cyprus, after all, is the home of Aphrodite, the ancient Greek goddess of love.

I was tempted to put the shard in the little purse I wore across my chest. I justified to myself that no one would probably want or even care about this piece of clay, otherwise it would have been picked up already. Its evidence under my foot was proof enough that it wasn't even as valuable as a pretty shell.

I looked at my young husband, who had been silently watching me. He was a rule-follower. I admired that about him.

I did not tell him my thoughts, but I suddenly felt that it was wrong to take this piece with me. I believed in right and wrong, too. It would have felt as if I were stealing a treasure, even if it wasn't one.

I dropped the piece where I found it, pushing it a bit under the sand among the beach grass, and caught up with the others.

I wonder now, fifty years later, about that beach, and if it's become overcrowded and touristic. And I wonder if the shard remains, or is now ground up under a nightclub or highway. Or if it's in someone's collection.

Thirty years later, divorced ten years from that husband who stood with me on the beach, I was traveling to Egypt with the man I was living with in Washington, D.C.—a different kind of man than my ex. We wandered near a construction site in Alexandria and found a bunch of terra-cotta shards in a pile of rubble. One had a circular handle that looked like it had been on a cup.

My companion picked it up and placed it in his pocket, without a word. I thought about saying something, but then figured it would probably be destroyed anyway. And maybe it wasn't even that old.

We took the shard back to the hotel and didn't think about it until we were flying home. My companion placed it is his underwear, just in case, and I laughed about it.

The cup handle is now on my coffee table, an artifact of my past relationship with the man. I never found out if it is ancient or not, because I didn't want to know. When I look at it now it not only brings back a memory, it reminds me of how I've changed through the years.

And I'm not sure how I feel about that.

CZECH REPUBLIC

Hot and Cold, and a Lot of Bull

Soon after the Velvet Revolution, when Czechoslovakia peacefully split into the Czech Republic and Slovakia, Prague became the darling of backpackers, and its streets thronged with tourists. "The City of a Hundred Spires," spared destruction countless times, seemed perhaps the fairy-tale capital of all Europe.

I enjoyed walking in Prague: over the pedestrian Charles Bridge, completed in 1402 and lined with statues of Catholic saints; around the Old Town Square; and by Baroque buildings, Gothic churches and the medieval astronomical clock, with its animated show on the hour.

My favorite space was tucked in a corner of the ground floor of Prague's Municipal House, a supreme example of Art Nouveau architecture. The room was a former confectionery, still unchanged after fifty years when I peeked inside it in 1993, and I was overcome by its preserved perfection. Dusty and closed off, it would reawaken after a long sleep, and has since become what some call the most beautiful Art Nouveau restaurant in the world.

My hotel room, however, was not as perfect, a quirky reminder of the shoddy buildings of the Soviet era. Two faucets stated "cold." A bit of a crapshoot when I washed up, half awake.

✳

I had just taken a pleasant train ride back to Prague from Karlovy Vary (Carlsbad), the charming spa town in the Czech Republic popular for its thermal springs since the nineteenth century. Filled with canals, cobblestones, fantasy turrets and lacy pavilions, this mountain resort still reflects an interest in nature and wellness that has thrived for hundreds of years.

And now my son Rand, who had been traveling in Europe, had come to visit me. Over beers in a dark Prague café he told me about his just completed experience at the Spanish Festival of San Fermin in Pamplona, Spain—that once-a-year, once-in-a-lifetime rite of passage—running with the bulls.

"I don't get it," I said. "I'm just glad you didn't get gored." We toasted with amber glasses of Pilsner.

"Well…," he answered, averting his eyes.

He looked and sounded fine, all in one piece. And then he told his story.

It seems that, costumed in traditional all white, with a red sash and red kerchief, he had completed the run without a scratch, although the half-dozen bulls running along had gored two locals and trampled twenty others.

Feeling lucky, he decided to again test fate and keep going until the run's end point, Pamplona's giant Plaza de Toros, where three small, fast bulls were let loose to wreak havoc on anyone in the way, for the amusement of 20,000 spectators.

"A few people were knocked unconscious," he said, casually. "But there's a five-foot-high outer wall, and most guys knew to jump up and over when a bull came looking for trouble."

One bull, however, figured this out, and used his head to crunch people against the wall, about ten feet from where my son was standing. And then he looked at Rand, who had to decide whether to use the wall to avoid him—or run away. And for some reason my son chose to sprint.

As the bull bore down upon Rand, he said that he felt forty thousand eyes watching him flee like a silent-film character. Then suddenly he was on the ground, and the crowd roared. Rand had run directly into a castrated steer that had been dispatched to calm the bull down.

And when the bull finally got distracted, Rand got up and found his chance to escape behind the wall.

Back in the café, he rolled up his sleeve to show me his badly bruised arm from bumping into the bystander steer. "It doesn't hurt now," he assured me. "It should be better in a month or so."

"I know running with the bulls was crazy," he added. "But I just had to. You can understand that."

And the thing is, I did.

DENMARK

Shucking, Slurping— and Melting

Tivoli Gardens, the old-fashioned amusement park in the heart of Copenhagen, sparkles at night when the buildings are outlined in lights. Near the city, at the house of Isak Dinesen, who wrote *Out of Africa*, I read the letters she saved from her lover, played in the movie by Robert Redford in his prime. Dinesen's house is close to the great Louisiana Museum of Modern Art—which has nothing to do with the state, which confuses everybody. And, of course, I visited Hamlet's supposed castle, Kronborg in Elsinore, even though most of us know it's a phony connection. These are things tourists know to seek out.

A lesser-known pleasure is the Wadden Sea on Denmark's west coast, the greatest continuous tidal flats system on earth, and home to migratory birds and seals. The invasive Pacific oyster is destroying the delicate ecosystem here, and the most delicious solution is to consume them.

With gloves and a knife at the ready, I joined a bunch of other hunters, scouring the bank for the bad-boy bivalves. In water lapping at my waist, we snapped open oysters as we found them, shucking and slurping in eco-conscious gluttony. Then

someone popped open a bottle of champagne, and we sipped as well as slurped.

After an hour in a rising tide, sated with oysters and champagne, we returned to reality. We had helped the environment in the most decadent way possible, and I had enjoyed one of my most memorable lunches.

I did not travel to Greenland, the world's largest island and a Danish territory, just to see the Midnight Sun or Northern Lights. And not because I could fly-fish, whale-watch, dive, hike, photograph sunsets or ride snowy hills behind an Inuit driver and racing dogs (although I was fortunate to experience many of these things).

I went to bear witness.

In February 2008, I cruised near 70 degrees latitude south in Antarctica. And that April, eager to explore the polar-opposite region, I traveled to Greenland, 70 degrees latitude *north*, 250 kilometers above the Arctic Circle. (Friends said I became "bipolar.")

I flew via Copenhagan (you can fly from Iceland in the summer months) to the coastal air hub of Kangerlussuaq on the west coast of the island. From there you can drive to a remnant of the Ice Age, the southern edge of an ice sheet fourteen times the size of England, containing ten percent of the world's total reserves of fresh water.

It was melting heavily when I was there, but not even close to July 2019, when Greenland's ice sheet lost almost two hundred billon tons of ice—the equivalent of eighty million Olympic pools.

Greenland is over two million kilometers in area but claims only about sixty thousand citizens, most of native Inuit or Danish heritage, sprinkled about in tiny, colorful hamlets along the coasts.

Roads are rare outside of settled areas, so vehicles mostly include small planes, helicopters, fishing boats and dog sledges. I boarded a cherry-red Dash 7 turboprop airliner and headed for Nuuk, Greenland's capital city. We taxied from the little airport straight to a lunch of cold-water cod and shrimp.

At the open-air market, whale meat and seal meat are displayed in all their bloody reality, legally hunted and carefully regulated. I sampled raw whale blubber, chewy, with a not-unpleasant flavor of hazelnuts touched by the sea. Veggies are few, and to make up for vitamin deficiencies, locals traditionally eat raw seal liver.

I decided to forgo that taste sensation.

Central Nuuk offers a cathedral built in 1846, a capital building with muraled chambers, and the National Museum. The Cultural Center houses a thriving art scene, theater, workshops and café—a light-filled, Danish-designed space for all.

Nuuk seemed a livable town despite the harsh weather, and at my comfortable hotel I dined on musk-ox, which does *not* taste like chicken. Meals throughout my visit included Greenlandic coffee drinks, but my favorite fiery concoction was called "Northern Lights."

On a two-hour flight up the coast to Ilulissat, Greenland's third-largest town, I gazed down at thousands of icebergs that looked like white polka dots on blue velvet, shed from glaciers and formed from compacted snow that fell perhaps fifteen thousand years ago.

The town's six thousand residents live in Lego-like, multicolor houses perched against ice-flecked waters. Working dogs sleep in special outdoor areas, ready to get going.

Dog sledging is the best way to explore Greenland's towns and terrain during most of the year. So suited up in rented sealskin, after a brief orientation (basically, "Hold on!"), I sped behind a fan of fifteen Greenlandic dogs, reclining on a blanket on the narrow sledge, clasping a thin rope.

I often closed my eyes as the dogs pulled me up and down endless, ice-covered hills with the Inuit driver steering and—too infrequently—braking as we coursed over glistening snowfields in and around nearby Aallaniarfik. (Bet someone that they can properly pronounce that word. You will win.)

Then on to the Ilulissat icefjord, where the fastest moving glacier in the world also produces the most ice—twenty million tons a day. But the glacier has retreated tremendously since I was there.

You can hike to the edge of the fjord, or hop onto a fishing boat for hire in the picturesque harbor, to sail into Disko Bay. We floated past icebergs as big as islands. Openings in some seemed to tempt our little red fishing boat to sail through (we didn't), and our boat crunched over ice the size of cars.

Aqua water outlined bulky bergs below the surface (seven-eighths submerged), and small, clear bits—frozen rain trapped maybe thousands of years ago and now freed—floated like crystals. Some of this ice slowly drifts far south, in the path of ships like the Titanic, before finally melting back into the sea.

At Oqaatusut, a still-inhabited whaling outpost, I walked gingerly from the boat onto frozen Rodebay Harbor, checked out a dozen or so old settlement buildings and patted a few Greenlandic dogs, before lunching on smoked whale meat and brown bread.

Fishermen warned that temperatures around Greenland have warmed several degrees in their lifetimes, drastically changing fishing patterns, and Ilulissat Harbor now rarely freezes over.

The melt has become drastically worse since my trip. As a witness to increasingly fragile ice shelves, ice caps, glaciers and icebergs near both of our poles, I can't help being humbled, frightened—and more vigilant. We *must* heed the warnings.

DOMINICA

The Professor of Empathy

South of Guadeloupe and north of Martinique in the Eastern Caribbean, Dominica is far enough from the U.S. mainland to not yet be inundated with tourists. I was looking forward to the beauty of natural hot springs and tropical volcanic peaks, waterfalls, streams and rainforests. Our four-masted clipper ship docked at Dominica's capital, Roseau, near colorful timber houses and botanic gardens.

After my divorce in the 1980s I was single for over twenty years, on and off. I traveled solo much of the time. But not always. Thus, my remembrance of Dominica is not of diving, whale watching or canyoning adventures. I remember a jerk.

My edgy companion and I considered lazing on the island's black sand at Mero Beach, or maybe spending a day at Morne Trois Pitons National Park. I was eager to experience the Boiling Lake, heated by a volcano.

But I realized we needed less heat and fewer boiling points. So we chose a bamboo raft ride along a narrow, winding river fringed with tropical foliage. I sought calm after being cooped up

with this professor of philosophy, whom I had been seeing for a few months.

My companion seemed a brilliant eccentric on land, but became a hostile kook when sharing a tiny cabin. He lectured around the world and wrote books about empathy. Except that he had none. Professor Non-Empathy sulked and demanded and fumed and complained. He insulted the crew and insulted me. He was late, grumpy, grungy—and gassy.

The quickest way to learn about people is to travel with them, and the very best way to do that is to cruise. You're stuck with each other—and what can take months to figure out on land can emerge in a couple of nights at sea, especially if the toilet clogs or the waters get rough.

When we got back to Miami, we didn't even share a cab to our homes. Who knows how much time I would have wasted with him if it hadn't been for that cruise to Dominica?

DOMINICAN REPUBLIC

The Columbuses and Give and Take

Christopher Columbus' brother Bartholomew founded Santo Domingo, the oldest European city in the Americas and the capital of Spain's first colony in this part of the world. From this base, Spain managed conquests of Mexico, Puerto Rico, Cuba, Guatemala, Peru, Florida, Colombia and Jamaica.

The private home of the first governor of the colony, Diego Columbus—Christopher's son—is an exceptional example of classic Spanish-colonial architecture, and the Columbuses also built a customs house, a hospital, a cathedral, a university and a library.

Christopher Columbus' crypt is in the cathedral here. Except that Seville, Spain, claims to have his remains, too. I've visited both cathedrals, and have no idea who is correct or if they are someplace else entirely. I just know that the Columbus family sailed across the Atlantic, discovered this place, and called it home.

⁂

I admired a small painting while browsing through an open-air show in Santo Domingo. The artist sold it to me, and then we talked for several minutes about art and creativity and island life and our families.

As I was about to move on, he said, "Wait," and reached behind his table. "This painting is torn, so I can't sell it."

The very top of the large canvas was peeling, but the bottom part was perfect, an expressionistic market scene painted in bold primary colors.

"I haven't fixed the painting for months," he shrugged. "I think you could make it work." And he placed it in my hands.

He was right. I had a framer trim the top, and the bright, happy painting now hangs without any obvious flaws over my desk. When I admire it, I think about the Dominican artist, and the smile on his face when I accepted his generous gift. Small moments like that in my travels through the years are the most cherished of all.

In 2016, a ship named Fathom was branded for "voluntourism," the new hybrid of having fun and doing good as you travel. Cruisers would be spending big bucks to cruise from Miami to the

Dominican Republic, helping out for most of their vacation, to better the country in-between playing trivia and cards and lounging around the pool.

A group of us were sent down to preview this idealistic experiment. Cruisers could choose among three programs: teaching English to school children, helping to process clean drinking water, or assisting local businesses.

We stayed in Puerto Plata, near the new port where Fathom would be docking. We learned a bit about each program, visiting a school, attending lectures and hanging out at a small chocolate factory.

As the upcoming cruisers would, we also had some downtime, and were entertained by local dancers in traditional costumes, visited a farm and climbed to the top of a fort overlooking the Atlantic.

The cruise line was excited about this new wave of do-good tourism. But, alas, Fathom failed almost immediately. Caribbean cruisers seemed to prefer fun in the sun, period, and weren't willing to pay to volunteer, at least in this form, at this place, at this time.

Whether this kind of voluntourism will work in the future is still a question, but travelers can find other ways to give back. For example, websites offer carbon-reducing projects, an easy way to effectively fight climate change. Carbon-mitigation projects across the globe include planting trees in Africa and India, putting up wind turbines in Costa Rica and creating cleaner cookstoves for use in China.

Voluntourism will continue to develop, no doubt, as our earth struggles to survive. But for now, in the Dominican Republic I have received a painting from a generous artist. Far more than I have given back.

ECUADOR

God in the Galapagos

When we married late in life, my second husband, a congregational rabbi in Westchester County, New York, had accrued two three-month sabbaticals, so we had time to travel together to places where he had never been, in what we didn't realize would be the last three-and-a-half years of his life.

I would research and coordinate the travels, and then write about the experience. He would ask questions, amuse me in ways naughty and nice and carry my bags, so to speak. In our short time together, we flew out of New York to visit the Grand Canyon, the Amalfi Coast, Rome and Bruges. We enjoyed tulips in Holland and fruit beers in Brussels.

We traveled to the Isle of Skye in Scotland and to Miami and Sarasota, and to Berlin and Leipzig, where he got to hear a recital on the harpsichord that his idol Johann Sebastian Bach had played himself. We revisited London, where, not knowing each other, we had both lived with different spouses at about the same time.

Chaim would relax and absorb things like a precocious kid; he hadn't had the chance to travel much in years past because of his rabbinical duties, and he was loving the opportunity to experience the world with me.

Because he wrote much of the liturgy for the reform movement of Judaism, when he intro-

duced himself people would often recognize his name from the prayer books, and then keep asking him all the profound, unanswerable questions they could think of: "Does prayer work?" "Is being Jewish a culture or religion?" "What is God?"

It got so distracting that on a couple of trips he used an alias (George) and a fantasy occupation: He'd say he was a sports agent!

We booked a trip to the Galapagos Islands, off the coast of Ecuador, and chose the smallest boat possible, holding about twenty people. We figured that way the odds were that no one would know him and we could relax in the isolated island chain that Darwin studied in his *On the Origin of the Species*, enjoying the giant tortoises and blue-footed boobies, pink flamingos and red Sally Lightfoot crabs.

And when we learned that only seven others had signed up, Chaim decided that he wouldn't even need to become George, the sports agent.

When we walked onto the boat's deck for the first time, we were handed a glass of Chilean red wine as we introduced ourselves to fellow passengers. The last to come aboard was John. He paused after the introduction.

We held our breath. We squeezed each other's hand. Would we be able to crack jokes and hang out by ourselves among the marine iguanas, or would Chaim have to be on best behavior, looking neat and answering Talmudic questions?

The moment, blessedly, passed. We spent days swimming among sea lions and penguins, rays and sharks, and stepping gingerly among nursing seals. An albatross couple performed a mating dance like Fred and Ginger, and we met Lonesome George, the last of the giant tortoises, who, soon after, lumbered over the Rainbow Bridge.

But then, about halfway through the cruise, in the bobbing little boat in the middle of the Pa-

cific off the Ecuadorian coast, John showed a dangerous gleam in his eye that we recognized immediately.

"I hate to bother you, Chaim, but I've been holding off on a question that has nothing to do with the Galapagos, but I can't wait any longer…"

Damn!

EGYPT

Sketches and Palms

I spent a month in Egypt researching a guidebook in the 1990s, visiting sites throughout much of the ancient country. Some of the world's greatest antiquities are here, but my impressions are both glorious and dismal.

Cairo. The city sprawls low and wide, neighborhood to neighborhood, millions upon millions. Gated mansions and leafy, exclusive streets run along the Nile, and high-rises and hotels mix among vast slums.

Horns honk in a cacophony composed by frustrated Cairo drivers. Vendors sell tissue on the dusty streets for drivers who blow their noses and wipe their sweaty faces, then toss the tissues out the windows. The snotty papers swirl like huge snowflakes as cars pass on the hot pavement.

The neighborhood called City of the Dead is piled with rubbish. A synagogue is empty, with an old Jewish man guarding the entrance.

The Seven Ancient Wonders of the World were compiled by Philon of Byzantium in 200 B.C.—essentially a travel guide for his fellow Athenians. These were the Lighthouse of Alexandria, the Temple of Artemis, the Statue of Zeus, the Colossus of Rhodes, the Hanging Gardens of Babylon, and the Mausoleum of Halicarnassus. The only one that remains is the Pyramids at Giza. Today, hawking and tourism surround the pyramids just outside of Cairo. Within a pyramid, in a close, crowded space, we climb at an angle like crabs to a stark tomb on the apex, then turn back after a minute, dreading the crawl back down.

Luxor. Obelisks covered in hieroglyphics tower like a stone forest, ancient even when Romans in togas stood before them. Awestruck visitors—kings, generals, emperors and their retinue—have come here for millennia, the original tourists.

A few of these obelisks now grace traffic circles and parks the world over. Monuments like the one in Washington D.C., emulate and amplify the shape.

Egypt's dynastic royalty lies silently in caves amid splendors collected for their time in the underworld. Beyond the ruins and the riverboats, farmers plant on the green ribbon between the desert and the Nile. And beggars hide in the shadows.

Alexandria. A ghost library filled with the knowledge of the ancients looms in imagination where the sea now washes. What could we have learned had that repository not been destroyed? What information will never be retrieved? *(And what future treasures will be lost after the seas wash over the coasts, as temperatures rise?)*

Art Deco buildings curve along the Alexandria waterfront, and date palms soar by King Farouk's former palace. The fat playboy, last of the kings, was renowned for having romances with movie stars when I was a child.

※

The Red Sea. I am on a strange, stressful drive for a couple of days on a narrow road along the Red Sea. Parts of the scenery remind me of Big Sur along the California coast. The driver is a young military man who leaves the car's main headlights off as he speeds through the dusty evening.

I have long wanted to snorkel among the unique fish here, but the driver has a girlfriend waiting, and bullies me to skip the adventure. I sense danger and reluctantly comply.

He is frightening me. When I ask to stop at a gas station for a toilet break, he does not listen, and I am forced to pee near the side of the car, in the desert, with him facing away. When I return to the rental car company, I complain, but they do not seem to care.

※

"Are you from California? I have a cousin in California." These are common lines preceding a request for money: *baksheesh*, tips. I hear this even from the guards in the Egyptian museum when I ask a question about a mummy.

I walk alone, and am besieged by a group of boys who grab my arms and insist I let them hoist me over a curb that I could easily step over by myself. I seem to have no option. There is a need for them to make work, to survive, and pressure for me to comply.

A dignified older gentleman in a suit and tie says something softly to the boys that makes them scatter. He walks me fifty feet or so to the steps of my hotel, and bows. At last I have found someone who is not scrambling for money. I thank him and offer my handshake.

He extends his hand as well, palm up.

FINLAND

The Mole in the Sauna

I was on a press trip in Finland in the dead of winter with five other American travel writers and one Finnish reporter who wrote features for Helsinki's leading paper. The trip was led by a tough public relations rep who lived in New York. Leena looked more like a Russian than a Scandinavian; not surprising, as Finland is tucked between those two areas, even though it is often grouped with Denmark, Norway and Sweden.

The Finnish language is unique and most comparable to Hungarian. (I remember only *"oli kiltte"* (please) and *"kiitos"* (thank you). Our press group couldn't read any signs, which made us dependent on Leena to translate, so we followed her along like shivering ducklings.

Days were spent at double-speed, as press trips tend to be. You sample things from morning through night—experiencing in a week what would normally take a couple of weeks or so.

I do remember riding a rogue reindeer named Rudolph in a race around a ring. I also steered a dogsled over snowy fields and snowmobiled with Lapps, who talked on cell phones. This was back in the early 1990s, before these basic, not-yet-smart phones were popular in the States.

We hung out on lakes, ice fishing, but really drinking beer the whole time because no fish was stupid enough to wake up in frigid water and nibble. Later, in smoky tents with our Lapp hosts we ate smoked reindeer (the slowest of the ones we raced?) with tart red cloudberries.

I wanted to tango, as I knew the otherwise standoffish Finns are tangophiles, happily locking knees and dipping in sexy Argentine moves, but we were too busy waiting hours for a fish to bite on a frozen lake.

And then there was the sauna.

The typical Finnish sauna, as small as a closet and cedar-lined, is found in most hotels and homes around Scandinavia. Placed somewhere near water, this dry-heat box or cabin is where you sit and sweat out toxins.

In the real deal you get naked and thrash yourself with birch sticks so that your blood gets circulating, and then plunge into a cool pool, or an icy lake if you happen to be in the Finnish countryside, as I was. Some choose to immediately return into the heat and repeat, sweat, and rinse until they are satisfied or exhausted—or faint.

The Finns pronounce it SA-oo-na, and it's as much a ritual in Finland as churchgoing is in the Bible Belt. Part of the obsession is the health aspect, and part is the communal aspect of sweating and letting it all hang out with other naked people. There's something bonding about that, I'm told.

Leena was obsessed with saunas, and bossy. "We will be going to the sauna before dinner," she would shout. "And I mean *everybody.*"

The first night in Helsinki I sat in the sauna, as instructed, sweating away, avoiding a glance at the naughty parts of my fellow writers, which would often slip out from the towels we draped over ourselves in a pathetic attempt to remain semi-clothed.

Men were in another sauna, although there was talk of mixing, but that was thankfully nixed by Leena. Unlike public relations people, travel writers are not a particularly pretty bunch.

The Finnish reporter, sitting in her towel among us, was friendly and full of questions. Throughout the trip she took lots of notes. I took some, too, but I never wanted to see another cloudberry or reindeer. And I especially never wanted to feel the claustrophobic heat of another sauna.

A couple of weeks after we returned to the States, another writer from the trip called and announced that our Finnish press trip compatriot was not a travel writer at all, but an *investigative* reporter.

Sure enough, she had written a front-page piece in the Helsinki paper about how the Finnish Tourist Board had wasted millions of dollars on press trips over the years, where drunken writers guzzled beer and ate themselves silly, and then sat in saunas grousing about the heat.

Luckily, there were no photos!

To an outsider, that's what a press trip may look like: hedonistic gluttony. You don't see us checking on notes, pounding out articles in the early morning to stay on deadline for very little payment. Losing luggage, jetlagged, missing husbands and cats. (I know, tiny violins.)

What was troubling was that when I looked at those untranslatable Finnish words in the newspaper article, every so often I would see *my* name, with long quotes after it.

What had I said? Why was I quoted so often? Was I woozy from the heat of the sauna and the beer? Did I gossip about Leena and complain?

I called Leena but she wouldn't tell me what was in the article. Her voice got quiet, she changed the subject and left it at that. And, to tell the truth, I didn't want to know.

So, I never translated the article. Let it be. I might have been quoted saying, "I hate saunas

and I'm getting bored by this cold, reindeer-filled country with unpronounceable words." Or maybe, "I've never seen such healthy people as the Finns. I admire their love of saunas." Or, maybe, "This is the ugliest group of naked people I have ever seen."

I haven't stepped into a sauna since.

FRANCE

The Righteous Village

Many memories. Short trips and long with friends (but never long enough). Press trips. River cruises on the Seine, Rhone and Saone. Family trips with parents, husbands, children and grandchildren. Hotel openings. Even trysts in Paris in my glory days.

On my first visit to Paris, in 1965, I stayed under the eaves of a small hotel on a side street on the Right Bank. On some visits I stayed deluxe—at the Bristol and historic Meurice. And in the last ten years, I chose annual stays at the charming little St. Paul Rive Gauche near the Luxembourg Gardens.

I drove with my young husband throughout the French countryside in an MGB roadster, like Audrey Hepburn and Albert Finney did in *Two for the Road.* (Their chemistry—they were lovers as they filmed—wafted through the screen like Chanel No. 5. Ours, I remember, was more like Ivory soap and water.)

I remember joy in Paris the day Macron was elected, when the French high-fived with me in a café, relieved that moderation had won out. And at the historic restaurant Polidor on the Left Bank, the setting for Hemingway and Dali and all those creative types in *Midnight in Paris,* toasting a new year with a group of Israelis at a communal table.

In June 2019, Bill and I drove with my son Cary and his Significant Other to visit the trenches of the Somme and the beaches of the D-Day landing in Normandy, on the 75th anniversary.

Cary doesn't remember, but when he was a baby I had climbed up and down hundreds of steps of the nearby monastery at Mont St. Michel, maneuvering him in a stroller. Almost fifty years later, to get to the top, he'd probably have to maneuver me in a chair. But I'd go.

✳

But all is not perfect, even in France. Bill and I once booked a hotel room in a provincial town after reading a couple of glowing reviews online. The proprietress, a talkative woman with a tangle of blond hair and heavily accented English, met us at the car and helped us unload our luggage. She led us into a store on the town's main shopping street, with her sculptures displayed in the window.

It turned out that the musty store was our room, with a bed and a small bathroom in the back. This "hotel" had three "rooms" in total. When I mentioned that it seemed to be a rather odd B&B situation, the owner shouted. "No, Madame, this is *not* a B&B. This is … the smallest hotel in France!"

The one storefront window just let in light and there was no air-con, so in the morning we had

to open the door to the main street to get some air. Window shoppers admiring the sculptures would come in inquire about the artwork while we were going about our private business.

One man rushed into the shop/room several times while I was in various states of undress, yelling, "I can't find my wife!" We later found out she was upstairs with the proprietress, drinking wine.

I could laugh about this experience, except that this was the most expensive stay of our trip, including at my favorite hotel in Paris.

We had paid in full ahead of time, and, as there was no reception area, we just left the keys in the store/room and escaped.

Driving away, we got a call. "Bonjour! You still owe $10 tax!"

Too few reviews? Lesson learned.

AIMEZ-VOUS LES UNS LES AUTRES

※

Bill and I had an extra day to spend in Lyon, and when I looked at a map I noticed that Le Chambon Sur Lignon, a rural village on a plateau in the western foothills of the French Alps, was just seventy-five miles southwest.

My son Cary had curated an exhibit about the town at the Kupferberg Holocaust Center in New York, called "Conspiracy of Goodness: How French Protestants Rescued Thousands of Jews During WWII."

In 1940, days after Nazi Germany's invasion of France and the establishment of the Demarcation Line separating Northern Occupied France from unoccupied Vichy France, the pastor of Le Chambon rallied the villagers to action: "We will resist without fear, without pride, and without hatred."

The parishioners of Le Chambon took this measure to heart, welcoming Jewish refugees—mainly children—into their homes, educating them in their public schools and hiding them from periodic raids.

Here and in the surrounding villages, residents joined together to conceal, rescue and provide false documentation for Jews and French Resistance fighters, at great risk to their own lives, saving 3,500 from Nazi Germany and the soldiers of Vichy France.

Perhaps they offered sanctuary and kindness to refugees in part because Huguenots (French Calvinists) had lived under oppression themselves and were targets of religious persecution for hundreds of years.

Their actions have been noted at the U.S. Holocaust Museum, and the entire community was awarded the Medal of the Righteous, Israel's highest civilian honor for the largest act of communal righteousness during World War II.

Bill and I wanted to visit the town, and we drove about an hour-and-a-half from Lyon, on a highway for half the time and then onto winding roads, increasingly rural: cows munched languidly, mountains fringed the plateau, and tiny villages popped up every so often.

Le Chambon looks much the same as it did in the photos from the 1940s. The two obvious reminders of the war years are a small modern war museum on a side road and a 400-year-old Protestant church across the road called The Temple. The Bible verse engraved over the church's doorway is "Aimez-Vous Les Uns Les Autres"—Love One Another.

Museum exhibits focused on the inspiration and leadership of Pastors André Trocmé and Edouard Theis, who led the townspeople in this Haute-Loire region.

After the museum, we lunched at a small restaurant filled with regulars. An older man with his dog came by to say hello. He would have been a young man during the war. He had kept the secret.

We were the only non-locals, and the table next to us was occupied by a group of older women, who were young during the war, and no doubt a part of the righteous community. Did they play with the hidden children? When we got up to leave, they smiled at us, and as we left, one called out, "God bless you." And we were not surprised.

※

If the Eiffel Tower is France's spirit, Notre Dame has been France's soul. The first image of Lord Kenneth Clark's famed British series *Civilisation* was Notre Dame. "I'm not sure how to define civilization," he said, standing in front of the cathedral, "but I'm looking at it now."

From my favorite hotel on the Left Bank I could easily walk to Notre Dame—gray and grand by day, luminous at night. One rainy twilight I brought a friend who had never been to Paris, and we took photos of the light-washed stone facade reflected in the puddles.

I enjoyed visiting the gigantic north Rose window on sunny days, when colors streamed into the cathedral like multiple rainbows, and I remember an extraordinary Christmas concert under Notre Dame's glowing stained glass, with voices soaring high into the Gothic arches.

Before the 2019 fire, tourists visited the spiritual citadel towering above the Seine more than any other of the many masterpieces of Paris.

Like Shakespeare's works, or the music of Bach, Notre Dame represents humanity's ability to create beauty. Even more, it is a symbol of collaborative art.

And now it reminds us hauntingly that our own beautiful works, along with earth itself, are precious and fragile.

GERMANY

Back to the Future

As I write this, Germany is a beacon of democracy, welcoming refugees more than almost any other country. But I first traveled there when bombed-out sites remained throughout Europe, and the country was still recovering from World War II, just coming to terms with the horrors that had been exposed.

In Frankfurt I visited the area where my grandmother had grown up before she came to America at seventeen, on her own, to escape an arranged marriage

in the late 1800s. Before there even was an Ellis Island, she arrived at Castle Clinton across New York Harbor.

Grandma wanted me to take a photo of the street in Frankfurt where she had grown up so long ago. But the area had been bombed to rubble during World War II, and a parking lot was now on the site. When I got home, I said I didn't have time to find the block. And she pretended to believe me.

In 1965—only twenty years after Adolph Hitler died in his Berlin bunker—I visited the town of Berchtesgaden, and the house where Hitler met heads of state, Eagles Nest, high in the Bavarian Alps. Newsreels show him cavorting with his mistress, Eva Braun, patting his dog and greeting emissaries on a terrace surrounded by mountains that seemed a backdrop from a Wagnerian opera.

Hubby and I rode the same outdoor elevator—furnished in brass, mirror and leather—that British Prime Minister Neville Chamberlain had taken when he arrived for talks. Maybe the prime minister was lulled by the lush setting before appeasing the dictator. Hitler, we were told, disliked using the elevator. He worried that its mechanism would attract lightning.

The place was called "Kehlsteinhaus," and we saw no sign, brochure or guide mentioning Hitler's name. Germans were having trouble facing their immediate past.

On that trip in 1965, the concentration camp at Dachau had just reopened as a museum. Locals filed in front of the displays and photos, shaking their heads as if none of what was documented could be true.

Years later, on a trip to Munich, I would visit nearby Buchenwald. My handyman, Walter, in Westchester County, New York, a non-Jewish Pole, had been imprisoned there as a young man, and had escaped through a hole in the barbed wire. Living in trees during the day and walking through the night, he eventually joined the Allied forces and was sitting on top of an American tank as they liberated the camp.

Walter was matter-of-fact and understated, and never complained about his past troubles. I would offer him a scotch and an occasional dinner and TV show after, when he worked for me. One evening, while watching The History Channel, the screen showed a photo of a cruel woman known throughout history as "The Bitch of Buchenwald."

Walter said calmly, "I remember that woman. Mean as hell, but good-looking."

It seems that fifty years later, Germans and prisoners alike faced the past in their own ways.

※

Short takes of Germany, in no particular order: In 1970 my husband and I picked up a car in Stuttgart with our kids in tow, and drove it to London, where we lived for a year in Hampstead Garden Suburb. As we passed though ancient towns along the Moselle, my young son commented on the buildings made of "sideways trees with no leaves." I still think of that phrase when I see timbered houses.

On that same trip, I took my toddler son in with me to the ladies' room in a train station. When an occupant left a stall, she opened the door for us to enter, and a woman official ran over and insisted I pay the equivalent of a few cents to use it. I made hand gestures to say I didn't have any change with me. She pulled me aside and blocked the door to the stall with my crying son inside. We tussled and I ran out with him. I brought back a man with an important-looking cap, who entered the ladies' room to bring the woman out, and he came back defeated, with his cap askew.

Later, walking with my husband and two sons, I saw the woman walking in the station. Away from the toilet stall she looked like a sweet little old lady. Without much thought, still furious, I went up to her and yelled in her ear, "NAZI!"

A smile crossed her face. And I realized that she must have taken it as a compliment.

※

Germany is repurposing its past in Berlin. In the decadence of a 1920s-style cabaret scene with a transvestite chorus in a restored café. In the ferocious remembrances at the stark, chilling Jewish Museum. In remnants of the Wall, once separating East and West Berlin, now considered by some a brutal work of art.

I felt the shock of past and present in 1995 as I viewed the Reichstag—the German House of Parliament—burned down by the Nazis when Hitler's government took over, later bombed by the Allies and redesigned by British architect Norman Foster. When I was there, the artist Cristo had wrapped it in silver fabric for two weeks, and it looked like a giant aluminum packet.

Repurposing is all around. On a round-trip Spree River boat ride from the Hauptbahnhof pier in the city's historic center, I passed a restaurant inside a repurposed railroad storage facility that juts over the river. And I glided by the Tränenpalast (Palace of Tears), where for years East Germans parted from their Western visitors at the Friedrichstrasse station border crossing.

Berghain, a converted power plant in the formerly Communist east, is the venue for week-long techno-music raves. At the end of the day you can sleep in the Titanic Deluxe Berlin, a landmarked nineteenth-century building that once housed the costumes of the Berlin State Opera.

Past and present together, into the future. Things change.

✳

Erfurt, in what had been Eastern Germany, is where Martin Luther had lived and preached. It was 1995, I was traveling solo on a segment of a three-month trip to Russia, Scandinavia and Germany, researching for a guidebook. I was staring at a Max Ernst painting when a man introduced himself as the director of a European travel show doing a shoot on the museum. He said that he was delighted to see a solo American tourist and would like to create a segment around me, on the spot.

I was skeptical, of course, but then spied the crew. Okay, I thought, it beats going back to the room and writing a hotel review. So, all day long I explored the city, followed around by camera and sound people. They patted my face with powder, and interviewed me and we all ended up at a merry dinner at a medieval castle.

That evening I thought about the joys of solo travel. I've traveled with lovely people, but also with duds: an ex's cousin who bossed me around like I was her child; my doctor's receptionist, who drank from daybreak to bedtime; a young tenant who had never before traveled overseas, and who wouldn't eat anything but clear soup and bread.

There was the woman who was supposed to be my assistant driver and navigator as I drove through Eastern Europe reviewing hotels. I should have guessed there would be trouble when she got to the airport and took the last upgrade on the plane, leaving me in a middle-coach seat. She emptied the minibar, skipped the bills, and let me know at the last minute that she couldn't drive our stick-shift, and didn't read maps.

That serendipitous day in Erfurt convinced me once again that traveling alone isn't just a different way to travel. It can be the best way.

GREECE

Ancient Wonders, Stingy Friends, Hotel Stories

An Athenian lady with a dog walked me blocks out of her way rather than just give directions. A woman I laughed with on a ferry invited me to stay in her inn for free (I didn't care for the room, but assume she meant well). I did accept the invitation of my (reputable) guide to enjoy coffee and honeyed pastries with his grandmother, who toured me around her house and garden, and showed me family photos.

I love Greece.

In the 1990s I was writing guidebook updates on the Greek Islands, and I found that of the more than 300 isles, I especially favor less-visited ones: Alonnisos, with its haunting hilltop town. White-washed, craggy Skyros. Kimolos, greenest of the Cyclides ("my heaven," as locals say). Paros and its fishing boats. Tiny Koufonisia, with tavernas on alleys by the sea.

And then there's little Chios, closer to Turkey than the Greek mainland. I loved the black-and-white stenciled buildings in the village of Pyrgi. But the magical thing about the island is a precious, gooey resin called mastic, found in local evergreens.

Ancients referred to mastic as the "balm of Gilead." And locals still use it in creams to heal wounds, powder for irritable bowels and ulcers, smoke to ease asthma, soap to clean. They chew it as gum, drink it as coffee or liqueur, and eat it with cereal, pasta, tomato sauce, eggplant sauce, olive oil, salt, and jams.

When Chios was governed by the Republic of Genoa, thieves who stole ten pounds of it would lose an ear. More than two hundred pounds, and they'd be hanged. But the product has become even more precious, and may be life-saving. The mastic of Chios is in clinical trial in the United States for vision problems, stroke and Alzheimer's. Pharmaceutical companies are watching.

And I still have an old pack of mastic gum somewhere in the back of a drawer!

On one research trip, a perfect month in May, two men kept me company in Greece, each for two-week segments, and neither knew about the other. The first was a British friend who wanted benefits; the second, a boyfriend upon whom I bestowed them.

The Brit named Brian lived in New York. I forgot what he did for a living but it must have been lucrative, because he sailed a vintage wooden boat and flew a Cessna. Brian was easy on the eyes but not on the ears, as he bragged more than a bit, untypical for an Englishman. I was not smitten, yet he agreed to help me out with research, so we decided to travel together, as friends.

We split bills for hotels, food, tolls and gas for our rental car. He made reservations and kept records, and at first, things worked fine. In Mykonos, we visited clubs and lingered by the row of 16th-century windmills on a hill above town. In Crete we hiked the Samaria Gorge, visited the Bronze Age settlement of Knossos, and wandered alleyways in the harbor town of Chania.

According to Greek myth, Zeus—god of the sky, lightning and thunder, and king of the gods on Mount Olympus—was born in a cave on Crete. When Prometheus gave fire to humanity, Zeus got mad at him for being so generous. He chained him to a rock and had an eagle eat Prometheus' liver every day for eternity.

On Crete I found out that stingy Brian, although no Greek god and without access to an ea-

gle, could certainly begrudge me. And when he realized early on that—yes, indeed—we were going to remain "only friends," he got cheaper and meaner. He booked rented rooms by ferry ports with saggy twin beds and scurrying six-legged critters on and below them.

By the end of the two weeks, Brian argued for hostels with bunks, and obsessed about splitting gum, stiffing me whenever possible—but only in the money sense.

I was delighted when Brian packed his duffle bag for the final time, although he left me footing the bill for the last night in a seedy Athens inn. What he didn't realize, and what I was gleeful about, was that in the airport he might have passed right by the next guy who was coming to be with me.

I can visualize their yin and yang: one, a horny, miserly Cessna-flying British wannabe lover—tall and gray-haired—passing a short, funny Jewish suitor who was about to whisk me off to the finest hotel in Athens. Yes, as parsimonious as the first guy was, the second was the opposite. We dined that first night on our elegant balcony overlooking the Parthenon, and he hired a driver to take us on our research trips.

This still-early relationship would eventually fade, but at this moment—after Lord Cheapo—it bloomed as beautifully as the wildflowers in the Greek isles. And to this day, whenever I think of an eagle, I think of skinflint Brian.

Lodging also played a big part two years later, when I revised those chapters on the Greek Islands. (This time no men.)

I waited until the last minute to book a hotel on the island of Limnos because I figured I would easily find a room. But I wasn't aware that I had arrived a week before hotels were opening for the season. After calling around, I found one hotel that was willing to let me be the sole occupant besides the maids and skeleton crew.

I slept well, breakfasted on yogurt, honey and walnuts in the hotel's huge, empty stainless-steel kitchen, and let myself in at night. At times I felt I was in *The Shining,* but without Jack Nicolson around the corner and with the blue Aegean beyond.

I will never forget that place, and although I have stayed in far better lodgings, never before or since have I run around hotel halls in my bra and panties singing Tom Petty songs as loud as I wanted.

GRENADA

Adopted

The Caribbean island of Grenada, with swaying palms and starry skies, is often confused with Granada, the city in southern Spain. The island is *Gren-ay-da.* The city in Spain is *Gran-ah-da.* (Let's call the whole thing off?)

I was invited to the island on an independent press trip right after I was separated from my husband, after twenty years of marriage. I was forty-two and this would be my first real solo trip. Unfortunately, I picked the wrong place to spread my wings.

I would eventually travel alone from Antarctica to Zanzibar. But this virgin time I had yet to figure that a Caribbean island in winter is not the best place to be alone unless you don't mind retreating to your room overlooking the dark sea with only the company of a scorpion in your closet.

During the day I lounged by the pool reading a British novel set in the 1930s, and the first evening I gorged on banana pudding and mango ices in bed. The next night, itchy to get out,

I donned big sunglasses to hide behind, and ventured to the just-opened terrace dining room for an early dinner.

I propped up a book about tropical fish (fascinating how some of them manage to puff up), and looking around, realized I was the only person sitting alone—probably on the entire island.

When a passion-fruit drink with an umbrella swizzle appeared, I looked up hoping for a longing gaze across the room. But no, the drink came from the bunch of young people in flowered shirts and flip-flops at a table across from me.

They were a crew, in Grenada for an underwater film shoot. And by the end of the dinner they had adopted me, and throughout the next days I was an "assistant." (Maybe it was the book on fishes that had impressed them.)

And I had a great time.

Similarly, on an Alaska cruise I was adopted by two psychiatrists and learned about borderline personality and manic depression between spotting bald eagles. How she wound up there I'm still not sure, but my niece Erica, traveling solo, hung out with a 91-year-old monk in a Swiss monastery, who challenged her to ping-pong. You never know.

You can find friends. If you get out and smile a bit and look clean and read something interesting, you just might get adopted, if you want to be. Even in a romantic place like Grenada.

GUADELOUPE

Island Reverie

The French overseas territory of Guadeloupe is shaped like a butterfly. Grande-Terre Island, one of the wings, has the softer terrain of beaches, hills and sugarcane fields. Parc National de la Guadeloupe on Basse-Terre Island is on the wild side, with Carbet Falls and La Grande Soufrière volcano.

I enjoyed both wings, maybe because I too am a combination of soft and wild, although the softer side has naturally predominated for many years now.

Sailing on a four-masted schooner, I also visited nearby islands in the southern Caribbean where larger boats can't dock. I was most impressed with Îles des Saintes, or Les Saintes, the dependency islands of Guadeloupe's coral-rich waters and palm-lined bays. The language, the food, the attitude: I felt as if I were in France, but with tradewinds.

※

Like Les Saintes, small islands can provide powerful memories.

At the phosphorescent bay on Vieques island, near Puerto Rico, the stars above seem to fall into the water. I flew there on a small plane from a resort community called Palmas del Mar, in Puerto Rico. Charles Fraser, the developer of Hilton Head, Amelia Island and Kiawah Island, had read my first travel piece in a magazine, almost fifty years ago, and invited me to visit the resort.

On little Montserrat, in the Caribbean, locals speak with an Irish brogue. With a strong sense of Irish heritage, Montserrat is also the only country outside of Ireland where St. Patrick's Day is a public holiday. My guide there, who sounded as if he were from Dublin, taught Sting to windsurf; and, yes, when he proudly played a Sting song for me, he smiled when he heard his name mentioned in it. (Elton John also recorded music in Montserrat, but I see him more surfing channels than wind.)

I remember the craggy mountains, dense forests and remote beaches of Corsica, the French island in the Med where Napoleon was born. And the nearby Italian island of Elba, not far away in the Tyrrhenian Sea, where he was exiled for a year.

And then there are the archipelagos, clusters of delight: The green San Juan Islands, outside of Seattle, green in gray mist. Sunny ferrying though the Finnish archipelago. The Thousand Islands in northern New York State near Canada, where the rich of the Gilded Age built summer homes on private islets to escape the heat. In Nicaragua, too, hundreds of houses built as getaways on tiny lush islands.

I remember Flintstone-looking granite boulders tumbled on the beaches in the Seychelles, with huge turtles camouflaged in the crevices. Also in the Indian Ocean, the clear waters of the Maldives, where I snorkeled in late-afternoon light. And in Southeast Asia, the pretty, mainly undiscovered Philippine Islands, including the Palawan archipelago of nearly 2,000 islands. Here there are secret lagoons and one of the longest underground rivers in the world, five miles through karsts and natural rock formations. As beautiful as the islands off Thailand's coast, but less crowded.

On and on, in reverie. The outer islands of Malta, the varied isles of Greece and Madagascar. The Pearl Islands of Panama. The Galapagos. Others I can return to. More than enough to remember sweetly for the rest of my days.

GUATEMALA

Fragile Beauty

Guatemala, just south of Mexico, is perceived right now as a country of crime and poverty, with heartbreaking photos and stories of Guatemalan parents and children seeking asylum

in the United States. A potentially top-level travel destination, it has struggled to break away from the stigma of "Banana Republic" shared by some of its Central American neighbors. *(See: Honduras.)*

I spent weeks there in the early 1990s, reviewing hotels for a travel-agent publication. The government was iffy then as well, but I went about my business solo and safe, discovering new foods, practicing Spanish with shopkeepers, impressed by the land, the culture and the people.

I was overwhelmed by one of the largest Maya cities in the Americas, Tikal, which rivals Machu Picchu *(See: Peru),* with limestone palaces, temples, pyramids and sports complexes. On the altar of Tikal's main plaza, Mayas still burn copal incense, light candles and make flower offerings to their ancestors.

These ancient remains are set in one of the last patches of pristine rainforest, among 300 species of birds, several species of anteaters, and numerous caterpillars. To explore Tikal in the early morning—when animals are most active and visitors are still asleep—I stayed at one of the hotels just outside the park.

Although I did not see a rare jaguar in the night, I felt I had awakened in Eden.

Lake Atitlan covers nearly fifty square miles, with a backdrop of three perfect volcanoes. Beachside villages are easily accessible by boat, and I remember eating traditional sugar cookies on the docks. The stepped pools and waterfalls, caves, underground rivers, orchids and butterflies of Semuc Champey—"sacred water"—are still unknown by most tourists.

At the highlands town of Chichicastenango—Chichi—smoky incense rises from the steps in front of the church of Santo Tomás, as Guatemalans from surrounding villages gather on Thursdays and Sundays to trade in leather, carved wooden masks and textiles. Each village boasts its own traditions, foods, weavings and dress, and vivid fabrics woven by local women now cover pillows on my sofa.

The Maya culture is based on achieving balance and harmony with the universe—people, plants, animals, and even stars. I hope that the country can be inspired by its amazing heritage, and find its way forward and upward.

I returned to Guatemala on a day trip off a cruise in 2019 to revisit Antigua, once the capital of all Central America. I first visited that beautiful city to attend language school, as Spanish spoken here is considered among the best and clearest outside of Spain.

Set at the base of active volcanoes, Antigua was practically destroyed by an earthquake in 1773, and the capital was relocated to Guatemala City. But blocks of Spanish Colonial architecture remain among the best-preserved anywhere. At the main plaza, flowering trees bloom year-round, children play and laugh, and women bring goods to sell to locals and tourists.

Antigua was preparing for its famed Easter celebration when I arrived. During Semana Santa, Holy Week, the streets are covered in handmade carpets, *alfombras,* designed by Guatemalans months before the celebration. Layers of sand are placed on the cobblestoned streets within a 24-hour span, and then covered with multicolored sawdust, pine needles, flowers and such.

On Good Friday, floats with the fourteen Stations of the Cross are hoisted by thousands of purple-hooded devotees and carried along the carpeted streets, sometimes half-a-mile long. The processions walk directly over the alfombras, destroying them as they pass. A cleaning team then sweeps up all signs of the works of art.

The symbolism is beautiful and fragile. And in many ways that sums up Guatemala today.

HOLY SEE

One Degree of Separation

Vatican City, often referred to as the Holy See, the smallest country in the world, is about a third of a square mile, a few buildings and parks in the center of Rome. It has its own government, army and diplomatic missions, but no permanent native population; citizenship is granted only to people who work in the Vatican and its missions abroad.

The Holy see is the universal government of the Catholic Church and operates from Vatican City State, a sovereign, independent territory. The Pope is the ruler of both Vatican City State and the Holy See.

On my first trip to Vatican City, I spied Vicki, a classmate I had not seen since high school in Miami Beach. Seeing her waiting on the stairs to go into the Sistine Chapel, so far from home, I remember pondering the likelihood that we would be in the same place at the same time. And wishing that I had a better haircut.

I've learned since that the world population is about six billion, and yet there are supposedly no more than six degrees of separation among all of us. Guglielmo Marconi, in a 1909 Nobel speech, suggested the number six (well, 5.83) as connecting everyone together in a radio network—long before the Broadway play of that name or spin-off "Six Degrees of Kevin Bacon" game.

Stanley Milgram later measured connectivity in Americans and indeed discovered that only a small number of connections interlink the entire population, especially through hubs and portals like the internet.

All of us have examples of surprising connections, but my favorite began at Heathrow airport, outside of London, in 1984.

I had flown to England with a group of travel journalists, to accompany Richard Branson a few days later on the inaugural flight of his airline, Virgin Air, from London Gatwick to Newark Airport. It was a big deal, and Branson was having us over to his houseboat on a canal and even to his estate in the English countryside.

I was first visiting a friend before going on to the festivities. Queueing for a cab, I began talking with a friendly guy, a graduate student from Texas. We found that we were both going to northwest London, so we decided to share a ride. And to our pleasant surprise, we found that we were both going to Hampstead Garden Suburb.

But we were shocked as we realized that the two of us, strangers from across the Atlantic who had just met while standing in line, were both going to the same little dead-end street with an unforgettable name: Wild Hatch. Wow. What was the chance of such a thing happening with two random people?

And then, to our astonishment—as I gave the address to the driver—we realized that we were going to the very same house!

The friend I was visiting had been my neighbor when I lived in London, and I hadn't seen her since then. She knew I was coming, but her mouth was agape when she saw both the student and me, two people she had known years before but who had no connection, geographic or otherwise, standing together that sunny day at her door.

My friend's daughter was the student's friend, and she knew he was coming. But as she and her mum now lived in separate residences and had lots going on, neither had remembered to mention our planned visits to the other. And when the daughter came to the house, she was just as shocked to see me as her mum was to see the student.

So, we did what the Brits have done for hundreds of years through joys and sorrows. We drank tea and talked about the weather. And when it was time to leave, the student and I bade farewell and drove away in separate cabs to our separate lodgings in London, and I never again saw him, or my friend from London, for that matter.

HONDURAS

Illusions and Blow Darts

Honduras in Central America is one of the most dangerous countries in the world. Beyond the gangs who extort money from working people, corruption extends to ghost teachers who take pay but don't show up, hospitals that provide tainted drugs and inferior medical care, police, the courts and Congress.

But I saw none of this. When you travel in groups you're usually steered to areas where hotels are clean, sites are prepared with tourists in mind, and visitors can leave with a positive impression.

The weather was perfect, and from our limited touristic viewpoint it was a pretty and peaceful place. And on this tour off a ship, it was a pleasant experience.

Should I have stayed on the ship? Did we help the economy? Was it a moral issue? I'm not sure.

✳

The Honduran native show reminded me of another dance experience that wasn't a typical tourist production and that I will never forget.

On a day trip with a press group, hacking our way through vines and ant-infested foliage to visit a tribal village along an Amazon tributary in Peru, word was that a nice lady from Connecticut recently visiting this tribe with a tour group was hit in the hand with a poison blow dart because she hadn't been sufficiently respectful to the chief. (Should she have curtsied? Offered a fist pump? Said "Chief," like you say "Chef"?)

Our group spent quite a while discussing whether this awful poison-dart event could be repeated, but, taking no chances, we agreed that we would be extra-respectful. The male-dominated tribe seemed to notice our deference, as they immediately started beating drums and demanding that we run around a pole in the middle of the hut.

Then they placed a large rodent that looked like a blown-up rat in the hands of one unlucky member of our group, and the rest of us were grateful just to run around the pole as many times as they asked, sans rodent. We were most afraid that

On Roatan, an island off the coast of Honduras, our cruise ship docked in a crescent turquoise bay where musicians in colorful outfits greeted us with local music. I bought a bright geometric painting and a ceramic pot at a harborside shop.

Two-lane roads were edged in purple and red bougainvillea, with open-air restaurants and shops scattered in small villages at the base of the hills. In a straw-roofed pavilion I attended a traditional ceremony with drumming and costumed dancers, then boarded a small boat and floated past a rusting hulk of a ship. The water was especially clear, with many hues of blue, and I realized that I probably should have snorkeled, as the reefs near Honduras are exceptional.

the chief would have us pass it around like a football. And then, what else might he want us to do?

The indigenous group began chanting faster and faster, so we increased our speed, and I became out of breath, running in endless circles around the pole. After several minutes, the man holding the rodent had the sense to gasp a request for us to present our gifts. Thankfully, the chief nodded.

We dug into our backpacks but the tribe did not seem impressed with our assortment of sunglasses, lipsticks, T-shirts and other trinkets. Except for one offering.

The chief himself came forward to acknowledge a man who had brought a present grabbed from his wife's drawer as a joke for the tribe that had everything—a pair of (lightly) used control panties.

The chief looked annoyed. He pulled on the panties like a slingshot. And then, as we waited anxiously for the poison blow dart to possibly appear, he smiled—and put the panties on his head.

After that, the mood changed, and the chief showed off his storage area filled with other gifts left by nervous tourists, including dozens of tees with sayings like "I Love NY." When we left, thankfully unhurt, the Amazonians probably got comfortable in their jeans and tees, joking about our stupidity and bad taste.

HUNGARY

Remembering Nathan

When I visited Hungary, I thought of a woman who had lived there as a teenager. I had worked with her in the early 1980s, ghostwriting her memoir.

Cecile Klein was in her fifties then, fragile and intelligent; a Holocaust survivor finally ready to share her experiences. She had written some narrative and had shown her poems to Elie Weisel, who had encouraged her. She now sought a writer to help her.

For almost a year we spoke and met. I edited her prose and poems, sorted through the remaining pictures of her family, and talked with her for many hours about her early years. We polished three chapters and several poems and sent them to a few editors. Some expressed interest, but some were abrupt: "Too many Holocaust stories coming in right now," one editor wrote back.

Cecile was put off by this and didn't want to face possible rejection, so the project ended, and I lost touch with her. But I never forgot her remarkable story, which started in Hungary. *(See: Poland.)*

When Hitler came to power, Cecile was a sensitive girl living with her sisters and brothers and her widowed mother in the mountains near the border of Czechoslovakia and Hungary. A couple of her siblings moved to Palestine. One brother became politically active and was sent to a concentration camp early on.

As the Nazi menace flared in Hungary, Cecile's young, well-off boyfriend asked her to join his family, who had paid a farmer to hide them. She wanted to be with him, but decided she couldn't leave her mother, and said no.

Not long after, that farmer betrayed her boyfriend's family, and they all disappeared.

Cecile stayed with her mother for months, and then, to hide out more safely, she moved to Budapest with some Catholic friends, slept with a cross over her bed and worked in a dental office. A clever, bold teenager, she'd walk around with an anti-Semitic newspaper to throw the authorities off.

But eventually the police brought the girls to a station and queried them, one by one. Cecile was last, afraid that she had been outed as a Jew by her friends.

But she not only got through the interrogation, she persuaded a policeman to walk her home, figuring they would never again suspect her if she actually wanted to extend time with the Gestapo.

I visited Budapest, where Cecile had hidden as a Catholic, living with her girlfriends. This grand city in the 1990s probably looked much the same as when she survived there in the early 1940s, still emerging from years of Soviet domination.

Unaware of exactly where Cecile had lived, I wandered by the rail station and thought of the Hungarian Jews rounded into transports going east to Poland. And when I visited the main synagogue, still standing, I realized that she would never have entered there, as she had been hiding as a Catholic.

In 1944, time had run out for her. Hungarian Jews were the last to have escaped deportation. Cecile was rounded up, along with her mother, her sister, her brother-in-law and her two-year-old nephew, Nathan.

One of Cecile's poems describes seeing the stars through slats in the cattle car on the transit east. She writes of the darkness, and throwing out the buckets of waste. The stuffy heat and fear of the unknown. The fainting, frightened captives and slivers of sky and clouds above.

When the train stopped at Auschwitz, Cecile's brother-in-law gave away his hidden watch to a worker in stripes, who rushed the Jews out of the train. The man whispered, "Have the old woman hold the little boy! Otherwise, your wife will die along with him."

Cecile's sister didn't hear those dire words, but her mother did, and she pleaded to her older daughter. "Let me have little Nathan. I'll take care

of him. Otherwise they'll assign me to hard labor." Cecile's sister resisted giving up her son, but to save her daughter's life the grandmother took her grandson in her arms, aware that they were soon to die.

Cecile and her family lined up for selection before Dr. Josef Mengele, just beyond the train. Her mother, still holding Nathan, was sent to the left. Her sister cried, but still did not fully understand what would be happening to her son and her mother.

(One day when we were working together, Cecile called me in a strained voice. "Look in *The New York Times Magazine*. The story about Raoul Wallenberg." There, spread across the page, was a rare grainy photo taken by the Nazis, of bewildered people walking on a train platform. The focus was a sweet-faced older woman in a head kerchief, carrying a little boy, sucking his thumb. That woman was Cecile's mother, holding her grandson, hours before their extermination. Cecile had never before seen that photo.)

Although the rest of her family perished, Cecile and her sister managed to stay together at Auschwitz, surviving, day by precious day, through luck, cleverness and support. Sixteen-year-old Cecile volunteered to write love poems for the Jewish leader of her block, to arouse the woman's Nazi guard lover. When the affair ended, the despondent woman cried in her arms, "We're doomed."

At one point, Cecile actually stood at the door of a gas chamber, awaiting certain death. But at the last minute her group traded places with another group, and she was sent away to dig potatoes. She often kept a few of them to supplement the watery soup that barely sustained her and her sister. One day the guard asked the laborers to empty their pockets. Those who had potatoes in their pockets were shot.

Cecile had hidden her potatoes in her cap.

The sisters stayed alive through the degradation, illness and constant danger. Even at the end, after their camp was destroyed and they were liberated, many of the starved victims ate their fill, became ill and died. Cecile had cautioned her famished sister not to gorge on the food provided, and they remained safe.

But the story is even more remarkable. On the train taking them to their freedom, Cecile recognized one of the fellow passengers, the boyfriend who had been betrayed by the farmer and who she assumed was dead. They had both somehow endured Auschwitz, living close to each other in the death camps for months and never knowing it.

They fell in love and married, but returning to a now Communist Hungary, where they encountered anti-Semitism once again. They eventually managed to get to America, but were treated poorly by their sponsors, and lived for a long while on scraps such as beef lungs and wilted vegetables.

Years passed, they raised a family, worked hard and prospered in suburban New York. Her husband lived the American Dream, and put the past behind as much as possible. But when I met Cecile, the sadness in her eyes still reflected the loss of her siblings and her mother and nephew and the relatives and friends who had perished in the Holocaust.

So yes, when I visited Hungary I thought of Cecile's story, of her mother's harrowing sacrifice, and of the millions who perished without having their story told. And I especially remember the millions of children like Nathan, the boy who perished in his grandmother's arms. He was only two.

ICELAND

Outrunning the Volcano

A volcano was rumbling in Iceland, and our travel writer's conference was in danger of being called off. The risk-averse among us—yes, travel writers can be wimpy—cancelled the trip.

Not my husband Bill and I. We decided to take our chances. Volcano reports warned us—on whiteboards in lobbies, and on the car radio (spoken in Icelandic, but we would figure out if there was an eruption soon enough). And then? Run to the coast and hijack a fishing boat? Hide under a desk, as I had in elementary school when we practiced surviving an atomic bomb attack? Hang out in a thermal spring until the ash blew over—*us?* We'd figure something out.

Anyway, despite the possible danger, we decided to stay apprised and continue with plans to sightSee: in Reykjavik, and then drive around the country for a week along the Ring Road.

On the first day in the capital city, we rode a double-decker bus for an overview of the old town, visited the Hallgrímskirkja concrete church, and a bunch of museums, including one dedicated to, of all things, the penis. We atoned that evening by attending a proper choral concert in Harpa, the arts center by the harbor.

sandwich, followed by tomato cake with tomato tea. Fortified with Vitamin C, at Thingvellir National Park we walked in a rift where the continents are shifting, watched Geysir spew right on time, walked along the wet edge of spectacular Gullfoss waterfall, and then ate caramel-tasting bread baked with thermal heat.

The volcano still dormant, we continued forth past grazing horses and rushing rivers along the south shore, to Skogafoss and Seljalandsfoss waterfalls, and walked behind the falls to feel the power of the water.

The wide black sand beaches around Vik were especially beautiful, but the volcano was rumbling. Reports were heating up, and ruins on the road from a previous eruption made us understand how dangerous it could be. Risk-reward, risk-reward. Onward.

❊

The drive reminded me of another dicey car trip near Carlsbad, New Mexico. My first husband and I had detoured in iffy weather to view thousands of bats emerge from the caverns in the evening. But in the middle of nowhere a wind suddenly whipped up so hard that we stopped in the road, and became soaked even though the windows were up.

The blast lasted a minute or so, and to this day I think we were in a tornado, but we didn't realize it until later when we dried off in a motel. As a treat we placed a quarter in a slot by the bed, and had a fifteen-minute mattress massage, which we decided after all was far preferable to dodging bat guano.

❊

But back to the Ring Road. Skaftafell National Park, a green oasis below Vatnajokull glacier (which covered the sputtering volcano), is surrounded by black desert sands, and we paused to

I would have loved to have dived in a dry suit in the cold waters, the only place in the world where you can touch two landmasses—Eurasia and North America. Instead we went whale watching in the harbor, and didn't even see a dolphin.

At the Blue Lagoon, for a few extra bucks, we splurged on a private room, one of only six, which had an indoor pool fed by the springs, so we didn't need to expose our silica-covered bodies. After, in our bathrobes, we lunched at the fancy restaurant overlooking the lagoon, like in an upscale hospital dining room.

The first night on the Ring Road we stayed in a village directly on top of a geothermal area, and the hot water from nearby springs heated both people and plants. At night the sky glowed yellow. Why, I still haven't figured out. It wasn't because of the volcano, although it was still sputtering.

On we went. We enjoyed lunch at a greenhouse consisting of tomato soup with a tomato admire ice chunks on the beach, like diamonds on velvet. At the Jokulsarlon Glacial Lagoon, we took a short boat ride among the icebergs, right where a James Bond movie was filmed.

Langoustines are served fresh off the boats here, and at a charming place called Humarhofnin, we ate a bunch of small claws, not even thinking of the volcano for a few delicious minutes.

Driving got more challenging on a steep gravel shortcut to Egilsstaoir. Eastern Fjord scenery is vast and empty, with towering mountains and quaint fishing villages. At the town of Petra we admired a mineral collection. In summer you can take the boat tour to Papey Island to see the clownish little puffins, the real elves of this magical country.

Things now got more interesting. We were supposed to go to Egilsstaoir-Lake Myvatn. The stark highlands lead to Dettifoss, the most powerful waterfall in Europe (sounds like dental floss—one of the few words I could pronounce). There's also a horseshoe-shaped canyon, and whale watching in Husavik on the Tjornes peninsula, a bird museum in Myvatn, and nearby volcanic formations, pseudo craters and colorful, sulfurous slopes.

We had planned to drive to Gooafoss waterfall, and Akureyri, the capital of the north. In that area we could have seen the plume from the erupting volcano. And we wanted to finish at Sauoarkrokur-Stykkisholmur, the horse-breeding area, to enjoy the beauty of the Icelandic horse, with its extra gait called a tolt. And there was the farmstead at Glaumbar, a great example of old Icelandic architecture. And river rafting, and seal watching.

But … we didn't get to do any of these things. Because those last three days the volcano finally caught up with us. And so did the risk.

In the southeast part of Iceland, we had started to smell sulphur. The air was getting dangerous, as the wind was bringing the poisonous fumes in our direction. And that was enough. We decided to skip the northern area and fly back to Reykjavik.

The volcano sputtered and threatened and occasionally passed gas throughout our stay and in the weeks after, and then calmed again and didn't blow its top. It fired orange, but never spewed red.

In the end, we couldn't outrun the volcano and so we compromised. We wanted to be comfortable and safe above all. We had nothing to prove, and we gave in to the power of nature. And for a treat, in Reykjavik we relaxed and ate as many Icelandic hot dogs as we wanted.

INDIA

Once a Decade, Mummy

I first traveled to India in 1984, with a friend, my senses overwhelmed. Spicy aromas burst from foods. My skin felt misted in humidity. Orange and saffron, turquoise and purple saris swished by at street crossings, and vendors with blankets covered in trinkets and smoking incense sat cross-legged on curbs, yelling of their wares. At a bus stop, a rooster sat atop a girl's head, and crowds passed without notice.

We visited the Taj Mahal in the afternoon, but it was crowded. The next dawn, on my own, I visited again—the silent, calm Taj turning pink to gold in morning light. What a difference. Timing, my friends. Seek to avoid crowds, and go alone if you must.

※

Which reminds me of another trip to India, exactly thirty years later, when I couldn't do much about the crowds.

I was on a cruise with Bill from Dubai to Cape Town, via coastal India and the Arabian Sea. In Mumbai we walked through Gandhi's house in quiet respect. A group of us went to a Bollywood movie and dined at our seat (and left before the movie's big music and dancing scene began. Dumb). And we crashed one of the many weddings we passed along the way, affairs of maybe a thousand guests each, with elaborate food, decorations and dress.

In Goa, to the south, we toured a macadamia packaging factory, where women selected and separated towering piles of nuts while their wide-eyed children played nearby. And we visited Old Goa, the capital in the early days of Portuguese rule.

The Portuguese-Baroque Basilica of Bom Jesus, a UNESCO World Heritage Site, holds the mortal remains of St. Francis Xavier, said to have had miraculous powers of healing. Every ten years, on the anniversary of his death, the cathedral opens a vault and takes out his remains for public viewing.

That must be really something, I thought. Every ten years. Walking to the basilica with our busload of cruisers, I noticed we were swept along with dozens, and then hundreds, and then thousands of others, a stream pouring into a tributary of worshipers that seemed as wide as the Ganges as we pushed toward the church.

Yes, that day in 2014 when we were out touring, by chance was the very anniversary, ten years in coming, that the mummy was displayed!

Our guide shouted through the multitudes, "Meet up here at this first door in twenty minutes," and we kept that in our minds as the crowds got even thicker.

I got disoriented, so for the entire time Bill and I just stood in the place the guide left us, afraid of maybe being left behind in Goa until the next boat came by and we could join a group and get out, hopefully on one of the days in the ten years before the next mummy extraction.

I did take a minute to photograph a girl who was bent at a prayer rail in supplication, her eyes downward, seeking a quiet moment of piety in a sea of chaos.

I stood in the same place until it was time to leave, like a dog on a leash waiting for his person outside a store. Eventually all of the group —although perhaps a couple didn't make it, I'm still not sure to this day—threaded through the throngs and back to the bus.

Later that evening in our stateroom on the ship, after a shower and a meal on the balcony—by ourselves, of course—I looked at my photos and realized that I never did see the mummy, just the mayhem. But I could feel the spirit and the faith of the people who traveled there, all of them making the journey to honor the saint, except probably our clueless busload from the ship.

At least there was my photo of the kneeling Indian girl, taken as I waited by the door. She seemed so pious amid all the frazzled pilgrims and tourists milling around. She would be my spirit animal, my takeaway memory from an overwhelming experience.

And then I looked closer, and noticed that her eyes were not gazing downward in religious supplication. The Indian girl in the cathedral—on the one day in ten years when the mummy was displayed—was texting on her smartphone.

INDONESIA

So You Think It's a Dance?

Tiny example of how things have changed over the years: Flying on an Indonesian airline to Jakarta in 1989, most of the male passengers were smoking, even though the "No Smoking" sign was evident. When I complained to the flight attendant that the cabin was filled with smoke, she said, "Mind your own business," scowled, and walked away.

Another change in this current world? I'm reading that Indonesia plans to move the capital to Borneo before Jakarta sinks into the sea.

✳

On a solo excursion to Borobudur, the towering hill of Buddhas near the royal university town of Yogyakarta, I remained for an hour in a half-covered courtyard where rain gushed into gutters. I had longed to see the famed monument, but instead was trapped by the weather. A man sat nearby, staring ominously, although we never once talked.

When the rain stopped, the religious site was closed. A $20 bill convinced a gatekeeper to take out his heavy iron key, and he let me climb to the very top of the monument, as the sun fell below the horizon. I remember the sound of the wind and the vastness of the earth below. I was surrounded by hundreds of Buddhas in a pink haze, not a living thing near me except birds flying high above. The rain gone, the man from an hour before gone. I felt at peace. One of many moments in my travels when I was grateful to be alone.

✳

My book *Solo Traveler* was published in 2005, not long before Elizabeth Gilbert's cult-inducing phenomenon, *Eat, Pray, Love.* Like her, I wrote about the freedom and joys of traveling alone. Besides selling reasonably well, my book spawned a website, Solo Lady, and besides offering how-to's on eating alone and packing and such, I included a few dozen personal essays, including ones set in Italy, India and Bali. I can't complain.

My experience in Bali could not have been more different from Liz Gilbert's. We both found the place enchanting. But she left with love, and a book influencing a generation of women. And I left with welts.

My boss in DC, who produced some of the first interactive videos ever, had assigned me to overSee: a video shoot for the military, and I was in charge of a cast and crew on location in the Philippines and Thailand. I was exhausted, and, on a much-needed break, flew solo into Bali without a reservation on a moonless night.

To avoid the crowded coast, the cab driver suggested I settle in the center of the island, and drove me a couple of hours to a tiny converted temple overlooking a misty lotus pond.

Awakening early, I found at my door an exquisitely carved offering of fruit on a leaf. The Hindu custom of appeasing the gods meant that these offerings would be placed all around throughout the day.

I became enchanted with the gentle beauty of the people and their ways, and I hired a driver who sped me around the sinuous roads, past hills of green rice paddies and plunging gorges. Among the stops, we visited a temple where women prepared the offerings, each a fragile, temporary work of art.

Nearby we spied a line of people heading toward a clearing, carrying silver vessels atop their heads. A cremation ceremony was in progress, one of many each day on the island, the biggest of them celebrated with food hawked and funeral pyres built high above the crowds. Strangers were welcomed, and the long ceremonies ended with ashes thrown into the sea.

But the cremation before me now seemed as simple and natural as the wind. An old woman had been placed on a bed of branches under a grove of trees, and the mourners were tossing petals until her body was covered in pink, like the ground under a dogwood in late spring.

I stood back on the grass, wearing a traditional black-and-white sarong tied around my waist—a garment given to tourists entering Balinese temples or attending ceremonies. The mourners acknowledged my respectful presence and garb, and beckoned me forward.

And then came moments I will never forget. The wood under the dead body was lighted, and as the flames crackled, I felt sharp, painful sensations, and realized I was standing on a nest of *fire ants*. I hopped away too late, as the insects had already crawled up my legs, biting and stinging as they climbed.

I jumped around, scratching and rubbing myself in a contained frenzy, all the while trying not to disrupt the solemn cremation.

The mourners, confused by my sudden activity, couldn't help turning from the pyre and staring at the sight of a Caucasian woman shaking and wiggling up and down and side to side in some strange ceremonial dance. They seemed to regard my movements as my way of showing respect to the lady going up in smoke, so they continued to watch me intently and with appreciation, as I writhed around, slapping the ants, hopping on one foot, then the other.

I didn't want to embarrass the mourners by screaming obscenities, so I just kept moving and

scratching, hopping and jumping, finally trying to ease the itch by rubbing my legs together, as if I were trying to start a fire, an irony not lost on me, even in my intense pain.

Still unaware I had ants in my pants, the congregants turned back to their smoldering beloved. They must have thought I was one of the weirdest strangers they had ever seen, and that I certainly had an unusual way of paying respect.

Grimacing, hopping and rubbing, I finally stumbled back to the van led by my convulsed driver, his hand covering his grin, while my ill-fitting sarong unraveled around my splotched legs. At last I could remove the damned sarong, scream "F**k!"—and scratch away.

IRELAND

Journaling an Irish Ramble

Journaling is a terrific way to remember your travels, and I was a note-keeper long before I was a professional travel writer. *(See: illustration facing the table of contents.)* The important thing is to write down specific observations and emotions as soon as you can. Until recently you would need pen and paper near you, but today you can keep notes on your smartphone or even dictate.

With freewriting you don't have to be concerned about grammar, punctuation or form, so that you can concentrate on getting your facts and impressions recorded. Even jotting key words is okay. Later you can clean up the words and fill in the secondary details. Especially if you are writing for yourself, you can leave your journal in any shape you want.

In the fall of 2007, I joined a walking tour of western Ireland. The following—sometimes raw, sometimes edited—notes give you info about my trip. They also are a good example of how to capture specifics of a trip without worrying about the specifics of the writing. *(See: Colombia.)*

The first three paragraphs are left as I originally wrote them. The others have been edited, to show how you can develop the writing.

Although there are many useful facts and observations throughout, note how the "voice" and the "tone" and the flow differ in the first section from the rest of the piece.

Arriving at The Ring of Kerry

Flight was just over five hours from NYC, with the wind at our back—an Irish blessing. 6 am. Waited two hours for the pickup, then a couple of hours from Shannon to Glenbeigh on the Ring of Kerry—the SW Irish coast, by the Bay of Dingle—fields shimmering green, towns prosperous and tidy.

Cozy little hotel between the Bay of Dingle and the mountains. A cup of nettle tea in the parlor, a shower, a three-and-a-half-hour (!) doze. Then dinner, meeting my dozen companions, mainly women—ages 30s to 70s—from the US, England, Canada, Belgium, Scotland, Ireland and Germany.

Three of them—one married, two divorced—met on other walking trips and reunite yearly on another. Two guys will be cycling tomorrow and rejoining the group on the last day.

First Walk Near Glenbeigh

A ramble on the beach and through the boggy countryside. My fellow walkers were in better condition and had better equipment, but I managed to complete the seven miles, the last in the soft, steady rain the Irish call "mist." A collie joined us and ate much of my packed lunch, and a bull in a field had his eye on me. At an old inn called The Red Fox, I celebrated my accomplishment with an Irish coffee.

Dawdling in Dingle

The weather this morning was rainy and cool. Typical. I joined an Irish friend and we drove along the winding roads of the peninsula to the town of Dingle. Road signs are only in Gaelic, as a local pol is on a mission to keep the old language. Locals put up signs in English which he takes down, so most tourists get lost and the Dingle shopkeepers are furious.

We visited a humped, stone Celtic chapel from the seventh century, and lunched downtown in a wood-paneled pub. The facades along the main street are brightly colored, similar to the doors of Dublin. Flowers bloom from boxes and Dingle is filled with good restaurants and over fifty pubs, many featuring local music.

Drove back on a typical day of sun, rain, hail and rainbows. The wide valleys roll down to the Atlantic, and cliffs and sheep added to the scene. I figure I walked several miles sightseeing without realizing it—my favorite way of all!

A Solo Walk

Fresh-baked soda bread, mussels, fish and lamb are Irish favorites, but last night we enjoyed melon, beef stew and cream puffs with chocolate sauce and fresh cream; none of that squirted stuff. Walkers eat with gusto and without guilt.

Another on-and-off rain this morning, so I chose to walk on my own into the nearby town and saunter along the wide Atlantic beach. On the other side is the east coast of America, where many Irish arrived during the nineteenth-century potato famine. Autumn colors show in different guises here: orange, fuchsia, yellow gorse, red holly.

The group is hiking for ten miles along a mountain pass. But my body and gut, not my pride, dictate my actions, so a wimpy ramble around Glenbeigh for me, into tiny shops and along the coast, along a river and past a graveyard with a ruined castle above and a sheep field beyond. Around two hours, I'd say. Ended up in a pub, and ordered a pint of Guinness and a local crayfish.

The Skelligs

Five of us taxied to Portmagee on the Ring of Kerry road, and boarded a fisherman's boat to the craggy Skellig Islands. Over an hour on deck in rough waters each way, no life vests—but well worth it. This UNESCO World Heritage Site is rarely publicized, but was a setting in *Star Wars*. The smaller island protects thousands of migratory gannets and puffins nesting in the whitened rocks. Birds screech and wheel overhead, and the air is tangy with ammonia.

The larger Skellig was home to a thirteenth-century monastery with over three hundred worn, uneven steps, until you reach the ruins, with magnificent views of the Kerry coast. This rough walk without rails tested my fear of heights.

I managed the ascent, slow step by step, looking at my feet, but the scary, hurried descent to catch the boat was on my banged butt for some of the way.

We rewarded ourselves with tea and pastries at a harborside bakery before catching the taxi back to the lodge in the late afternoon.

Walks, Drums & Pubs

Today was a "gentle" walk of four miles, with an emphasis on Irish culture. In the morning we visited a ruined stone fort where a German/Irish harpist named Adolph (?) plucked away as we sat in the stone circle built in the sixth century in the midst of farming fields.

Later we walked among the ivy-covered ruins of a fourteenth-century castle, then drove on to the seaside town of Waterville, where Charlie Chaplin once lived.

The ramble today was perfect—out to the end of a peninsula: dunes covered with purple heather and autumn wildflowers. We lingered in a ruined abbey and an old cemetery above the sandy beach, framed with mountains. I found an iridescent mother-of-pearl shell, which I intend to make into a pendant.

We ate our packed lunch as the guide told us some of the long history of Ireland. The day was perfect—cool, and not a cloud. We later toured the house of freedom-fighter Danny O'Connell and then drove to a pub for a lesson on the Irish drum.

After dinner some of us visited another pub near Glenbeigh, and sang along to more Irish music; I now appreciate the difficulty of

the drum. A ruddy-faced Irishman offered to buy me a drink, but I passed. Although I understood only half of what he said, I could tell he was full of Irish blarney.

Lakes, Castles, Pony Jaunts, and Goodbyes

Last day of the walking tour—and I didn't walk. It was cool and my knee hurt. I joined the group canoeing through three lakes leaving from Ross Castle in Killarney. Gorgeous hour and a half. The fisherman guide told tales of how St. Patrick drove the snakes from Ireland.

I opted for a pony cart (called a trap but actually a way out if you don't want to hike) for seven miles through the rugged Gap of Dunloe, carved by ancient glaciers. Fields, waterfalls, stony glacial moraine—I heard my echo from the cliffs.

At dinner we said travelers' goodbyes—"we'll stay in touch"—to ward off the sadness of our ended bond. One nice note: A shy English guy and a sweet German gal were holding hands on the last walk. Off into the Irish mist...

ISRAEL

Desert to Forest, Plane to Ship

My younger brother and sister and I were brought up in a secular household where we displayed a small Christmas tree, even though we were Jewish. But I was a curious girl who wanted to explore my religion, so I attended classes in the nearby reform temple.

The country of Israel had been born only six years after I was, and it felt to me like another younger sibling that needed attention and care. I gave allowance money every week to go toward a tree fund that our class presented to the Israeli government at the end of the year.

When I was in my twenties, I visited Israel for the first time and was amazed at Jerusalem, modern Tel Aviv and the beauty of old Jaffa, with its ancient alleys. Desert and sandy scrub covered most of the country, and I remembered my tree and wondered if it were growing somewhere out there, but there was no way to know. I thought of that question regarding observation and perception: "If a tree falls in a forest and no one hears it, does it make a sound?"

When I returned forty years later, Israel was carpeted in green. All those trees donated by kids in Sunday school had now grown tall, and helped forest the hills. A lesson in patience. And so I planted another evergreen, this time myself, in a grove of baby trees. I dug a hole and placed the tree carefully into the ground, patted the earth around it and watered it lovingly.

Long after I am gone, this tree will stand tall to shade and cool Israel, just as my first tree has. Small plantings do become big forests.

※

On that first visit to Israel in the early 1970s, Husband Numero Uno and I were taking El Al, known for its tight security at a time in the Middle East filled with hijackings. Flying from London to Tel Aviv, attendants announced that all passengers' pockets, purses and carry-ons would be searched onboard for possible weapons before deplaning.

My purse held embarrassing things, including used tissues, business cards I had never thrown out and the remains of gooey, unknown snacks. But one proper Englishwoman's upended purse exposed a couple of butter knives, probably removed

from a high-end restaurant that still used that kind of utensil. The officials grabbed the mini-weaponry from her and held it up with some glee, and she huddled in shame for the rest of the flight.

Her exposure reminded me of the time I was sitting next to a well-dressed Englishwoman on a flight from London to New York who wouldn't even look at me. That is, until the plane dropped precipitously in turbulent air and she grabbed my thigh, and held on tight, screaming with each dip. I had more public affection with her on that flight than I'd had with any man on any plane, ever.

When the turbulence abated, she apologized, retreated to the lavatory to compose herself, and then went back to ignoring me.

✳

On that first trip to Israel, hubby and I booked our first cruise without much research, because of the dreamy itinerary from Haifa to Istanbul. We were shocked when we boarded a soon-to-be-mothballed, decidedly disgusting Turkish ship.

I have cruised many times since then, and have even written a book about cruising. There was nowhere to go but up from this clunker.

Our cabin, a triangle no bigger than a walk-in closet, was at the ship's bow. You could see through the linens, and they were so stained that I went to bed in my coat. I actually didn't sleep, as I heard something that sounded as big as a sailor scurrying in the darkness. And whenever we docked, usually before the sun was up, the cabin shook and the anchor scraped and turned in deafening rattles just beyond the wall.

We suffered in our bed but did attempt to upgrade to the better dining room. A thick chain and a bearded bouncer with crossed arms kept us out at the entrance, and I wouldn't have been surprised if he had brandished a whip if we insisted on entering.

Bathrooms? Public ones, of course. Toilets? Holes in the floor, with the biggest flush in the world visible below us—the sea. When the weather got rough, it became literally hit or miss, and I imagined my obituary: "Young American drowns by falling through toilet into Mediterranean on her first—and only—cruise."

ITALY

Heartbeats

My first trip to Italy, just before graduate school, included the must-sees I had read about since I was a little girl. The Roman Colosseum. Leaning Tower of Pisa. Bridge of Sighs. Michelangelo's David and La Pietà.

My young husband and I were dazzled by everything, from the Forum's tumbled antiquities in the middle of Rome traffic to porcini a thousand times earthier than the pale button mushrooms of my life until then.

We marveled at the perfectly preserved, domed Pantheon, thousands of years old, looking like it was built yesterday. In Murano, one of the Venetian islands, we walked among brightly colored buildings and arched bridges, and glided in a gondola with a man singing "O Sole Mio," a few years before tourist crowds would inundate this timeless land.

We didn't stay in hostels, although that would have been just fine. We were lucky that my husband's immigrant father found success in America, and funded our dreamy stay at a marble palazzo, a former convent with a facade by Michelangelo, a timbered lodge overlooking alpine meadows, and a grand hotel perched on cliffs above the Mediterranean.

I never had it so good.

Dreams don't last, of course. We divorced, and as a single mom for many years, I watched my pennies and curtailed travel until I figured out that I could see the world by writing about it. And that's what I did, traveling again when my children went to high school and my ex could be with them whenever I left.

Grazia Italia! That fairy-tale first odyssey inspired a fairy-tale career. And perhaps Italy, more than any other country, led me to travel the world.

＊

When my older son was entering high school, he expressed an interest in trying out for the football team. Hubby and I, ahead of our time, were worried about him getting banged up. So—surprise—we brought both our sons, thirteen and fifteen, on a cheapo bus trip around Italy just when football practice would be taking place.

We stayed in musty lodgings on the outskirts of towns and budgeted carefully. The boys climbed a dozen bell towers, fed hundreds of pigeons, played bocce with local kids in piazzas, gorged on pasta, risotto, pizza and gelato, and fell stickily into bed each night with big smiles.

Sitting in cafés, sipping wine and people-watching, we toasted our clever proactive investment. And sure enough, Rand skipped football, joined the ski team, and avoided being crunched and tackled.

＊

Which brings to mind another Italian trip with a purpose. I was researching chapters for a guidebook on Sorrento and the Amalfi Coast,

and drove myself in a rented Fiat along all thirty-three miles of narrow, winding cliffside roads to discover the best hotels, restaurants and activities along the route.

Many times I would spot a cute little restaurant and immediately *back up on the Amalfi coast.* It seems idiotic now, but with the traffic roaring around the curves, there was no way to make a U-turn except miles ahead at the next village. I had lots of nerve then, and more than a little luck.

＊

When I traveled to Europe in the 1960s, twenty years after the Marshall Plan, and just before the Vietnam War, Americans were particularly beloved. And in parts of Europe where

Americans liberated the population in wartime, we still are respected today. But bad politics and bad people can ruin things.

Right after 9/11, along with a few others, I was a special guest of Florence, Italy, representing New York City. We were symbols of eight million inhabitants: a deputy mayor, a city worker, a service man, an artist, an actor, and so on. I was "the writer."

Florence flew us in and put us up at a grand hotel on the Arno. We were hosted at the townhouse of the shoe-magnate Ferragamos and driven to the birthplace in Tuscany of Giovanni Verrazzano, the first European to explore the Atlantic coast of North America. The locals were so proud that New York City had named a bridge after him.

The city opened the Pitti Palace at night just for us, and the mayor cried as he said, "We love America. We are you."

That was a moment. They felt our pain. The world no longer feels it. Many feel us a pain. And some even wish us pain.

✳

I woke up in Rome with my heart racing. The hotel recommended a cardiologist, and I taxied to an ancient building by the Borghese Gardens. There was no elevator in sight, so I climbed flight after flight of stairs, huffing and puffing, step by step.

The waiting room was filled with patients breathing with oxygen tubes. I had seen no elevator. Is it common, I wondered, for a heart clinic in Rome to be reached only by stairs? The patients may not have needed oxygen until they arrived at the office.

During my electrocardiogram, connected to a bunch of wires, I gazed up not to fluorescent lights and popcorn ceiling, as I often did in the States, but to a frescoed ceiling from centuries past, painted in pastels with clouds and fat, pink cherubs.

And then a doctor who looked more like George Clooney than Dr. Wexler at home, assured me in sexily accented English that my heart was healthy and I should go back into Rome and treat myself to a *limone gelato.*

I can almost hear those angels on that Roman ceiling singing on high to this day.

✳

Leaving Rome on a Mediterranean cruise, my friend Irene and I stopped at Propriano, Corsica, and hiked in the rocky interior. We disembarked on the island of Elba, where Napoleon had been in exile for ten months, and shopped in glam Portofino.

In gorgeous Cinque Terre on the Ligurian coast south of Genoa, I stayed in the stateroom, finishing a deadline for a writing assignment. I had been there before, and was content to sit on the balcony gazing at villages spilling down the cliffs to the sea.

Irene decided to hike on her own along the popular Via dell'Amore, about a mile of trail winding along rocks overhanging the water, and famous for its kissing statue, and a tunnel covered in declarations of love. I told her it was a just-right walk even if you had no one to smooch.

But she changed her mind and decided to take the Sentiero Azzurro route, spanning the length of *all five villages,* the longest trail in the Cinque Terre. Walking it takes about six hours if you take short breaks, and of course she did, and she wasn't around when the boat was about to leave. And this was before cell phones.

I remembered when I had almost missed a mailboat on the Norwegian coast because I misread the return time and was wandering in the shops. When I heard the ship's warning blast,

I figured I wouldn't make it back by running. I went into fight-or-flight mode, and jumped into the middle of the road and stood in front of the cars coming down the road, and screamed, *"Please get me to the boat. Help!"*

And sure enough, a kind woman told me to get into her car and she sped me to the dock. And truly, the gangplank was slowly going up as I hopped aboard, like in a movie.

Irene's knees hurt for the rest of the trip, but she, too, made it back onboard. It's fun to be independent and stretch yourself. But it's lots better if you keep a timetable and don't miss the boat.

JAMAICA

Breakups

My husband and I traveled on a long weekend to Jamaica in the early 1980s and I remember not-so-hot flashes: dreadlocks, reggae and the smell of ganja (not, unfortunately, the high), rafting on a river, climbing up rocks in a slippery waterfall, hazy mountains in the distance, flowering vines and long Caribbean beaches.

But the hotel restaurant seemed to be running out of fresh food, and if we ordered something that wasn't grown on the island it was "unavailable." Servers gave lots of side-eyes. Crime was talked about in the hotel and the mood seemed dark, despite the sly sense of humor evident in the smallest ways (Jamaican speed bumps are called "sleeping policemen").

We were traveling with another couple. A few years later the man became a big deal and left his wife. I wasn't surprised, as I had heard him yelling at her through the bathroom vent. Soon after that weekend, on our twentieth anniversary, my husband took me out to dinner, gifted me with a little vintage purse, and the evening ended with plans for a divorce.

Jamaica remains a pretty place that holds few pleasant memories for me, and I became aware that you can be heard by others through bathroom vents and thin walls.

*

I remember an even worse short trip a few years later, when Murder Mystery Weekends were popular, loosely scripted plays that took place at theaters, hotels, resorts or even on boats and trains. Actors posed as guests, and one or more would be murdered, depending on the length of the stay and the availability of actors. On the last day guests got together to solve the mystery, and then, joined by the revived corpses, headed off to champagne brunch.

This was a great way to fill hotel rooms and pay minimum wages to amateur and unemployed actors. And guests found a clever way to interact with others before the onslaught of social media.

Offshoots included robberies. I remember a train from the Grand Canyon when outlaws boarded and assessed our goods in snarky ways. "That's a knock-off Rolex." "I don't need your chump change."

It ended with the sheriff saving the day, with the former outlaws now on guitars leading us in sing-alongs of Western tunes.

Anyway, my friend Gretchen produced Murder Mystery weekends in Cincinnati, and one day she called to ask if I'd take part in her event.

"Sure. I'll write about it."

"No, I want you to be *in* it. You'll get murdered."

An offer I couldn't refuse. Accompanied by a beau, I decided to fly to Ohio and take part. Gretchen said my friend could become whichever outlandish character he chose, as he wouldn't be murdered. Based on his wardrobe, he became an English riding instructor, which allowed him to wear his old horsey outfit and tall leather boots, and talk with a posh accent for a whole weekend.

We arrived at the grand old hotel a day before the guests, to learn our parts. I was to be an antique dealer who wore lots of clashing fabrics, which I did anyway, so that wasn't a problem.

At first I was relieved that I didn't have to act much, as I was to be poisoned by a cyanide-laced oyster within minutes of meeting the group on the first night. What I didn't realize, was that a corpse would have to hide in the room for the rest of the weekend. No lazing in the sun. No spa. I couldn't even sit on the balcony.

My companion, who was not to be murdered, could do whatever he wanted, parading around in his jodhpurs saying "Tallyho," and "I say, that was brilliant." His swaggering really pissed me off.

I read chick-lit, ate chocolate kisses and watched reruns of "M*A*S*H" for two days, while he brought me tales of flirty ladies and the mayhem and surprise when the other actors were murdered—one by drowning in the pool after being pushed in wearing a heavy skirt, the other by choking on a chicken bone despite a mock Heimlich maneuver.

To top the lousy weekend off, Gretchen (some friend!) gifted me with a rubber dagger, which caused quite a fuss going through airport security. My companion, who wore his riding outfit on the plane, was convulsed with laughter, and I decided he was a pompous ass, and ended things when we returned home.

JAPAN

All Shook Up

The Tokyo fish market bustles with fishmongers cutting quarter-ton tunas as customers check out stalls laden with octopus, mollusks, salmon, sea urchin and eel. I maneuver around scooters, hand carts and tiny trucks moving massive ice blocks to keep the fish cool. Frogs, sea snails and unidentifiable edibles surround me with the smell of the Pacific. A fascinating, overwhelming experience of everyday life, as I often find in Japan.

✳

Traveling solo on a subway, back in the 1980s, I couldn't read the signs and couldn't understand English spoken by well-meaning commuters. (Language translation apps and GPS were not around throughout most of my travel years.) At rush hour, I squeezed into a subway car nose-to-neck, and wound up riding all around Tokyo because I had no idea where to get off.

A young Japanese woman who had attended college in Boston finally got me to my destination at the Shibuya station. At the crossroads outside, probably the busiest in the world, vehicles in all four directions stopped at the same time, and pedestrians converged around me, scrambling like spilled marbles before the lights changed again. I just moved among them.

When I got to my hotel, I ordered room service sushi, and let a lousy in-room movie put me to sleep. I felt as weary as Bill Murray in *Lost in Translation*.

✳

Japan also offers peace and beauty. I remember with pleasure a rickshaw ride through the rustling and creaking of Kyoto's towering bamboo forest. Buddhist temples fringed with cherry blossoms by a reflective lake. Choreographed tea ceremonies. Awakening on a mat in a *ryokan* to a tea and seaweed breakfast by a garden. Dance movements of pale-faced geishas in Tokyo, and geikos in Kyoto. The spare elegance of low furnishings and single-flower arrangements. The artfulness of parasols displayed in front of a shop.

Eating a traditional *kaiseki* meal, I learned that flowers and leaves adorning the seasonal ingredients represent forests, mountains and islands. My food and tableware contrasted in color, texture, flavor, consistency and shape, just as in nature. In Japan it's about simplicity and details, in just about all things.

And then there's the quirky side. Japanese enjoy anime films and Miss Kitty. And some patronize Maid's Cafés, where ultra-cute young women dress and act as fantasy maids and adorable characters. I was curious and visited a couple of the establishments. One was soothing—*iyashi*—with soft music and voices, and patrons building computer models. But the other was a haven of childhood fantasy, with comfort foods plated with positive messages written in ketchup. A maid placed pastel rabbit ears on a customer's head, and served him a neon-colored drink. Then we all played childhood games and sang silly songs, complete with hand movements.

I felt out of place, but childlike getaways may be a way to wind down from Japan's tough work ethic, strict norms—and busy crossroads! To each his own.

As in many Asian countries, the Japanese wear medical face masks in public to protect themselves and others from germs. I've worn one, and after a few minutes forgot I had it on. When I return to the States and someone coughs in my face, I wish we both were wearing masks, and I now carry them in my backpack, although I haven't used them yet, except in Asia.

Cleanliness, hygiene, propriety and technology meet in Japanese public restrooms. Toilets may offer dozens of options, including a "power deodorizer" function. Many play a flushing music called *otohime*, literally "sound of a princess," to mask embarrassing noises that princesses would never, ever want to make.

The trouble is that if by mistake you push the emergency button (usually red), you'll have someone come get you, which would be the most embarrassing thing of all.

As you travel there's an array of new things to learn, starting with the toilet. Do you pull up or down on the plunger? Is there a foot pedal? A button in the wall? A pull chain overhead? And is the sink automated or does it have a small lever to pull up?

The other extreme, and sometimes the only option in much of the world, is a hole in the ground, and once you figure out how to position yourself, it is, excuse the expression, a piece of cake. I've learned to use non-Western toilets, especially when I'm with a group and they're lined up at the Western-style stalls, and I'm outta there.

The nuts and bolts of life offer a constant intelligence test as you travel. I've felt great pride in having figured out shower fixtures, keys, checking in by computer, thermostat settings, TV remotes, balcony doors, light switches, safes, adapters, pillow choices.

In Dubai, an ATM not only withheld cash, it kept my credit card like a sneaky thief. "Have a nice day" on a screen did not substitute for having no way to pay for anything. (Hours later I managed to cajole a bank to help out.)

Technology can challenge even the sharpest among us, especially when you add a bit of jet lag.

When I visited in the 1980s, my forty-something guide told me that Japanese women her age (my age, at the time) were considered over-the-hill, expected to wear dark kimonos. She lamented that married men could get drunk at dinners with geishas, while wives were expected to stay home with their children and often their parents.

Also, the walls at her home were not only paper-thin, but actually paper. She would book into a "Love Hotel" for privacy, amid ropes and swings and all kinds of paraphernalia.

"I'm jealous of Western women," the guide said. "You can wear what you want, and travel by yourself. You have privacy."

Forty years later, things have modernized in Japan. Social media and feminism have helped open the world to all people. I hope that the guide was caught up in the movement and was able to put away her drab kimono. Norms are better for her daughter, I'm pretty sure.

In 2013 I was sitting at a round table on the top floor of a skyscraper, sipping hot sake and schmoozing with a couple of fellow travel writers, enjoying the late-afternoon panorama of downtown Tokyo through floor-to-ceiling glass. Suddenly the chandelier above my head started tinkling. The scene looked calm outside, but the building began swaying like a ship on a swelling sea, and I felt seasick.

A recorded voice shouted, "Earthquake! Earthquake!" and lots of Japanese words, and kept it up, over and over. None of us knew what to do, except back away from the windows and the chandelier. We huddled in a corner, holding hands for what seemed like an hour but was probably a minute or so. And then, just like that, it was over and everyone who had scurried from the windows went back to work.

We found out later that the strong temblor was centered outside the city, and that because we were in a tall building, we felt it more than people on the ground. In fact, when we told our friends who were out walking, they thought they were just a bit tipsy from too much sake.

JORDAN

Wonder of the World

Petra in Jordan, hidden to the western world from about the fourteenth century until the early nineteenth, takes some effort to get to. I crossed the border from Eilat, Israel, to Aqaba, a popular Red Sea port, then rode a bus for a couple of hours through sandy scrub, passing shepherds with their flocks, as at the times of Jesus and Mohammed.

I could have overnighted in the desert, trekked on a camel or taken a four-wheel drive excursion at Wadi Rum, the Valley of Romans. But I went ahead, stopping only at the mountain village of Wadi Musa, the Valley of Moses.

The choice is then to walk or take a donkey or horse-drawn carriage almost a mile through a narrow canyon. Traders with precious frankincense, myrrh and spices did exactly this, thousands of years before.

I walked slowly in the shade of the canyon, and when it finally widened, there stood the Treasury at Petra, almost 150 feet high, carved into the limestone cliffs. As I walked into antiquity, the rock carvings and tombs turned reddish in the late-afternoon sun.

This has to be one of the greatest entrances on earth.

Petra is considered one of the *New* Seven Wonders of the World. *(See: Egypt.)* "New" is relative, as Petra may have been settled as early as 9000 B.C., and was possibly established in the fourth century B.C. as the capital city of the Nabataean Kingdom.

Other New Wonders are a mix of natural and man-made sites. Here they are, with my candid opinion:

The Great Wall of China is over 6,000 kilometers long. The closest section to Beijing, Badaling, has been open for the longest time (since 1957), but is crowded with Chinese tour groups. Check out the dozen other sections that are a bit farther away.

The Statue of Christ Redeemer in Rio de Janeiro overlooks the city from the top of Corcovado Mountain. *(See: Brazil.)* Visitors to Rio make their way to the top via a cogwheel train, a taxi, or by walking on the five-mile-long path. Its size commands attention, but the setting below—of Rio, Sugarloaf Mountain and Ipanema and Copacabana beaches—is the most impressive aspect.

Machu Picchu in Peru was probably deserted by the Incas before the Spanish arrived, known to only a few Peruvian farmers until 1911, when American historian Hiram Bingham found it while searching for the lost city of Vilcabamba, later found deeper in the jungle. In 1986, archaeologists found an even larger city than Machu Picchu just five kilometers north.

Machu Picchu *(See: Peru)* is perhaps the most dramatic site of all the New Wonders, an important ceremonial center with exceptionally high-quality stonework. But cloud cover can be iffy and altitude can be a problem.

The night before we visited the site our guide in Cuzco told us to rest. Half the group didn't listen, took a short walk, and were so sick the next day they couldn't leave their rooms, and missed the whole thing. I'd stay an extra night if possible, to acclimate, and to allow you to get to the site early to avoid crowds.

Chichen Itza in Mexico is a complex of Mayan ruins on the Yucatán Peninsula. A massive step pyramid, known as El Castillo, dominates the ancient city, which thrived from around 600 A.D. to the 1200s. Graphic stone carvings survive at the ball court, Temple of the Warriors and the Wall of the Skulls.

Grand as Chichen is, I'm even more impressed with Tikal, an ancient city abandoned in the tenth century, set in a rainforest. It just isn't as easy to get to. *(See: Guatemala.)*

The Colosseum in Rome is an antiquity worthy of this award. Add on the nearby Forum, a good map and a good guide or guidebook, and you have a day-long, remarkable experience.

The Taj Mahal, the tomb commissioned in 1632 by the Mughal emperor Shah Jahan for his favorite wife, Mumtaz Mahal, is even more beautiful than I expected. The proportions and the semiprecious jewels embedded in the marble are close to perfect. But the scene degrades when hordes of people are in your view, taking selfies.

As for other wonders, I'd add the ruins at Angkor Wat *(See: Cambodia)*, Jerusalem, Bagan *(See: Myanmar)*, the Terracotta Warriors at Xian, the Mosque at Abu Dhabi *(See: UAE)*, and the Moai of Easter Island *(See: Chile)*.

I'd visit the most difficult to maneuver, most far-flung places first, while you have the energy to get there to explore them fully. You can always visit cities and cruise around when you're older. Wonders await.

LIECHTENSTEIN

We're All Special, and Travel Games

The alpine landscape dotted with medieval castles and snug villages reminds me of a setting in an operetta, or, maybe in the shadows of the night, the perfect place for the Frankenstein monster to be created, instead of in nearby Germany. (The monster even shares the same last syllable, which reminds me that my friends on a ship were known as "Frank and Stein," because that was how their last names were announced when they checked in.)

I visited Liechtenstein back in the 1960s, walking trails and visiting a modern art museum. I went out of my way to get there, in part to add it to my list of countries. Like other small European countries such as Andorra, San Marino, Monaco and Vatican City, Liechtenstein is easy to add on when you're heading somewhere else, if that kind of thing is important to you, and I guess it was to me when I was a novice.

I try to experience a place for as long as possible, but obsessive travel enthusiasts are sometimes content just to put their feet on a country's soil, and then move on. Or they take non-direct flights so they land in a new country's airport maybe at three in the morning, half asleep and never leaving the plane. Whatever fills your passport and your scratch-off travel map.

Anyway, overlooked Liechtenstein does stand out as one of the world's two landlocked countries surrounded by landlocked countries (the other is Uzbekistan). And it's the sixth-smallest independent nation in the world by area, at 25 kilometers long.

But I am sorry to report that Roy Lichtenstein, the American pop artist, was born in America. Otherwise, I know of no famous Liechtensteiners. And that's all I've got for now.

Liechtenstein is often misspelled. (The worst I've seen is *Lickdensteen*, written by an otherwise intelligent adult.) And to add to its identity problem, the country is sometimes confused with nearby Luxembourg, which is much larger, although it is also small and somewhat baffling.

Which starts me on a tangled tangent of my travel-writer mind. I've created a fun game to play with travel-loving friends, and you can add your own entries, with Google as your fast friend.

- Most people pronounce the country *Angweela*, but Anguilla rhymes with vanilla.

- Some rhyme Qatar with guitar and some with cutter. The Arabic is somewhere between the two, kind of "gutter" but with a sound you can't easily replicate without seeming like you're spitting up. Also, people want to spell Qatar with a *u*—but that's incorrect; typical Arabic words don't use *u* after *q*.

- Antigua *has* a *u*, but leaves out that sound, although most people pronounce it incorrectly, like it's written. I know someone well-schooled who pronounces Thailand *Thigh-land*. That sounds like a porn video, so I did correct him, to which he responded as if I had told him his fly was open. (I myself have had some pronunciation problems with Thai words. *(See: Thailand.)*

- Myanmar is *Mee-en-mar*, not *My-ahn-mar*—but who cares? They are having more serious problems right now and I hope they solve them, as it is a beautiful destination.

- The correct pronunciation for Uruguay in Spanish for an English speaker would be: *ooh-roo-goo-eye*, not "You're a guay" (as opposed to you're a guarl?).

- Since Xian, China, is where the thousands of ancient Terracotta Warriors were found in the fields, I feel I should mention that Xian is pronounced something like *She-yen.* I've heard American tourists say Exxon, and "Exxon Warriors" sounds ridiculous.

- And regarding China, is it Beijing duck or Peking duck, Beijing opera or Peking opera? Both terms are used.

- Near to China, Macau is a country, pronounced *Ma-cow* like the bovine, and not like the colorful bird.

- Chilly is a feeling and a sauce. *ChEE-lay* is a country.

- Laos is not a louse, but it's pronounced that way.

- Can you pronounce these African countries? Namibia, not *Nambia*, like Game of Thrones' Narnia. Cote d'Ivoire or Ivory Coast. Mauritius is not Mauritania, Malawi is not Mali, Tanzania is not zany—it's *Tan-za-KNEE-a.*

- Benin is Beneen not Ben-In; Togo is not a Roman robe. It's South Sudan, not Sudan (there is no North Sudan, I guess, unlike the Dakotas and Carolinas—more like there's a West Vir-ginia and a Virginia but no East Virginia).

- And the pronunciation I consider the hardest of all countries is Niger. Not like Tiger—but is it *Niijer*—or *Nee-Jere*? I have no idea, as opinions and languages vary. Just don't mention these places if you don't have to.

Odd geography facts could make another game:

- Yugoslavia begat several countries: Croatia, Serbia, Montenegro, Kosovo. Also, Slovenia, which is often confused with Slovakia, which was begat from Czechoslovakia. And Bosnia and Herzegovina is one country, home to Bosniaks, the largest group of three; Serbs second; and Croats third. Natives are identified in English as Bosnian.

- The ancient kingdom of Macedonia was a crossroads between Mediterranean and Balkan civilizations. Since the formation of the Republic of Macedonia in 1991, Macedonians and Greeks have sparred over which country gets to claim the history of the original namesake. A large part of Macedonia became Southern Serbia, including the territory of what today is the Republic of North Macedonia. Aegean Macedonia became Northern Greece. Got that?

- It would be understandable if you made a plane reservation for the wrong Macedonia. I know someone whose assistant booked Athens, Greece, instead of where she was headed—the University of Georgia, although she would have been happy for the difference. A friend once booked a room in Arcadia Florida when she and her husband were heading for Acadia Park in Maine. I guess that's one reason there are travel agents.

- Dominica is a separate island in the Caribbean and has nothing to do with the Dominican Republic, which shares the island of Hispaniola with Haiti.

- And don't get me started with the five mysterious, unpronounceable "stans": Kazakhstan, Kyrgyzstan, Tajikistan, Turkmenistan and Uzbekistan. (Afghanistan and Pakistan are the two other familiar ones we can pronounce.) The suffix comes from the Persian root *istan*, or "land"—hence the "land of the Uzbeks," "land of the Kazakhs," and so forth.

- And have you heard of these African countries? Lesotho, Berkina Faso, Eritrea, Eswatini, Djibuti, Comoros, Burundi and Réunion (with an accent!)? Neither have most people, although I am curious about all of them.

These may be helpful or confusing factoids, but they tell you lots about how a traveler's mind can work with time to waste.

LUXEMBOURG

Third Time's a Charm

"If it's Tuesday it must be Belgium" was our style in 1965 as my husband and I whizzed through much of Europe, including an edge of little Luxembourg, before digging in at graduate school back in the States. Back then we had to show our passports and change money at the borders, and we got lost on the byways, and couldn't speak the languages, and the challenges made it all the more fun.

Five years later, still in my twenties but now with two toddler sons, we were preparing to live in London, where my husband would be finishing up his Ph.D. Icelandair offered bargain airfares from New York to Luxembourg, close to Germany, where we would be picking up a more family-friendly vehicle than the MGB from our honeymoon.

And, as a bonus, the airline offered a free stopover in Iceland. In 1971 nobody we knew had been there, and I imagined it was covered in ice. (I soon would find out that Iceland is green and Greenland is icy.) We marveled at spewing geysers, bubbling mud, lava landscape, and few tourists. *(See: Iceland.)*

When we flew on to Luxembourg, the wooded hills and sturdy houses seemed mundane compared to Iceland's moonscape. And anyway, I was more intent on picking up our new car and driving on to London.

※

In June 2019, almost fifty years later, I returned to Luxembourg for a day trip off a river cruise on the Moselle. Wind turbines turned like giant white pinwheels against the blue sky. Temps climbed to over 100 degrees in the new normal of global warming, and vineyard-clad hills shimmered in the heat.

On the way to Luxembourg City we stopped at the cemetery where over 5,000 service members lie, many of whom died in the Battle of the Bulge and the advance to the Rhine River. Grave markers fan out in the grass, interspersed with fountains, majestic trees and rose and rhododendron beds.

The cemetery was established on December 29, 1944, while Allied Forces were stemming the Ardennes Offensive, a critical World War II battle. The city of Luxembourg served as headquarters for George S. Patton's U.S. Third Army, and the general is buried here, as are his wife's ashes.

Approaching Luxembourg City, I noted a narrow bridge constructed over the highway specifically for wild animals to pass over. The city's historic center, over a thousand years old, displayed spires and old walls, but much of the rest of the city was glass and steel.

Besides French and German, I heard people speaking Portuguese, as many workers come from Portugal and the monarchy has connections to that country. And then there was *Luxembourgish*, a dialect I had never heard before. Our guide told us that it has become an official language, taught in schools since the 1980s. Because it came from traditional rural communities, this shy language doesn't even have a word for "love." I guess you would have to say, "I like you very, *very* much." Which would suit noncommittal types quite well.

＊

And then I met Charlotte, the statue in the main square, and the country's heroine. She was an inexperienced princess, in her early twenties when she took to the throne as grand duchess. In 1940, rather than cooperate with the Germans, Charlotte established a government in exile in the United Kingdom, and began to broadcast from London to rally support. The Germans retaliated by annexing Luxembourg and incorporating it entirely into the German Reich.

When she returned after the war, her reign continued until 1964, when she abdicated in favor of her son Jean; the current grand duke is her grandson Henri.

Under Charlotte's rule, the monarchy was saved, Luxembourg was finally liberated from German occupation, universal suffrage was rolled out, new labor and housing laws were passed and the often-violated status of neutrality was dropped.

In other words, Charlotte *ruled*.

Macau

Tastes Like Chicken

Macau was a Portuguese territory until 1999, and today is a tiny island country. It has giant casinos and malls and a tall tower.

But I was there on my own in 1982, before Macau became the biggest gambling venue in the world. Back then, going from Macau was the only way for Americans to get to mainland China for a day trip, and so I traveled from Hong Kong to Macau and then ferried to mainland China.

Returning to Hong Kong, I was invited for a special dinner at a new restaurant on the Kowloon harbor, along with a rather snobby writer for a science magazine whom I dubbed Macho Man.

Before the meal, the restaurant owner toured us through a kitchen that looked like a doomed petting zoo, with caged bunnies, birds, turtles and such, and an aquarium full of colorful, presumably delicious fish. I felt squeamish and guilty, as I don't like to be introduced to my meal, especially when the victim could be my pet.

Our pre-chosen menu that evening was highly unusual, considered an honor, and I knew I would be consuming things I would never eat again. The starter was sashimi of geoduc, a bivalve big as a pizza. The waiter wheeled it in and sliced

it up. Ouch. Shark-fin soup followed. I hope this is no longer served, because the entire shark is sometimes thrown away just to get the fin, considered an aphrodisiac. I did not need nor want that.

The restaurant owner sat, Buddha-like, with Macho Man and me, eating nothing, saying little. His wife picked at tea and rice, silently, head down. Macho Man bragged throughout the feast of the many icky foods he had eaten, including monkey brains and locusts.

He downed the first course with gusto, and I liked him less and less with each showy bite. When he learned that dessert was to be sea fungus in milk, he exclaimed with delight that he had recently enjoyed it.

The main course was a mild-flavored sliced meat. Macho Man chewed carefully, but couldn't recognize the taste, and finally asked our host what we were eating. The restaurant owner's wife, who had been silent throughout the meal, looked up from her rice and whispered, "deer penis."

Macho Man threw down his chopsticks.

"Absolutely delicious," I remarked, slowly chewing and then poking at the meat for another bite. "If you're not finishing yours, I will."

I have happily ordered escargots and frog legs, and, in my Julia Child phase, when I worked my way through her cookbooks, I prepared calf brains, veal kidneys, tripe and tongue. As a travel writer I've consumed local products around the world that only someone with the guts of food-adventurer Andrew Zimmern might ingest, including wild boar, air-dried whale blubber, zebra, fermented shark and dried puffin. I've told myself it was for research purposes, and yes, I have had my share of *turista*.

I usually at least sample whatever is put before me, even if it's oxen ear with mango coulis. As a last resort I might say something like, "I'm allergic to ears," or "I can't eat ears for religious reasons."

I've consumed proteins connected with exterminators, sometimes by chance. In a café on the Pan American Highway in Mexico, a crouton in my bowl of tomato soup turned out to have six legs. And in a well-known Washington, D.C., restaurant, a baked cricket was an unwelcome addition to an otherwise ordinary beef casserole. (After the apoplectic owner comped the bill, I mock-whispered to my friend, "Good work! We need another cricket.")

In Bangkok, our group of Thais and Americans working on a video project made faces as we ate shrimp. The Americans removed the tops and consumed the bottoms, and the Thais did just the opposite.

"How can you eat the eyes and brains?" asked the Americans. "How can you eat the intestinal tube?" asked the Thais. We wasted nothing by exchanging parts.

Worms to some are as delectable as eels to others, but many of us can't stomach either. I have passed on sheep eyes, grubs, ants, Amazonian rodents and cat. In the northern hills of Vietnam, I admired and nuzzled dogs that I learned later were raised to be eaten. That would be a no!

On the other hand, pigs make smart and affectionate pets. They are just unlucky that they taste so good.

I have eaten alligator and iguana, which, yes, taste like chicken. (Would people used to eating those creatures say that chicken tastes like reptiles?)

In Chiang Mai, in northern Thailand, after a trek on an elephant named Sarah, my friend and I chose a restaurant with a snake pit at the entrance, placed much like a lobster tank at a neighborhood seafood joint. The boa ended up as a burger, filled with what tasted like pebbles. Were they the undigested bones of rodents? Ick. The cobra was tender, but the ribs left on the plate were scary. And yes, snake also tastes like chicken, perhaps because reptilian dinosaurs were the precursors of birds.

In Tokyo I savored a porcelain bowlful of blush-pink jelly that turned out to be jellyfish. But that's nothing compared to my dinner of *fugo*, a potentially deadly blowfish prepared by only a few registered Japanese chefs.

I lived to write about it. And when I have a choice and read a translated menu, I am careful to ask for details. Thus, I did not eat what was described on a Vietnamese menu as "soft-boiled baby chicken in a spoon." Fetus gives me gas.

And at this point, older even than the lady who sat quietly at our table in Hong Kong so long ago, I'll take the rice and tea when they pass around the mystery meat.

MADAGASCAR

Looking for a Lemur

In the Indian Ocean east of Mozambique, Madagascar—the Red Island, the Rainbow Island, the "Eighth Continent"—is the fourth-largest island in the world, chock-full of wild and wonderful things.

You'll find dry desert, towering octopus trees with spindly cactus-like branches, white sand beaches and gigantic baobab trees. Around eighty percent of the island's natural wonders, maybe 200,000 species, don't exist anywhere else. Here are half the world's chameleon species, and glorious birds, bugs like tiny giraffe-necked weevils, and amphibians including the painted Mantella frog—fluorescent green and bright pink, with yellow stripes.

Madagascar's customs are equally unique. *Famadihana,* the "turning of the bones," is a funerary tradition of the Malagasy, who remove their ancestors' bodies from family crypts, rewrap them in fresh cloth, and rewrite their names on the cloth to be remembered. And sometimes they dance with the remains.

My grandmother loved the waltz, but I can't imagine dragging her corpse around to "The Blue Danube." Also, since dancing in faraway places has sometimes brought the unexpected *(See: Malawi)*, and most of my partners dance as if they are dead anyway, I'll pass on that goal.

※

I remember reading in elementary school in Miami Beach about furry animals with long arms and huge eyes, that hang in the crooks of branches—monkey-like creatures ranging from the large, wailing indri to the tiny mouse lemur.

Through the years I'd seen a couple of lemurs in zoos, and their look and their behavior reminded me of my uncle, who liked to sleep on his stomach on the couch after a Thanksgiving meal, with a hairy arm dangling to the floor.

I longed to see lemurs in Madagascar, their only natural habitat. With few predators, they are relatively fearless, and I was told a close-up encounter in the wild would be easy to come by. And so, late in life, I sought to find one.

I arrived in a speedboat across turquoise shallows to Nosy Komba, one of hundreds of islands that make up the island-nation of Madagascar. Along the shore, batik cloth in primitive patterns rippled on lines; cottages with palm-frond roofs seemed cozy; a woman in a sarong, with markings on her face, looked bored as she waited for Instagrammers to take her photo; and vanilla beans were displayed in plastic bags, ready for foodies to purchase as hostess gifts for people with open kitchens and farm sinks.

But I had only one goal. I trekked into a jungle where I was told they hung out, and heard a conspiracy of lemurs—yes, that is the group name—squeaking in the faraway trees.

After about half an hour, there it was, my first—and, as it turned out, my only—lemur, dark and furry with big orange eyes, hanging directly above. A slacker if I ever saw one. And yes, it did resemble my sleepy relative, so I called him Uncle Artie.

I got closer to take a photo, a life's dream. I sighed, and knew I would remember the moment forever. And I certainly did.

Uncle Artie pooped on my head.

Malawi

He Never Calls, He Never Writes

I was in Malawi in 2004 with a group of journalists. We visited Lake Malawi and held some meetings with government officials to help them with their tourism industry, which was minimal because of poverty and the scourge of AIDS, which had hit this African country hard.

"You need more directional signs on your roads," I offered.

"We had many signs," said the officials. "But people stole them to make shelter."

Tough realities. So I hardly expected the sweet surprise of the following night, a short tale befitting the duration of the experience.

A Malawi dance group was performing at an official function. A man in white asked me to join in a ceremonial dance. I was reluctant, but threw off my shoes, joined the man and moved with him as best I could to throbbing African drumbeats.

The dancer gestured, I gestured. He sat me down and danced around me for a few minutes, waving his hands above his head, and I remained seated, but copied his hand movements.

This went on for several minutes, waving and tapping my feet, mirroring his hands as he whirled.

Suddenly everyone clapped and laughed. It was the end of the dance, so I stumbled, exhausted, to a group of people standing on the sidelines the whole time, with big smiles remaining on their faces.

"What's so funny?" I asked. I knew I wasn't much of a dancer, but still….

"Oh," an official smiled. "Your new name is Ngunda. You two danced very well together. You two are now married."

Malaysia

Stinky, Sad and Surprised

In 1989 I was executive producer of an interactive language project for the Defense Department in Thailand. Most of the crew headed off to dive in Indonesia, but I chose to go solo to Malaysia for a couple of days during the Thanksgiving break.

In Kuala Lumpur I hired a car with a driver who could speak some English. We traveled throughout the countryside, past endless, neat groves of palms grown for oil, and tiny indigenous communities with houses on stilts.

I tasted my first durian on this little trip, bought at a roadside stand. Southeast Asians love the huge, spiky fruits, supposedly able to fire up libido and cure just about any malady. But as the driver took out a knife and whacked through the hard shell, the stench was a combo of stinky cheese and dirty feet, with a wisp of used diapers.

I was repulsed, but the driver offered me a piece of the fruit's creamy interior. I sampled it out of curiosity, holding my breath. The durian tasted slightly better than it smelled—let's say peach and onion, with a whiff of socks.

The driver ate his fill, and I happily gave him my share.

＊

The durian may have been the worst smell I'd encountered, but not the only unpleasant aspect of that Malaysian road trip. At a busy crossroads I saw a man with a captured bat, its wings pinned to a stake as it struggled in the sunshine. Animals are symbols of reality as you travel the world observing other cultures. I remember a pig squealing as it was knifed behind a shed. I've seen lambs gamboling onto trucks driving them to slaughter. Bony horses whipped to move. A lost donkey wandering on a highway. A bear chained to a rail. A lone elephant, used for rides, rubbing against a wall. A dying sea lion, lost among penguins.

We travelers often confront the weak and helpless, and things that challenge and even disgust us. We can learn from experiences that push the limit, and come out stronger and wiser for it, and perhaps more compassionate. And hopefully we keep going.

＊

I arrived at a timbered lodging in the Cameron Highlands, in the cool, green Malaysian uplands where I was staying for the night. My room overlooked row after row of tea plantings threading the hills.

At dinner I sat alone in a dining room that looked like a transplanted public house from the English countryside. As the only Western woman in the room, I felt all eyes on me, and was especially sorry that the driver didn't want to share the meal. It happened to be Thanksgiving, but he was tired and didn't realize that this memorable day when he ate a durian was also a holiday back home in the United States.

My discomfort was brief. The server brought my meal with a big smile, And then I grinned back, and felt thankful. He had stuck a little paper hand-colored American flag in a chicken thigh. He knew it was Thanksgiving.

That's life on the road—good, bad, ugly, surprising, stinky and, sometimes, kind.

MALDIVES

Not Pilates. Pirates

A few years ago, Bill and I were cruising on an elegant ship in an upgraded stateroom, cosseted by a butler, fed by toqued chefs, pampered by staff and crew at every turn. Lucky us. Our ports of call in the Middle East, India and Africa included Dubai, Abu Dhabi, Oman, Mumbai, Mangalore, the Maldives, the Seychelles, Zanzibar, Madagascar, Mozambique and stops down the East African coast to Cape Town.

An itinerary to die for. Figuratively speaking, I assumed.

Heading toward the Maldive islands, I looked forward to crystalline water and white sand, and visiting the mosque in the capital city of Malé. I knew that these thousand islands comprised the smallest country in Asia and the ninth smallest in the world, as well as being the lowest and flattest. Dangerous superlatives in this era of climate change, and I figured I'd better visit before they were submerged in the Indian Ocean.

Bad thought. But then we received another one that evening in a message placed beside the chocolates on our pillows. We had been expecting it.

"We will be passing through an area known as High Risk Area (HRA) for piracy. … While sailing through the HRA we will be in permanent contact with an International Task

Force including US and UK naval forces that are assigned to protect merchant vessels from pirate attack by a United Nations mandate. … In the event of pirate activity, announcements will be made from the bridge."

Announcements from the bridge? The cruise director announced the daily trivia games and bingo. The captain let us know the weather and where we were located in the ocean. Which one was going to tell us about "pirate activity"?

At least they didn't put *Captain Phillips* on the in-house TV.

Yes, we were plying waters where Somali pirates had attempted to raid a few cruise ships and other vessels over the years. In fact, in 2008 this very ship had fended off pirates by simply outrunning them. Scars remained on the ship's side from the sparring, and word was that some passengers on that scary cruise stayed on their stateroom balconies as the race was taking place, taking photos of the pirate vessels to show the folks back home. Not. Smart.

At two (heavily attended) lectures about pirates past and present, we learned about assorted plunderers on all the waters of the world over thousands of years. Most of these guys from days of yore until today have been more interested in ransom than life-taking, a small comfort to those onboard with considerable bling.

For two weeks of high-pirate alert, by day we immersed ourselves in the normal indulgences of sunning by the pool, lunch buffets, dinners in the grand dining room, high teas, Pilates, games, ports of call and days at sea. But every night, after enjoying the magi-

cians and musical shows, we were required to close our curtains and keep our balcony lights off.

And when we took our half-hour nightly walk above the pool area, no festive string of lights celebrated our presence in the open waters of the Indian Ocean, heading toward the Maldives. Up there, we felt alone under a waxing moon, on a ghost ship.

We had several pirate drills at which we stood or sat in the hall in our life preservers, and we became more and more easily spooked as we passed through the zone. Could ship speed-ups be possible flights from danger? Strange noises got my immediate attention. Anyone who looked off into the hori-

zon drew a group looking in the same direction, as if we were spotting whales instead of pirates.

Just in case, every night I wore pajama bottoms under my usual nightshirt and placed my pills ready to grab at a moment's notice. My husband and I made sure to lock the stateroom door, and even measured if we could fit under the bed (not remotely possible after all those six-course dinners).

Cruisers joked about our captain turning into a modern-day Horatio Hornblower, with sonic noise weapon and fire hoses at the ready, fighting pirates who were probably wearing rain slickers with Bose noise reducers on their ears.

As the days passed, "Aaarghs!" punctuated conversations. One night my husband, who had a retina problem, put on his eye patch to much hilarity.

You can imagine how relieved and delighted we were when we finally came out of the pirate zone. Lights and and bling were on again. We made it.

But only a day later we found this on our pillows:

> "We recently received a U.S. State Department advisory regarding threats against foreign travelers. In an abundance of caution, we have decided to cancel...Mombasa, Kenya... We hope you're enjoying your cruise. Have a good night."

MALTA

Solitary Walks and Hello, Grandpa!

I ferried from Malta to visit mythic Calypso's Cave on the little island of Gozo, then returned to the capital of Valletta, built as a city-fortress following the Great Siege of 1565.

Malta's buildings range from the oldest freestanding stone architecture in the world to formidable defensive systems. Rulers here included Romans, Moors, Knights of Saint John, French and British, so the islands offer fortresses and megalithic temples—the most remarkable concentration of UNESCO World Heritage Sites in any nation-state.

In the cooler evening I walked through Mdina (yes, that's the spelling). This "Silent City" was Malta's capital from antiquity to the medieval period, when the Maltese archipelago, just south of Sicily, was strategically important for the domination of the Mediterranean.

Candlelight flickered against stones, and as my steps echoed on the enclosing wall I was transported to a time of knights and sailing trade routes.

I like walking alone. Some of us just do, although lately there has been more awareness of possible safety issues in this new normal. Throughout my life I have kept a low profile and done just fine. And here, the solitude was part of the magic, and that evening walk in Malta has remained a haunting memory of ancient times.

✳

On May to September weekends over the last four centuries, Maltese towns and villages each celebrate the feast of their patron saint. Fireworks on the town square light the night, and bright banners and handmade statues atop wooden columns decorate the main streets.

Locals cover their balconies and rooftops with festoons—blue, red, green—according to the feast they are supporting, and open their doors to show off their freshly cleaned main rooms.

On one early evening in an agricultural village, I entered several doors and looked around dwellings as Maltese hosts proudly displayed their well-used furnishings and family photos. (I encountered lots of people sitting in their kitchens and lots of cats, but I realized later that I did not see even one Maltese dog.)

At one house I was handed a sweet almond drink, then shown the living area and family pictures. I was then beckoned into a back bedroom, where a white-haired man in his pajamas was sitting in bed. We smiled and nodded to each other, and had a lovely hand-signal conversation, me pointing with approval around the room and he returning a kind of salute.

I returned to the street feeling warm and fuzzy, perhaps from the truly nutty drink, perhaps from greeting a stranger in his bed as if it were a normal occurrence. The homeowner and her father (husband?) were obviously proud of their home and their Maltese culture, and had picked up a friendly vibe from me, a solo traveler. Meeting people is one of the pleasures of traveling on your own, which if you choose, could take you into bedrooms around the world.

MARTINIQUE

Headless Josephine, Lucky Ludger

Martinique's capital and largest town, pretty Fort-de-France, has steep hills, narrow streets and a garden named La Savane, bordered by shops and cafés. A statue of island-native Josephine de Beauharnais, first wife of Napoleon Bonaparte, dominates the scene quite like an emperor's wife should.

Empress Josephine holds a locket with a portrait of Napoleon. Years ago, her head was lopped off and red paint splashed over her body, and she remains that way because she's not very popular. Islanders believe Josie was directly responsible for convincing Napoleon to reintroduce slavery in the French West Indies so that her family plantation would not suffer.

I feel for headless Josephine. No one wants to be considered an airhead for hundreds of years.

As I drove through this Caribbean island, I passed century-old mahogany trees, towering ferns, bamboo, ixora, heliconia and porcelain rose. Rushing streams overhung with rope and wire suspension footbridges punctuated valleys below volcanic peaks. But that lushness comes with a price, I realized, when I came upon a small marker near a rural road.

On May 8, 1902, Mount Pelée erupted, burning or suffocating over thirty thousand people, the highest death toll of any volcanic activity in the twentieth century. The water temperature in the crater's lake was near boiling, and the spreading wave of scalding ash destroyed the town of Saint-Pierre.

One man, Ludger Sylbaris, survived. He was a convicted felon arrested for beating another man, and had the good fortune to be thrown in a single, underground cell with stone walls and no windows, one day before the volcano erupted.

Ludger was locked up for four days before rescuers heard his cries and found him burned, but alive. When healed he was pardoned, and toured America with the Barnum and Bailey circus as "the man who survived doomsday," and the first black man ever to star in "The Greatest Show on Earth." He died of natural causes at age 54.

Mount Pelée is expected to erupt again, but scientists don't know exactly when. The moral of the story, if there is one, is that if you act up and are thrown in jail near a volcano, it might be the safest place around.

MEXICO

A to Z

Frida Kahlo fascinates me. French surrealist Andre Breton called her paintings "a ribbon around a bomb," and that could well describe the artist herself.

During her lifetime she was known mostly as muralist Diego Rivera's wife, but Madonna bought one of her paintings for $5.6 million, a record for Latin American painters. Frida's artworks hang in museums throughout the world, and her defiant gaze under that unibrow graces mugs and T-shirts, as well.

She contracted polio at six, and was bedridden for nine months. Kids called her "pegleg."

At eighteen, she was on a bus that collided with a streetcar, and was impaled on a steel handrail. Bedridden again for two years, she started painting self-portraits on a special easel, with a mirror.

I lingered at that bed in the Mexico City suburbs where she painted through her suffering.

The outer walls at Casa Azul are electric blue, the same color of fashion designer Yves St. Laurent's property in Marrakesh, Morocco. The tropical garden seems a smaller version of the late designer's extensive garden, as well.

Frida's house has green doors and bright yellow floors, walls and shelves. Her works, photographs and memorabilia are displayed throughout, with a few of Diego's paintings thrown in. More than a studio or museum, Casa Azul is maintained the way it was when Frida and Diego lived there, displaying personal goods, including sunglasses, corsets and specially designed clothing to hide her deformities.

Frida died in Casa Azul in 1954, where her ashes remain. "I want to live," she said, near the end. "In spite of all this, life is worth living." My visit there made me feel grateful for her fierceness, and for the opportunity to experience such power close up.

✳

Thinking of her house, I remember other artists' studios and residences I've been privileged to visit, among them Rembrandt's mansion on an Amsterdam canal, and Van Gogh's bare room in Arles and his asylum room in nearby St. Rémy.

At Jackson Pollack's working shed on his Long Island property, when the docent went to take a call, I was left alone on a floor swirled with his paint drippings and I felt as if I were in a cathedral. Outside Winslow Homer's studio in Maine I traipsed along the rocky shore he so often painted. In Paris I walked through Picasso's studio, and at Rodin's house I paused at The Thinker, and thought a bit more than usual.

In Tangier I tipped the doorman to stand by the hotel room window where Matisse painted a famed scene of marketplace and sea that remains much the same a hundred years later. In Cezanne's atelier in Aix en Provence, the cards used by the players in his famed painting are displayed on an original table, his hat and coat hang on a stand, and iconic Sainte-Victoire, the mountain he painted time after time, looms through the window.

All of these visits have increased my appreciation and understanding of these artists—and art.

And enriched my life.

At a lodging compound called Las Brisas, in Acapulco, Mexico, back in the 1960s, casitas clung to hills overlooking the Pacific. Every morning our private pools were sprinkled with hibiscus blossoms, and pink jeeps with striped awnings delivered goodies and deposited guests to the beach below. Butlers passed meals though a little opening in the door so as not to disturb whatever might be going on with the romantic occupants.

And yes, we were newlyweds, in bed almost the whole time, night and day.

Because we had dysentery. We never used the pool. We didn't even see it, all week. I do remember the rustic bathroom, and a doctor's visit to our bedside, and food sent in and rejected through the door opening, and darkness. Not exactly a fantasy suite. Sometimes that's the way it goes.

Two husbands later, I ziplined for the first time on a tour off a cruise ship in Cancún. The instructors spoke Spanish and heavily accented English. We were about to zip high above the trees, not quite understanding how to brake. I zipped, jerkily (or maybe I jerked, zippily). Bill later said he felt like a jerk, as he did not brake at all. At least he was stopped, legs askew with all hands helping. In the photo taken as we headed for our landings, he seems like a panicked elder Tarzan, flying into the jungle on a vine, never to return.

We stayed unzipped forever after, and vowed never again to do anything potentially dangerous without understanding the instructions.

Playa del Carmen is just south of Cancún on Mexico's Riviera Maya, on the Yucatan coast. Once a sleepy fishing town, the port was put on the map by Jacques Cousteau in 1954, when he filmed an underwater documentary of the Great Mayan Reef about twelve miles offshore.

But I flew to Playa del Carmen for the haunting festival *Dia de Los Muertos*—the Day of the Dead.

Painted in white masks and darkly lined, exaggerated faces, Mexicans acknowledge that death comes to all, and so they both celebrate and taunt it. Markets sell toys and candy transformed into skeletons, coffins, and death herself, *La Muerta*. Cheeky obituary poems criticize politicians or chide friends and family—an original form of tweeting, I'd say—written as if the person had already passed, mocking death.

On October 31, All Hallows Eve, children create altars to entice the angelitos (the spirits of dead children) to return, and go door to door asking for *calavaritas*, sugar skulls. On All Saints Day, November 1, deceased children are believed to return to life, and their graves are cleaned and decorated with candles, paper streamers and marigolds.

Loved ones gather at cemeteries to greet returning adult spirits on All Souls Day, November 2. I admired altars adorned with photos, lighted incense, candles, flowers, colorful cut paper and candy skulls inscribed with the names of the deceased.

Music, prayers and favorite meals of the departed are also a part of the ceremonies. On Halloween I usually eat too much candy, but here I enjoyed tamales and mole sauce, pumpkin and fruit sweets, and *pan de muerto* (bread of the dead).

With my face painted in stark white and black, at nightfall I joined a boat floating on a ce-

note, candles lighting the dark water with the heat of faith and life. A "Catrina"—a beautiful symbol of death—told us of other haunted women: *Xtabay*, who scares men; and *La Llorona*, a woman left alone to raise her two sons, and who in grief and anger drowned them in a river and has wandered for eternity looking for the bodies, causing misfortune to any who hear her wailing.

These myths scared the occupants of our little boat, but in a different way than in a Halloween haunted house. They were deeply psychological symbols. Death is neutral, an equalizing force for rich and poor, coming to all.

My celebration ended in darkness in the woods as a shaman, surrounded by flames, gave thanks for the sacred elements of water, sun, wind, earth and life. Villagers danced to drumbeats, and the community prayed for harmony, promising to continue feeding the fire of life.

At least once in your life, pass on Halloween to share this experience, to bond and have fun, and remember those who have come before. I can't think of a more ideal intergenerational trip.

I was cruising on a boat with seventeen others in Baja California, on the Sea of Cortez, watching dozens of pink dolphins following in our wake. Earlier I had snorkeled eye-to-goggled-eye with a sea lion in a humbling connection, while its mom (or pop—either was menacing) circled constantly. I thought nothing could top that.

But later, in the distance, someone spotted a blue whale, the largest creature on earth. We all ran to the starboard side, hoping the massive creature would breach from the water. And then, several minutes later we saw it twisting in foam as if rising in a myth. We clapped and shouted and waited some more. But that was it, and the boat moved on.

Jacques Cousteau called the Sea of Cortez "the aquarium of the world." I can attest that—along with Alaska and the Galapagos Islands—this area of Mexico is one of the best places to observe sea creatures. And just maybe, if you're lucky, an unexpected, faraway blue whale.

*

Driving in the Florida Panhandle, clusters of Monarch butterflies flew into my windshield. Through the day, thousands of them fluttered in weeds and around my head, pausing on their annual migration to the central mountains of Mexico, where they would soon feed and breed by the millions.

Butterflies are something of an obsession. *(See: Peru.)* A few years after that Florida experience, I was staying in colonial San Miguel de Allende, a few hours' drive from the Mexican highlands, where millions of the Monarchs rest, feed and breed.

I emailed a guide with qualms about the altitude, but he assured me I wouldn't have a problem, so Bill and I joined a group of half-a-dozen butterfly lovers on a trek. We drove seven hours total, walked an hour uphill and an hour down, rode a horse a half hour each way, and walked another thirty minutes.

Huffing and puffing, it took me twice as long as the rest of the group—including my even-older-than-I husband. And what did we see at 11,000 feet? Nada. The day was cloudy and cool and the Monarchs were sleeping it off. I've seen more butterflies on my flowerbed in an hour than I did on this debilitating, futile journey.

I have since satisfied my butterfly craving by watching thousands of Monarchs fluttering in Central Mexico—on YouTube. I sometimes enlarge the video to better immerse myself in the orange flurry, a magnificent wonder of nature, indeed. I repeat the videos often, over and over, as if I were right there, which I indeed was, to no avail.

MONACO

Not-so-Grand Prix

My friend and I were midway on a Mediterranean cruise, and the fully rigged five-masted sailing ship loomed like a ghost from another century in the Monte Carlo harbor.

The vast casino opened in 1863, when Vegas was just an outpost in the desert. We just peeked in at noon and then drove on the Grand Corniche, stopping to gaze at views of the French coast, and then headed up to Saint-Paul-de-Vence.

Years before, with Husband One, I had lunched on a terrace there, sipping local rosé to the sound of cooing white doves fluttering among the umbrellas. Within the inn were paintings by once-hungry artists, including a young Picasso. On this trip, the inn and the winding streets remained as charming as I had remembered from the 1960s, but with crowds snaking along the steep lanes, poking into artsy boutiques.

Back in Monaco, we walked along the harbor, people-watching. This showy principality is not everyone's flute of champagne, less than a square mile carved out of France, crowded with the biggest yachts and most expensive real estate money can flaunt. A "sunny place for shady people," crooks, socialites, hangers-on and the really wealthy, who sleep late and party early in this hedonistic tax haven.

Prince Albert, son of Princess Grace *(See: Bosnia),* is not only the royal head of this second-smallest country after the Vatican, he's the mayor and the CEO (but probably not the dogcatcher). The good news is that he's focused on climate change, which will drastically affect all coastal areas, including Monaco.

✳

For four days each spring at the Grand Prix de Monte Carlo, stripped-down Formula One race cars speed throughout the streets. And I have some idea how those drivers feel.

A friend of a friend was opening a Grand Prix track at a former pecan farm on the Colorado River in Austin, Texas, in 2008. Did I want to partner with a race car driver at 150 miles an hour in a supercharged, ground-hugging, open-to-the-elements hell-on-wheels?

"Sure," I said, before I realized I hadn't written a will. I go 75 miles an hour on the expressways, I figured. How bad could twice as fast be?

I met Jimmy a few minutes before entrusting my life to him, a former exec who scrapped it all to race Ferraris in Grand Prix events, and mentor wannabe racers like the actor Craig T. Nelson ("a brilliant driver") and the Tour de France cheater Lance Armstrong ("feisty with the ladies").

I helmeted up in the seat beside him with false bravado as he set a mic so I could scream to stop the madness, and then strapped me in a four-points seat belt. The race car was built so low that I felt I was sitting on the dusty ground, like in a streamlined bumper car. Before I had a chance to say, "Let me think a bit more about this …," the motor whined like a jet engine, the tires screeched, and my face felt like it was plastered to the back of my head.

I can't adequately describe the terror of immediately accelerating from 0 to 150, hurtling around a race course purposely set with unexpected curves, bumps and straightaways. It was the fastest I'd ever moved on the ground (except

maybe when I was running away from a bull in a pasture one time—another story).

Besides being impulsive, I'm stubborn. I was determined not to wimp out and push the panic button. When I asked Jimmy later, after my face returned forward, he said that the closest experience would be in an F-16 jet: G-forces, blinding speed, pumping adrenaline, the feeling of flying.

I will never experience a *Top Gun* moment, and I have never skydived or bungee-jumped or accomplished other breathtaking endeavors. I can only attest it was ten times scarier than the highest, fastest roller coaster I had ever been on. And a coaster is simulated danger. This was the real deal.

I hated every minute. Twice. Because when Jimmy, an exceptionally charming sadist, saw that I was petrified, he sped me around the track again. And this time we came less than a car's length behind another normal-looking car that seemed to be dawdling along, probably at 130 mph. Ever since

driver's ed I knew that you're supposed to leave two car lengths, even at normal speed. I began to question Jimmy's judgment, but it was too late.

And then there was the "J curve," a maneuver Jimmy teaches the military in case they ever have to get out of an alley in Kabul, fast. *Without stopping*, the car turns into reverse and speeds the other way. It was over before I had a chance to close my eyes. I just, and I mean *just*, managed to hold down my Tex-Mex lunch. (Yeah, I know. Dumb.)

Afterwards, "relaxing" with Jimmy in the trailer, I noticed blood on his shirt. I must have been in a daze, because I didn't see it before. I now also noticed a scar on the left side of his face, by his nose. He had said he always escaped mishaps. He just didn't say how many, and in what shape. Anyway, I do not recommend the race car experience to the timid or the sensible. Relieved that I was still alive, I flew home ready to face the biggest risk of all: driving in Miami traffic.

MONTENEGRO

It Takes a Village

In the 1980s I visited a fifteenth-century fortified village turned into a resort, on a little island named Sveti Stefan. Attached to a villa on the Montenegro coast by a narrow isthmus, this seaside hideaway with pink sand beaches was a picture-perfect combo of cobbled lanes and hand-restored stone buildings with shaded courtyards and red-tiled roofs. I drank from a stone well and poked around an old schoolhouse turned into a cottage in what seemed like a journey back in time.

Since then, when I pass rural, closed shops and abandoned buildings worldwide, often in highly scenic areas, I sometimes daydream of moving in—usually when I've imbibed an extra glass of wine.

Most intrepid travelers daydream. When I was single and in my fifties, I decided that when my sons were all grown I would settle in rooms overlooking the Bay of Naples on the fisherman's island of Procida. I could tutor English and write novels, and a handsome fisherman in turn could teach me Italian. I saw myself on a Vespa, going down to the harbor to pick up the day's catch and reading myself to sleep with a purring cat on my lap.

Actually, dreams are becoming realities right now as people are buying up forgotten areas at bargain-basement prices to stem depopulation and create jobs in fading or ghosted communities, and then repurposing potential lodgings.

Entire villages are being put up for sale, ready to be transformed. The Italians are leading the trend, with over a hundred towns-turned-resorts called *alberghi diffusi*, or "scattered hotels." In fact, in off-the-beaten-path Matera, in Puglia, chosen European Capital of Culture for 2019, cave dwellings are becoming lodgings, and one hotel is tucked into part of a former Benedictine monastery.

In the Jura region of France, or Galicia in Spain, whole towns can be bought for less than a modest house in the States: fifteen-hundred hamlets are for sale in Spain alone. In the Italian-speaking Ticino region of Switzerland, the ten or so remaining residents of Corippo are transforming their town into a luxury hotel, with rooms in once-abandoned stone cottages and a "lobby" in the main square.

In Kalopanayiotis in Cyprus, a man turned a dying town into a forty-room hotel and spa, and the president asked him to join the government and do the same for 115 other communities in the country. And Antikythera, eight square miles of loveliness between Crete and the Peloponnese, has only twenty-four residents, but is willing to give successful applicants—especially families with young children—not only a house with a plot of land, but also about $500 a month to live on for the first three years.

I've seen houses in Bulgaria that English friends bought up as summer colonies for very little. In Breb, Romania, where residents still ride in horse-drawn carriages, a bed and breakfast has taken over four houses near the reported doorstep of Dracula's castle. And in Sasayama Japan, a five-villa development in an Edo-era municipality known for its fine beef is now the flagship for a budding brand of village hotels.

I've read about movie stars and celebs discussing giving tiny, empty villages as presents to friends and family. And one of my online writer friends has messaged a bunch of us about getting out of the States and buying a hamlet to get away from the political mess, and live together in perfect harmony. (Dream on.)

Is this a cut-rate housing trend, like tiny houses, that burns out but changes how we look at our housing needs? Or will it lead a new movement of utopian living as a reaction to dark forces in the world, like communes in the late 1960s?

I can repurpose a teapot into a planter and a child's nursery into an office, but at this point, changing a cave into a house and a dead village into a money-making hotel is beyond me.

Renewing and salvaging are good, and I am pleased to know it's happening. But rather than moving to an isolated village far from doctors and cultural riches, my reality-based self understands that I'm better off staying for a while at magical places such as Sveti Stefan in Montenegro, and then moving on.

Morocco

Extreme Shopping

My first trip to Morocco with my young husband was a quickie hydrofoil jaunt from Gibraltar to Tangier. While browsing through a marketplace in that Mediterranean coastal town I found a lovely hand-painted chest, perfect to use as a coffee table.

I had no idea how to bargain, and the Moroccan vendor with the grizzled face had been at this for years. When I exclaimed how pretty the chest was, he could tell that I wanted it.

He asked $50, and I thought I would be getting a deal by offering $45. But then we decided the chest would be too heavy to take with us, and that the shipping cost would be twice the value, and we reluctantly walked away.

He ran out after us. "$40, just for you."

"No, thank you."

"$35!"

"No, thanks."

By the time I got to the bus, the lovely chest was $15.

We lugged that chest throughout Morocco, and my husband pulled a muscle in his back. But I did learn how to bargain.

On my next Moroccan trip, twenty years later, my bargaining skills were perhaps too good. Our group was driven deep into the desert for a shopping spree at a tiny outpost.

By now I had developed an interest in framed mirrors and had collected many around the world, examples of a culture's workmanship and materials that fit my budget, and my luggage.

In a vast, tented marketplace in the middle of nowhere, I strolled among vendors selling food and goods to locals at local prices. I wandered on my own to the crafts area and took my time considering brass, studded leather or painted frames, now expertly bargaining for a fair price despite language difficulties.

I especially admired one mirror with a tooled leather frame and an octagonal shape, and decided to buy it. After an elaborate give-and-take with the seller, I glanced at my watch and suddenly realized that I had missed the tour's departure time by twenty minutes. *They wouldn't leave without me,* I thought, racing to the meeting point.

Unfortunately, I was wrong.

The bus was gone, leaving me God knows where. This was in the good old days when you could get lost pretty easily, especially on your own—not only no smartphones, no phone service. I had been lax in details, as I sometimes get when someone else is in charge of herding me around. In my confusion I couldn't even remember the name of my little hotel, or the correct pronunciation of the small town where I was staying for the night.

"No worries. They'll come back and get me," I hoped out loud, sitting down in the heat.

As the sun moved west, I realized that nobody must have even noticed my absence. Now I was not only upset, I was insulted.

I sat in place, afraid that if I even got up to relieve myself I would miss the chance to be rescued. I thought of hijacking a camel and heading out, or maybe just living the rest of my life here in the desert, learning a craft. In summer camp I had woven a lanyard. Maybe that would sell here.

After an hour or so of my increasing paranoia, a car came by and picked me up with a guilty guide who insisted that they had looked everywhere for me, and then hoped I had gone ahead to the hotel. I felt like a lost toddler who had found his mommy in a department store.

Some tips so you don't spend your life in a desert outpost weaving lanyards: Carry a charged cellphone, with the phone number and address of where you're staying. Have a buddy who won't leave without you. Don't be late for pickups—in fact, be early, just in case.

And the worst of it, looking back, is that I didn't even get to buy that octagonal mirror.

MOZAMBIQUE

Hair and Fishes, Rain and Sun

Our guide was maybe twenty-five, and he was blunt. Standing at the front of the van he told our little group on the half-day-tour off the cruise ship that he wanted to move from Mozambique to Dubai, like so many others his age who were bright and strong but without much of a future. This country on the Indian Ocean had a corrupt government, he said. The recent election had been a disappointment.

People in Maputo, the capital, had some money, but most in the countryside remained poor. The Chinese were building resorts and shopping malls, and only the already well-off were benefiting. The country needed more opportunities, more housing.

The guide's bearded face remained sad. He would have been handsome if he were able to crack a smile.

He guided us through the bustling capital that looked much like a mid-size American city from the last century, to a sprawling downtown marketplace filled with neon-colored fruits, lean meats and household goods. One section was draped in a scary row of black hair extensions hanging from ropes.

This was our only shopping opportunity. We had chosen the museum tour and most of us were disgruntled, as the other group was going to a big crafts market and we would instead be dropped at a small park where a few sculptures were placed amid scraggly bushes.

The sky began dripping to match our mood. We had not brought umbrellas, and after dutifully poking amid the sculptures we returned to the van in a half-run, damp and ahead of schedule. As thunder rumbled, we figured this was one of those gloomy tours that return you to the ship weary and ready for the comfort of your stateroom and a buffet lunch with wine.

Nobody was excited about our last stop, but we climbed up steps, past an unexpected sleek, hand-crafted wooden boat.

A man in a suit welcomed us each with a handshake and a beaming smile. He gestured proudly toward a small room. "Welcome to Maputo's fishing museum. I'll answer any questions but I will let you look for yourselves."

Fishes mounted on a wall. A map. A canoe and another small boat. It was a paltry exhibit. The man in the suit gathered us after about half an hour to an even smaller space with a dozen chairs in front of a boxy TV. When we were seated, he turned on a video.

We wanted to get to the van, and back to the ship. But we dutifully watched the video, and learned of the potential of this poor country. It was in its waters.

Mozambique has one of Africa's longest, most biodiverse coastlines, one of the few places on the planet where whale sharks and manta rays can be found year-round. It's home to turtles, bottlenose dolphins, humpback dolphins and rare small-eye stingrays.

During Mozambique's winter months (our summer), humpback whales travel north to breed before returning with their calves to rest and teach

their calves to breach in Tofo bay, then continuing south to feed in colder waters. The Mozambique Channel, between mainland Africa and Madagascar, has current eddies that draw cold, nutrient-rich water, enabling zooplankton ("fish food" for our filter-feeding ocean giants) to bloom.

We were learning something new and important. At the end of the presentation there was silence, and then we asked about tourism, new marine industries, scientific studies.

The man was informative about fishing in the Indian Ocean and the country's potential, and we felt uplifted by his efforts in the face of obviously scant funds and resources. We lingered in front of the boats placed at an angle and the chart of fishes. And as we left, we held the man's hand and his forearm and thanked him and praised his venture and he walked us down the stairs and waved goodbye. And many of us dropped money into a container—not only informed, but touched.

As we were leaving, we looked more carefully at the hand-carved boat just outside the museum that we had rushed past as we entered. It was a work of art, magnificent as a sculpture.

We walked back to the van smiling, although our guide still looked glum. And the sun had come out, peeking among the clouds.

NAMIBIA

You Oughta Be in Pictures

I considered myself a writer/journalist, not a photojournalist. For most of my life I couldn't see spending money for complicated cameras, and I figured I didn't have the chops to deal with film processing and learning about focuses and lenses. I did, however, enjoy hanging out for hours with photographers, noticing details they sometimes overlooked, and enjoying beauty in the moment as they were capturing it on film.

But I never figured I was good enough. "I write guidebooks," I kept saying. "I don't need to take photos." Besides, photographers had "talent."

All those years, all those unphotographed people and places as I traveled the world from the 1960s. Historic remains, bombed-out sections from the World War II blitz, now gone. Varied sunsets. Signs of the times. Uncrowded vistas, now filled with selfie-takers. Festivals, parades, faces, clothing and torn-down buildings fading in my memory, and all could have been captured. How I wish they were photographed for me to see once again.

When I was a child, my Aunt Hilda bought me an unwieldy Brownie box camera, and I'm sure I took some photos, now lost; I often didn't even have the film processed. And then she bought me a Polaroid camera, which magically developed film right in the camera. But the photos faded, and so did my interest. Then there were the Kodak Instamatic, the point-and-shoots and the disposables, which I often carelessly disposed of with photos still in them.

My few photos over the years were snapped on the run, so they were blurry or had the shadow of my finger in the corner. I convinced myself I was a writer. Period.

Enter the smartphone, especially the recent versions, offering photos as sharp and clear as ones from great cameras, with just a touch, and with easy-to-use filters and effects.

I started to take pictures of my grandchildren, my husband, my sons, my cat, and then, finally, after fifty years, my travels. And I haven't stopped since.

✳

Namibia, west of South Africa, was the first country I traveled to specifically to take photos. I designed the trip to capture the highest, reddest dunes in the oldest desert in the world.

On a scenic plane ride from Walvis Bay, which had overflowed with seals and flamingos, we flew along the Skeleton Coast, peering at shipwrecks scattered along beaches where towering white dunes plunged to a turquoise Atlantic.

Then the Namib Rand Nature Reserve, covered in the legendary red sands of the Kalahari. I woke
before
dawn
at

a lodge in Sossusvlei, just before sunrise divided the dunes in black shadow and increasingly deep shades of magenta, apricot, ruby, scarlet and rust.

I had climbed dunes in Vietnam and on the north island of New Zealand, and in Morocco and Dubai. But here, all I wanted to do was take photos: bare, sculptural trees in the white salt pans. The dry Tsauchab River and rocky Sesriem canyon. On the dirt-road main highway to the capital of Windhoek, we passed the little settlement of Solitaire, and I took photos of a café and its famous apple strudel. And families of baboons that came down from the rocks onto the road.

I saw more, and observed more, so I came out not only with photos, but with memories of even small aspects of the trip.

I now often choose destinations with photography in mind. Slot Canyons with surreal swirls, tropical skies over the ocean, ornate ceilings, smiling children. I took a flight from Paris to Tangier and a long car ride into the Rif mountains, just to photograph the blue village of Chefchaouen in Morocco. *(See: Intro.)*

Even if you don't use a camera, observe—up, down, all around. Faces, spaces, storms, rooflines, crevices, alleys, souks. Think of different angles, try new things. Look outward, and cool it on the selfies. In the digital world you have the freedom to find what it is you love, and make mistakes you can immediately trash.

At this writing my Instagram gallery ("travelea") has about 5,000 photos, including two series I created: closeups of faces ("People of the World") and skies of all kinds ("Sky Series"). My cell camera remains handy to seek what's beautiful, different, interesting wherever I go.

Let travel inspire you to take photos or write, or paint or do something you haven't done before. It's not too late to find a passion, and travel can unleash it.

NETHERLANDS

Time-Travel with Anne Frank

Anne Frank has been a lifelong obsession for many Jewish women my age, and the timelines and connections with her are meaningful.

At Nautilus Junior High in Miami Beach, my English teacher, Mrs. Gelber, handed me a paperback book titled *The Diary of a Young Girl* ten years after Anne Frank's death in 1945. I was then thirteen, the age that Anne had been when she was given her diary, on her birthday.

Anne went into hiding two months after that birthday, in the secret annex where she and others hid for over two years above her father's office in Amsterdam. She died from typhus at fifteen, seven months after her arrest, in Bergen-Belsen concentration camp just before it was liberated.

I took the book home and read it through. I identified with the sensitive Jewish teenager who could write openly and freely, who didn't get along with her mother, who was feisty and flirty and curious.

I lived through the war as a baby in Florida, and my Jewish grandmother left Germany (where the Frank family had lived before resettling in Holland) to come to the States. I realized with a chill, perhaps for the first time, that "there but for the grace of God...." This was when the world was still discovering the horrors of the Nazi death camps. Many survivors of these camps lived in South Beach, and I had by then met a lady with a tattooed number on her arm.

Anne Frank's story was turned into a play on Broadway, and when I was sixteen years old, on my first date with the man who would become my husband, we saw the film adaptation of the book.

Five years after that movie date and only twenty years after she and her family were found by the Gestapo, my new husband and I visited the attic in Amsterdam above her father's office where Anne Frank and her family went into hiding. We walked right up the same stairs she had climbed to hide behind the false bookcase, the same stairs she was forced down by the Gestapo after being betrayed.

We walked alone through the cramped attic hideaway, with movie star pictures from 1940s fan magazines still on the walls above her bed. I remember a little bathroom, and stairs to a skylight.

The two-tone sirens I heard in the Amsterdam streets that day reminded me of a scene when Anne Frank heard them in the movie. In that dramatized version, when the siren sound stopped, Anne knew that the police had found their hiding place.

I've been back to the Anne Frank House a couple of times since that first visit in the mid-1960s, to the modern building with interactive displays and world viewpoints and quotations about goodness. The queue to get in snakes around the block near the Westerkerk, where Anne heard the steeple bells through the attic skylight. The canal scene remains peaceful, as it was, deceptively, when she was hiding.

More connections with Anne Frank: In a regional theater production in Atlanta, my niece, who has an uncanny resemblance to Anne, played her older sister, Margo Frank, who also perished. And a few years ago, I worked with a survivor Anne's age who had also hidden through much of the war, and I visited Auschwitz *(See: Poland)*, where that brave lady had survived hell on earth.

We who love the written word can only imagine what perceptive, creative Anne would have accomplished had she lived. Instead, she became a symbol of the horrors of war, an inspiration to millions, and perhaps the most famous child of the twentieth century.

New Zealand

Surprising Maoris

I was writing an article about New Zealand for an upscale magazine, and Neal, a young guide with an old soul, was accompanying me on an independent press trip for a couple of weeks. In the dining room of one lodge we noticed a trio of fifty-something, well-dressed women who kept staring at us. Here I was, doted upon by a Brad Pitt clone about thirty years my junior.

After a glass or three of New Zealand's fab Marlborough Sauvignon Blanc, Neal and I decided to up the fantasy ante the next night to amuse ourselves and the ladies. At that dinner, this good guide/guy was blatantly catering to my every whim. And, sure enough, one of the women heading to the restroom detoured to whisper in my ear, "Honey, I *need* to learn your wicked skills."

The next day, Neal scheduled a surprise lunch on a private island. On a nearby beach we met a barefoot boatman with a belly hanging over his shorts, like a rotund version of the cartoon sailor Popeye. He yelled, "We're going to paradise!"

He piloted us into rough Pacific waters on a beat-up hybrid vehicle that changed from a car on the beach to a small boat as it splashed into the waves. I gripped a rope to keep from falling into the ocean, sliding back and forth in the swells as we pushed toward the horizon.

The cigar-chomping sailor explained that the entire island, with its one sleek lodging, was rented out to only a couple or small group at a time, and guests could enjoy anything possible, included in the $15,000-a-day tab. One sheik asked for nothing but quiet. A rock group requested a chamber orchestra at dinner. A sultan wanted girls.

Holding onto the rope with both hands, I figured my request would be to make it to the island alive, and I practically kissed the shore when we arrived, wandering on a noticeably raked beach strewn with iridescent abalone shells.

After a tour of a spa and the lodging, I rested by an infinity pool, sipping champagne and watching whales pass by, far out in the ocean.

"The owner himself is cooking us lunch," Neal said.

A table overlooking the water was laden with local vegetables. And the grizzled sailor brought in fresh grilled fish.

Oops. Popeye was the *owner* of the island. And we all toasted, and the owner and his son later drove us up their private hill in an ATV. All in all, it was perfect, in part because of the surprise. Even the sail back, hanging onto the rope for dear life.

And this time it was Neal who whispered in my ear, "You must have wicked skills to get us to do this for you."

✳

In a sacred forest on the North Island, a young Maori man chants and prays each evening as ambassador and protector of a huge kauri tree. Kauris have been depleted by logging, and our small group had to hose our shoes and remove loose soil before entering the rainforest, as the few remaining giants are also threatened by disease.

We were careful to stay on the walkways as we entered the forest, and arrived in semi-darkness to a living giant: *Tane Mahuta*, "the lord of the forest." At over 150-feet tall and 55-feet wide, it is one of the largest kauri trees in the world. In Maori myth, *Tane's* growth broke apart the embrace of *Ranginui*, the "sky father," and *Papatuanuku*, the "earth mother," allowing needed space and light for life.

The stillness of the forest, the gigantic soaring tree and the man's moving chants brought forth tears. Walking back after the service, I asked the young man if he had ever wanted to live in a city, and he said that at one time he moved to Wellington on the South Island and he clubbed and fooled around for a year. But he needed to return to the forest and to *Tane*, where he belonged.

In the stillness of the rainforest under the canopy of the kauri trees, I could understand. They are the elders of nature, and they called him back.

※

A well-known Maori chef and I foraged for mushrooms and herbs, and he hooked some eels from a river, preparing them with fern fronds and Maori bush pepper, bush basil and potato.

He pointed out flowering plants and parrots—chubby kakapos—and sharp-beaked keas, which, he explained, were strong enough to attack sheep and yank rubber parts off cars.

After lunch, we dallied by a thermal spring, and he took my photo. The chef told stories of his grandfather teaching him *haka*, an ancient Maori war dance used on the battlefield.

"It's a display of pride, strength and unity," he explained. "We stamp our feet, stick out our tongues and slap ourselves while we chant. I've taken part in *haka* at weddings."

"A war dance at a wedding?"

"Yes," he said. "Our tradition." And then he told me of an even stranger one. When his great-grandfather, a Maori chieftain, had warred with his rivals, after one major battle he had eaten the rival chief.

"Your great-grandfather *ate* him?"

"He was honoring him, taking in the spirit of his foe. That act was fierce *and* respectful. It's been our tradition until the beginning of the

twentieth century." And then the chef paused and looked me in the eyes. *"He told my grandfather that people taste like pork."*

Words failed. I thought for a second about dietary restrictions, but no. Silence.

Later, as we rubbed noses, the Maori custom for saying goodbye, I couldn't help but wonder if the chef got into the food business subconsciously, in the spirit of his ancestors.

In a craft shop near Wellington, a beautiful Maori woman sold handmade artifacts. We talked a bit about the spirituality of the man I had met in the forest, and the Maori tradition of war-time cannibalism.

But when I told her that I had been, for a short time, a rabbi's wife, she beamed.

"You were a *rebbitzin!*" *(See: Curacao.)*

Whoa. This Maori woman from New Zealand had just used a Yiddish term.

"I know, I'm a *shiksa,*" she said. "But I picked up some Yiddish when I was an au pair for a Jewish family in New York, many years ago."

And in that moment, thinking of the people I had met on this trip to New Zealand, I realized more than ever that, despite varied customs and different spiritualities and interests, opening our hearts and respecting traditions helps us learn from each other and makes us better.

When I left, I said *"L'chaim."* To life. And, nose-to-nose, she said *"Shalom."* Goodbye, and peace.

NICARAGUA

Smokin'

As I write this, Nicaragua is going through a politically dangerous time, and Costa Rica's edgier neighbor is probably not the first place you'd consider for a fun-and-sun vacation.

But our small, four-masted ship stopped in Nicaragua in 2011, and left me with pleasant memories. We harbored in San Juan del Sur, set on a horseshoe-shaped bay on Nicaragua's Pacific coast, well-known for surfing, fishing, beaches, and a laid-back atmosphere.

Sandonista political history resonates in Managua, the capital, a noisy, messy, low-rise city, rough around more than its edges. Locals prefer nearby Montebelli and Chocoyero-El Brujo nature reserves, Pochomil beach, and El Trapiche hot springs.

Nicaragua has two rival colonial towns. Leon is the more political one, geared for backpackers, with loads of churches, art, cosmopolitan eateries, an intellectual atmosphere and local nightlife. Granada, on Lago Cocibolca, is the jewel, the country's oldest colonial city. Plazas, markets, pastel colonial buildings, museums and relative safety make it a popular and praised destination city. And sulphurous volcano Masaya looms in the distance.

I climbed a hundred steps or so along the edge of Masaya's huge active crater. Sulphur is not my thing, so I spent only a few minutes taking photos above the caldera. As I inhaled the fumes, I thought of other volcanoes I have ventured near— including in Italy and Saint Lucia. *(See: Iceland.)* All of them smelled like hell.

I remember back in the 1980s, when I flew with a friend in a helicopter over a still smoking

Mount Saint Helen's in Washington state, its top recently blown off. An iconic landmark changed in a few hours from a perfect peak to a decapitated, lopsided reminder that changes happen fast in nature. Americans who endure earthquakes and hurricanes don't expect a dormant mountain to explode.

Neither did the residents of the ancient resort city of Pompeii, near Naples, where you can see the charred remains of 2,000-year old couples holding hands. Nor, I'm pretty sure, did the people of St. Pierre. (*See: Martinique.*)

Volcanoes—beautiful, deadly, unpredictable—are metaphors for life.

NORWAY

Life Is Just a Sink of Cherries

Ferries in much of the world run on a tight schedule. Timetables rule. Show up on time or miss the boat, or even worse. I learned that the hard way, in Norway, on a June day long ago. Before cell phones, even before home computers, and before I knew very much about life's challenges.

Our young family—hubby and I and our two sons, four and two—had been camping in Scandinavia in a Volkswagen pop-top camper. The iconic two-tone van had a little sink and room to sleep four, just about, if you didn't mind folding yourself in two.

We were having a lovely time, rolling along and popping our top in any Scandinavian field we wanted—a traveler's right in this stunning part of the world, where villages are few and far between, mountain peaks rise into the sky from mirror-like water, and fields of wildflowers are open to campers as long as they're respectful of the land. I admit I once peed in the field just as a train roared right by, passengers waving at me, car after car. Was that disrespectful?

One sunny, perfect morning, driving along the Norwegian fjords, cherry trees were laden with red fruit, and we were rambling without a care. We decided at the last minute to drive our little camper onto a small ferry and cross a narrow fjord.

Our van was positioned first, so when we arrived at our landing about twenty-five minutes later, my husband drove right off the ferry to clear the deck while I lingered on the ferry stairs a few extra moments to tie one son's shoe while the other looked on. I would walk them off.

Suddenly I felt a rumble, and realized that the ferry was quickly moving away from the shore—with me and my two sons still aboard, and my husband on the pier. Hubby was waving his arms onshore, getting smaller and smaller, screaming, "Stop! Stop!"

I scrambled up the stairs to find the captain, and finally bumbled out our problem. He spoke slowly, as my husband became a speck in the distance.

"Sorry. We leave on time. We can't go back. You can meet your husband at the next landing."

"But he doesn't have a timetable and he wouldn't know where to drive."

"Then I hope he stays where he is," the captain said. "The ferry will return."

"When?"

"At the end of the day."

I had no money, no passport, no food. No diapers! And remember, this was long before cell phones. I felt as lost as a five-year-old at a fair, except I was the mommy. If hubby didn't meet us at one of these landings, I was in big trouble.

The boys started crying and I felt like joining them. I imagined that hubby would drive the van ahead to Oslo, and that I would never catch up with him. I'd become a bag lady without a country, with two sons who'd play patty-cake on the streets to earn us a few coins for food and diapers.

My husband did not show up at the next landing, or the ones after. I felt dread every time I did not see him, but I also wanted him to remain in place until we returned. I sat on the deck as the afternoon wore on, worried that he wouldn't know to stay where we had left him.

The captain offered the boys candy and I created diapers out of paper towels. They played with ropes. They napped. I told them stories. They seemed to be having a fine time.

But they kept asking "Where's Daddy"? And I said that he was shopping for our dinner.

I wished.

Throughout the day we completed the slow circuit from landing to landing, and the Norwegian fjord scenery was spectacular, but I couldn't enjoy a moment in this slowest day of my life.

We finally headed to the harbor where we had left my husband that morning. The boys were restless now and I kept straining to see him. As we pulled closer, I saw a bunch of cars in the distance, and then … our van, with the top popped! And then my husband, waving as wildly as when we had pulled away many hours before. In fact, he was jumping up and down.

And so was I. Even the stoic captain was happy to see him.

We made sure to be at the head of the line and ran off the ferry as fast as we could. And when we got inside the van, sure enough the little sink was overflowing with cherries. We gorged ourselves, faces smeared with cherry juice, laughing and hugging as if we had been separated for weeks.

Oman

My Favorite Travel Photo

I snorkled in the Gulf of Oman, walked amid the souks and fortresses of Muscat, the harbor-capital, and visited swank hotels and palaces with acres of soaring marble.

A sultanate with no evident poverty, Oman offers free schooling and free health care. The sultan's photo, and photos of his brothers and sons, peered at me from walls everywhere, but our guide did not seem to know much about him—or be willing to divulge anything. Is the sultan married? Does he have children? Is he alive? *Anything?*

In a world of tweets and Facebook, it seems especially odd that such privacy is possible. Our group asked questions and we kept getting vague answers and no information except that the sultan is a good man, and "very private." Okay, I figured. The Omani people are culturally different and I need to appreciate that.

Oman is a mix of desert and beach sands, green mountains with oasis streams, and a diverse ecosystem that includes hundreds of species of plants, mammals, birds and reptiles.

One afternoon I visited mountain-fringed springs, enjoying the cool greenery against the desert landscape. Locals were wading in the shallow water and chatting by the rocks. I walked awhile along the springs and noticed a group of Omani schoolgirls giggling together, as teenage girls do around the world. With their headscarves and smiles, I saw a chance for a magnificent photo to put on Instagram for my "People of the World" series.

I motioned to the girls and they gestured that I sit next to them to be in a photo *with* them. I rarely do that. I have rarely liked having my photos taken, especially late-in-life ones.

But one got up and indicated that she would take the photo on my smartphone, so I agreed and sat in her place in the midst of the girls. We all smiled, and the photographer took several images.

After I got up, I thanked her, took my camera and waved goodbye. Later, sitting in the van, I looked at the images of the springs and the mountains. And there they were—the whole line of girls

in head-scarves smiling at the camera, with me in the middle.

And then I looked closer and laughed. The girl next to me was grinning, and without my realizing it, had held her middle and index finger right behind my head in a universal sign of mischief.

That photo is on my wall and reminds me that although I have learned little about the mysterious sultan and how he governs, universal sign language and a sense of mischief transcend cultures and generations.

PANAMA

I'll Have What She's Having

I am on a press trip many years ago, rooming with a hefty Panamanian woman named Maria, who is our in-country representative, and she explains things to me about Panama that I probably shouldn't be hearing, including that she is the vice president's mistress.

As we drive on a tour bus, she gets off to buy us ice cream, and later points out her house, big as a castle on a leafy Panama City street. "I live there by myself," she says.

I have my doubts.

One night in a mountain inn where we are sharing a room, she asks, "Do you know Rojermo?"

"Rojermo?" I do not recognize that word. Is it even Spanish?

"Rojermo very good in bed."

I guess I look perplexed, so she whips out a faded photo of a svelte and sexy woman in a bikini, walking hand in hand on a rocky beach with Roger Moore, perhaps the most handsome of all the James Bonds. The girl is Maria, my roommate for the night, more than a few ice creams ago.

I realize that Roger Moore and I have something in common, kind of, as I look over at Maria in her nightshirt.

And I now believe her about the vice president and the house.

※

The San Blas Islands, a short flight beyond the Panamanian mainland, are home to a matriarchal society of native women who embroider *molas*, decorative fabrics in vivid tropical hues, sold for a good profit.

One of the photographers on the press trip keeps taking photos, and he realizes that a San Blas woman who has been following him around for the entire trip now blocks his entrance to the little plane that flew us here.

She gives him a paper on which she has marked down the number of clicks of his camera. He is forced to pay about $70 before any of us can leave the island. He is not happy.

We are on a tight schedule, and I realize that although I have flown in gliders, balloons and blimps, I have never flown before in a plane that is bandaged.

※

How many flights have I taken? One of the first was in a DC-3 from New York to Miami when I was a baby, and my mother tells our family that a grinning Mayor LaGuardia himself put me on his lap, and that I promptly spit up on him. (Thinking about it, LaGuardia Airport and messiness is not an unusual combination today.)

According to my mom, he immediately handed me back, cursing.

And on that topic, in one underdeveloped country, a woman in elaborate traditional garb that may never have been cleaned, caused many of us to gag when she walked past in the aisle. The attendant sprayed the cabin with air freshener with little success.

I remember when aircraft often flew half empty, and an eerie flight from New York to Miami in a huge plane with a handful of passengers. Lightning flashed the whole way and it felt like an episode from *The Twilight Zone*. In contrast, our small plane in Peru picked up people at a small airport in a jungle clearing, and the new passengers stood for the rest of the flight, as if in a rush-hour subway.

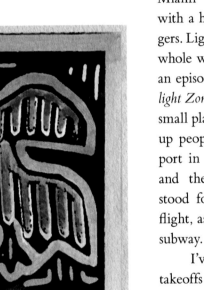

I've been on aborted takeoffs and rough landings, but most flights have been routine, which means they arrived safely. One flight from Cleveland to New York filled with smoke from a small fire in the lavatory, and we sped ahead of schedule, with yellow trucks awaiting on the runway. What I remember most was how blasé the weary business people seemed, as if showing panic was uncouth. I was acting cool along with everyone else, but I did clap loudly on landing and high-fived my seatmate.

But perhaps the oddest flight remembrance was from my sons' babysitter, who reported on her first flight ever.

"I liked it," she stated matter-of-factly. "Except when we had to put on our oxygen masks."

Thunderhead clouds tower over the San Blas Islands, and rain starts to pelt. I do not want to fly on that beat-up bus with wings, but my choices seem limited: board the bandaged plane or stay and live among the women of the San Blas Islands, embroidering and extorting whoever comes my way with a camera.

Clasping my seatbelt, I think, as I sometimes do in dicey situations, "Why didn't I choose a normal desk job? What's a nice Jewish girl living in the 'burbs of New York doing in a place like this?"

We take off and hit the storm. I notice below me on the side of the short landing strip the wreckage of a similar small plane.

I am really nervous, but Maria, our guide of "Rojermo" fame, is sitting next to me, reading a magazine and eating chocolate. She offers me a piece.

I take it. The cool that works for her might rub off, just a bit, on me. In this way at least.

PERU

Impressive Guys, Flutterbys

What I remember most about Machu Picchu is not just the splendor of the site, but the Peruvian boy who ran down the mountain from the ruins to beat the bus as we were leaving. There he was, running ahead of us at every hairpin turn, shouting as he saw the bus inching around the curve toward him.

And throughout the slow descent we were all laughing and waiting for him to greet us at the next turn, and we happily tipped him when the ride was over.

When people I know visit Machu Picchu, I ask about the boy. And for years they've said, "Yes, the boy who runs down the mountain, screaming!"

There have been, no doubt, many boys, and all these years later I imagine that they have invested their tips and are now living the good life in Lima, while other hopeful young entrepreneurs may still be screaming at tour buses in a proud tradition.

✳

I was drinking a pisco sour at a casual restaurant near the beach outside Lima, and started talking with a local surfer who told me that the longest waves in the world were on Peru's coast.

He explained that Peruvians have been surfing since at least 1000 B.C., and pottery from pre-Incan cultures along the country's northern coast even depicts a man on a log-like vessel riding the waves.

Peru's modern love of surfing dates to about 1942, when a socialite returned from Hawaii with a longboard reportedly given to him by Duke Kahanamoku, the godfather of modern surfing. Inspired by the gift, he founded Club Waikiki in Miraflores, which became a surfing mecca for wealthy Peruvians.

I had always thought that the Andes and the Amazon were Peru's natural wonders. But now I know to add the 1,600 miles of Peru's Pacific coast.

You never know what you'll find out when you sit at a beach bar and talk to a surfer dude.

✳

The Peruvian Amazon is a swirling, branching force in the jungle midway from where it first sweeps from a trickle in the Andes and rushes toward the Brazilian rainforest.

The rusty gingerbread buildings of Iquitos stand over piles of rotting bananas, and vultures swirl overhead. The sky often lights up and thunders from humidity released throughout the night.

The first day in Iquitos our group stayed at a hotel. I was talking to my friend Marilyn, watching an elderly, indigenous man in a hat fishing an iguana out of the swimming pool.

Suddenly the man, who was listening as we chatted, looked up at me and whispered two words: "White Plains."

I looked askance. And then he paused and said ... "Scarsdale."

Marilyn looked at me with her mouth agape. "How does he know you're from New York? And from Westchester County? Scarsdale is maybe ten minutes from where you live!"

We eventually surmised that the man had such an alert and refined ear from listening to jungle sounds that he perhaps could identify the accents of the many hotel guests he had heard over the years.

When we told our fellow travel writers about his gift, a couple of them talked to the man, and asked him to identify where they were from. But he just shook his head.

In my case, perhaps he made an educated guess that was worthy enough to be remembered here, so many years later. Or not. Marilyn and I still regard it as a bit mystical, and one of the highlights of our travels.

✳

Our group overnighted in a jungle camp on a tributary lighted by kerosene lamps, with cold-water showers and boiled drinking water.

Leo was our local guide, a tall Peruvian in his thirties with gleaming muscles. Leo had never been to Lima, but he knew all about his jungle. He walked us through the foliage, pointing out the flora amid the screeches of monkeys.

At dinner he announced that those of us willing to get up at dawn would be treated to a

canoe ride with him down a narrow tributary, to observe hundreds of awakening birds, insects and animals.

We all planned to join this special trip, but the night lingered late with dancing and laughter. Groggy-eyed, and dragging, I managed to show up by the canoes at sunrise. And I was the only one.

"Good," said Leo. "Leo and Lea. We'll go alone, and there will be more to see if we are quiet."

Indeed, there were birds, and Morpho butterflies as big as birds, which swarmed above my head, maybe twenty at a time, their iridescent, blue-violet wings shimmering like Tiffany glass in the rising sunlight.

I've always been enchanted by magical "flutterbys," the name I used when I was a little girl. *(See Mexico.)* And these were swirling clouds of the biggest, most beautiful ones I had ever seen.

"They like you," Leo said. "Make a wish now, and it will come true."

I closed my eyes and wished for a life filled with many moments as shimmering and peaceful as this.

The splash of oars in the water, the orchids and dense foliage and the sounds from the jungle beyond added to the experience, and the butterflies followed our canoe throughout that quiet morning.

At breakfast when we got back to camp, Leo told everyone what we had experienced, and the others seemed especially sorry that they had missed out. I explained how the butterflies hung above my head and that I felt a communion with nature.

One piqued man dashed the fantasy. "You're wearing a red shirt, Lea. Butterflies are attracted to red."

Leo just smiled.

Okay, so it wasn't exactly magical. But as I look back, I realize that the wish I made with Leo that early morning in Peru has come true.

PHILIPPINES

Business as Usual

In 1989, I was executive producer of a video project commissioned by the Army. The training company in Washington, D.C., where I worked as communications director, was one of the first anywhere to use interactive computer abilities, and the project was exciting both for us and the clients.

The Philippine dictator Fernando Marcos had recently been deposed, and a woman named Cory Aquino was president. We were relieved that Marcos' corrupt regime was over, but that relief was immediately dispelled when I arrived at the Manila airport and the customs officer made me open my suitcase.

"Nice T-shirts," he said, riffling through a pile I had brought for the Philippine crew that stated, "I Love the U.S.A."

The official proceeded to take them all. I objected, but the Philippine driver who accompanied me and would become my friend told me to let them go or there would be trouble.

Lesson learned. Price paid. Illusion dashed.

※

The video script I had written for the project—which would be used to teach the Tagalog language to military personnel and diplomats—centered around a week in the life of an American living in Manila. I found and hired an American actor who could speak Tagalog, local actors and crew, and we produced and shot in and around the city.

Filipinos went out of their way to be hospitable. We used the police force of an entire village to play the police in the film, and doctors, nurses, barbers and other workers to play themselves.

My driver-assistant instructed me how to work in a culture in which traditions were respected. I presented certificates to elders and usually got permission to videotape in their areas.

Our low-budget production used whatever, wherever, and I changed the script to accommodate what we found. An abandoned railroad car led to a scene in the video. The actors sat in the train car and the crew shook it back and forth to simulate movement.

Our one crisis came when the lead threatened to leave to become an extra in a Mel Gibson film that was shooting in the region. When I said I'd write him out of the script by having him die from syphilis, he reconsidered.

※

Sightseeing was not a priority, but I did visit the estate of the wicked dictator, Ferdinand Marcos, and viewed Imelda Marcos' infamous closets filled with thousands of shoes and elaborate dresses.

The couple's bedroom walls depicted Marcos as a sexy version of biblical Adam, and his wife as Eve. The Filipinos who visited the palace with me were laughing at a portable toilet Marcos had used, happy that the awful Marcos was no longer in power.

During the project I lived with the American crew at a budget hotel near the airport outside Manila, with no TV or radio. Electricity went on and off regularly, and the one dim bedside lamp made it hard to read. After shooting the video all day, I usually fell into bed, exhausted.

One morning I heard a sustained howling outside my hotel window, like an off-key kazoo played by a giant. I opened the drapes and saw trees bending, sheets of rain blowing horizontally and the ground littered with branches.

I rushed downstairs to the coffee shop, where people mentioned in an offhanded way that we were in the midst of—a typhoon.

I had heard nothing previously and neither, it seemed, did most of the people in that hotel. Groggy folks were eating cereal and drinking coffee. *Except we were in a typhoon.*

In the lobby I noticed that activity seemed pretty normal. There was no electricity, but, then, brownouts occurred every day. A group of Hong Kong tourists boarded a sightseeing bus, howling wind and torrential rain be damned. Others were entering cars, readying for business meetings in Manila.

At first, I was shocked. I grew up in Miami, where hurricanes mean boarding up, staying indoors or fleeing. Even back then, coverage in the United States was constant and warnings were frequent. But here in Manila there was no way to know what was happening because we had no advance warning.

We had planned to shoot a video segment at a bank with local actors. Losing a day would have been expensive and would throw off the rest of the schedule.

I thought about it. Others were out and about. I saw our van under the portico, and decided "When in Manila," so I ordered actors and crew to get in the van and go to the bank to shoot our video, come hell or high water, literally.

Traffic was snarled, with traffic lights out and trees down, but we eventually arrived at the bank and rode out the storm indoors, shooting the video with flickering power.

When I looked at the taped scene later, behind the blinds on the bank windows you can see the trees whipping about in the typhoon. Otherwise, you couldn't tell that we were risking life and limb for a storyline.

For months after, villages were out of power and cleanup continued throughout Manila. Going out in the storm was stupid and risky, but since everybody around us seemed to ignore it, we did too. I can't imagine I would have taken those chances had I been in the States. But we adapt to other cultures on the road. And in this case, at least I got the job done.

POLAND

Weeds and Ghosts

In the summer of 1995, I was on a two-month assignment in Russia and Eastern Europe writing for a travel trade publication. Feeling vulnerable, I found myself dreaming of Cecile, a survivor of Auschwitz whom I had worked with on her memoir. *(See: Hungary.)*

On this trip, fifteen years later, and fifty years after she had been liberated, I had the opportunity to follow in her footsteps.

The main square in Warsaw had been reconstructed to look exactly as it had been before being destroyed during World War II. It seemed like an elaborate stage set.

I remember wandering through a salt mine cathedral outside the well-preserved city of Krakow. And less than an hour away remained the most sobering memory of all my years of travels: the little town of Oswiecim, Poland—Auschwitz.

Auschwitz I was considered a labor camp, but over 70,000 were cremated near the neat brick administrative buildings that now house piles of hair, shoes, suitcases and other gruesome remains. In this surreal scene, most tourists are respectful.

But others now pose under the famous gate taking selfies, counting on high numbers of likes.

A few minutes away by car is the solemn vastness of the death camp at Auschwitz-Birkenau (Auschwitz II): the terminal, in a literal sense, for the 1.5 million people transported here in boxcars.

The camp remains much the same as it was when liberated by the Soviet army in January 1945. Overgrown paths wind between row after row of crumbling barracks stretching into the distance.

The friend I was traveling with was frightened by it all and didn't want to go into the camp. She asked to wait for me near the infamous railway watchtower entrance where the tracks ended, near where Cecile and the others had arrived for selection.

It was quiet when we arrived. The tourist buses had gone. By myself, with Cecile's descriptions in my mind, I walked through the gatehouse along the tracks and entered Auschwitz-Birkenau, among wildflowers and butterflies, in the stillness of a warm late afternoon.

After walking maybe twenty minutes I found the Hungarian block, the barracks Cecile had described.

Alone, I entered a building that looked like a parody of a house, the kind with two rectangles I used to doodle in class. The door looked like I was about to enter a cottage.

The space was now clean inside, but stacks of triple bunks still lined the sides, and I remembered Cecile's accounting of many people crammed together in a space for one. She described the bugs and filthy straw, and how when one exhausted person moved, all had to, so there was little sleep.

I didn't remember if Cecile and her sister were on the bottom bunk, right on the ground, which would have been frozen in winter.

In the sterile quiet I tried to imagine the fear and the stench that must have permeated this now-empty room. I wondered if this building might have been the very one Cecile had slept in, with dozens of other women stacked above and below her.

I walked to the huge open wash house/latrine that served the section. Benches with holes lined up along the center in a long double row, and I remembered that in the midst of horror, Cecile lamented about the lack of privacy. She had used the same bowl for washing herself and holding the watery soup she ate twice a day.

I walked in silence for maybe an hour to the back of the camp, to the crematoria now exploded into piles of bricks. I walked down broken stairs on which maybe a million naked men, women and children had trod, including Cecile's mother and nephew, their last steps into "showers," only minutes after arriving by boxcars.

As the last light faded I heard a rustle, and a deer bounded through the tall weeds. In the far distance I could make out the outlines of a factory in a nearby town, the tall chimneys reminding me of the smoke that had poured forth day and night in this hell on earth.

Other visitors had long gone, except for one couple, speaking German and shaking their heads. And I realized how long I had lingered, and that it was darkening rapidly. I walked as quickly as possible toward the front of the camp.

Auschwitz-Birkenau is a burial ground, and in the dark I was aware that I was treading on the ashes of the victims.

My waiting friend was beside herself with worry, and when I finally saw her again, I could hardly speak.

✳

You might wonder what became of Cecile Klein. Did she find a way to finally bear witness before her death?

In 1989 she published a slim book that you can find on Amazon, *Sentenced to Live*. And if you visit the United States Holocaust Memorial Museum in Washington, DC, you'll see one wall covered by the enlarged photo of Cecile's mother holding her grandson Nathan on their way to the gas chambers at Auschwitz-Birkenau. Cecile was chosen to go in the line to work until death rather than be put to death immediately, as her mother and nephew were.

And as you walk through the museum, the haunting, slightly accented voice narrating some of the exhibits is Cecile's.

Most amazing of all, in a short film at the end of the museum experience, Cecile is one of six survivors representing six million who were murdered. The six stories vary, each filled with indescribable horror, each told with dignity. In her

segment Cecile reflects quietly on the evils she experienced, and on her mother, who went to her death holding her grandson in her arms.

And I could feel the essence of those evils on the day I walked alone through the death camp, amid the weeds and the butterflies.

PORTUGAL

Madeira, M'Dear, and My Eff-It List

Travelers long to sip port and listen to mournful fado singers in Lisbon clubs, savor dried codfish, cruise on the Douro, buy hand-painted tiles in Sintra and laze in beach towns in the Algarve. Portugal is hot, and not just because of climate change.

At Lello, Porto's gorgeous Art Nouveau bookstore, I bought a ticket just to get into the place. Crowds pay to take selfies on the spiraling central staircase, walking right past the books.

This downside of Portugal's popularity reminds me of when I was researching Italy's Amalfi Coast for a new guidebook. I wrote about a charming boutique hotel, and specified the room with the best view. The hotel owner wrote to the publisher asking to please remove the entry. Not only was he having to turn people away, but guests were demanding the room I had mentioned, and were threatening him unless they got it.

Popularity can become physically destructive. More than a million people have visited Fjadrárgljúfur canyon in Iceland since Justin Bieber filmed a music video there in 2015 on the narrow cliff tops. The government had to close access. Venice authorities have voted to ban cruise ships

from the city center, and charge a fee for pedestrians. There have been crashes into canals, and crowds inundate St. Mark's piazza.

Other travel downers include theme parks and contrived entertainment versus the real deal. If possible, I'd rather see lions in the wild than a man in a lion costume—and anything to do with heights and/or ropes. *(See: Mexico.)* My theory on restaurants is if it revolves it's probably revolting. And I prefer a country's local foods to poorly adapted American food.

I much prefer beds with white duvets to maybe-washed-once-a-month bedspreads. And I choose small ships that hang around offbeat ports overnight over floating malls where you can forget you're on the sea. I do not like hunting, fishing and anything that exploits animals or our planet.

As for flying, I dislike most everything except the fact that it gets you around faster than anything else, and you get warm mixed nuts in the front of the plane.

Call this my anti-bucket list or, as some would call it, my "f**k it list." So there.

In Lisbon I placed my soft wallet in the hotel safe, along with other valuables. I usually leave myself a note on the floor by the door, or take my stuff out the night before so I don't rush and forget to open the safe.

But my husband gathered our things from the safe, and somehow pushed the wallet to the back.

We called the hotel right after we discovered it missing, but the wallet was not found. Lessons: Look carefully and don't rush when retrieving things. And take your valuables out yourself.

I had the opposite problem in Germany. I carried a stack of brochures and notebooks with me as I was checking out of an inn. I tucked the bundle in my backpack, and when I finally opened it on my return to the States, I discovered to my shock that besides my goods I had been carrying around a *hotel ledger*. Names, room numbers, dates in a notebook going back for years. (This was before computerized records.) I must have scooped it up by mistake from the reception desk as I was leaving. I airmailed the ledger back to the inn. Anonymously.

✳

Winter holiday season is one of my favorite times to travel. Christmas markets have inspired popular river cruises throughout Europe, focused on shopping and traditions. In Paris, the Champs-Élysées is lined with blue lights, stalls sell nougat and mulled wine, and the Eiffel Tower lights up with fireworks. London offers pantomime shows; New York City, creative store windows, ice skating under the Rockefeller Center tree and the New Year's Eve ball-drop in Times Square.

In Portugal, food is a big part of the festivities. On Christmas Eve, salt cod is traditional, and meat is served on Christmas and Boxing days. For dessert, crown-shaped *Bolo Rei* (fruitcake) offers a small present, like a fake ring. But get the raw bean hidden within and you'll have to buy the cake in the coming year!

New Year's fireworks displays light up towns, and traditional silly customs include jumping from a bench or a high stand, trying to place your right leg first on the floor to start the year "on the right foot." And I remember clapping kitchen pot lids together to bring good luck.

The Portuguese eat twelve raisins, with one wish for each month, and sip champagne to bring in the New Year. Long ago in a restaurant in Seville, we counted down the year in grapes, instead. Whatever, wherever in the world, it's a festive time.

✳

During the winter holidays on the Portuguese island of Madeira, off the coast of Africa, the harbor's natural beauty is adorned with lights and fireworks, and flowers are blooming.

I've visited Madeira on several cruise crossings from Barcelona to Miami. In fishing villages like Câmara de Lobos, nestled along the craggy coastline, men play cards in harbor cafés overlooking the Atlantic as they have for centuries, amid rose bushes, and bright blue and yellow boats. Winston Churchill painted picturesque harbor scenes from his apartment in the hills.

Madeira's interior *levada* trails follow narrow water channels through the mountains, so you enjoy views of cliffs meeting ocean with minimal climbing. Or you can hire a cab or take a bus to scenic overlooks and cable cars throughout the island.

The beaches here are mostly rocky; the best are in Porto Santo, a twenty minute flight away or a couple of hours by ferry. This peaceful little island offers a handful of low-key restaurants and hotels, and Christopher Columbus House, now a museum. If you ever need to hide, I assure you that no one will find you here.

Funchal is a dear little capital city, with lots of public gardens, restaurants and shops. I took the cable car up to the hillside chapel of Nossa Senhora do Monte, and then rode back down by traditional *carro*, a road-going wicker toboggan steered by strong drivers in jaunty hats. It started to drizzle and our toboggan skidded down the slippery hill, the wet drivers managing to stop it.

Later in a café on a pedestrian street where artists have painted the doors in creative ways, we paired sushi with Madeira on ice and watched pretty people walk by. Unlike Lisbon and Porto, Madeira has not yet been overrun. The sweet-spot time is now.

QATAR

Quickie

Flying back from Tanzania to Miami in 2016, Bill and I were planning a stopover in Turkey. But while we were in the Serengeti—trailing herds of rutting wildebeest and staring at leopards in trees, like my kitty in her cat tree at home—a political coup was developing around Istanbul.

If the coup erupted after we flew into Turkey, we didn't relish living in the airport like that Tom Hanks character in *The Terminal*. My husband, less of a risk-taker than I, managed to change our tickets at the last minute. We would now be changing planes in coup-less Doha, Qatar. We looked upon the stop as an unexpected travel opportunity.

I knew very little about this little sultanate except in terms of murky Middle Eastern politics, but when we arrived at the cavernous, gleaming airport, we noticed immediately that they don't just think big, they think humongous.

Qatar appears at first like a wannabe Dubai, a showy place rising from a desert filled with nomads and tents only decades before. The palace of His Highness Sheikh Tamim bin Hamad bin Khalifa Al Thani ("Tammy" to friends?) sprawls like a mall.

Doha's futuristic skyline along the Persian Gulf, built since oil replaced pearl diving as Qatar's major industry, seems a fantasy city, especially at night when the lighted skyscrapers dazzle in rainbow colors along the corniche. Seven-star hotels show acres of glitz and marble, soaring ceilings. Custom chandeliers that must weigh as much as a house flaunt the country's recent wealth.

Quirks and growing pains are evident. I ordered a glass of wine, and my husband, iced tea. The tea cost more than the wine—$20. And no refills! When we asked the restaurant manager about it, he said no one had ever complained before. Maybe because no one ordered it because of the price.

Daytime temperatures were so intense in Doha that you could probably fry not only an egg on the street, but a chicken. When we ventured from the hotel to our car, parked right in front of the lobby, we were immediately handed a bottle of water, and we rushed into the air-conditioned car to drink it.

The arts are blooming big-time in this desert. The I.M. Pei-designed Museum of Islamic Art's open floors exhibit a mix of art and history, with a permanent display about a visit from the American boxer Muhammad Ali.

The 2022 FIFA World Cup is spurring growth. The new National Museum of Qatar showcases film and art, artifacts and oral histories. Designed by Jean Nouvel, the French architect behind the Louvre Abu Dhabi *(See: UAE)*, it's layered to look like that gorgeous crystalline phenomenon, the desert rose. There's also the new Orientalist Museum, and the waterfront Art Mill exhibition space, plus a new underground railway system.

In the evening, when it cooled off into the 90s (!), we strolled through the Souq Waqif, Doha's traditional marketplace, checking out garments, spices, caged birds, handicrafts, foods and souvenirs. And after our walk, dined late into the night in a Persian restaurant with cut-glass ceilings.

Dress here is more traditional than in Dubai, but I noticed that many Qatari women wear designer shoes and purses. Their hair is usually covered with a black headdress (a *shayla*), their bodies with a black dress (an *abayha*). Some women cover their entire face with a black *burqa*, with only their eyes left uncovered. Qatari men look more colorful and less hot, often wearing a long white shirt over loose pants, and a loose headdress called a *gutra* made of white or red-and-white cloth, held on with a black rope (an *agal*).

The coup in Turkey never happened, but this unexpected stopover in Qatar offered much to remember beyond Middle East fashion and the most expensive iced tea ever. It was a chance to be surprised, and that's one of the most delightful aspects of traveling.

ROMANIA

Doggone

The palace in the Bucharest of the Ceausescus, former dictators of Romania, is bigger than the Pentagon. And the boulevard in front, lined with fountains, is broader than Paris' Champs-Élysées, on which they modeled it.

Our Romanian guide told us that when she was a child and these structures were being built, there was little to eat, and despite her parents giving her their food rations, she was always hungry. I've heard tales of starvation in so many countries, and realize that fasting for a day or cutting back on a diet gives no idea of the raw, hurting pain of hunger, often lasting for years, decades or a lifetime.

We stood under the balcony where students revolted, and eventually brought the evil dictator and his wife down, on Christmas Day in 1989 (the two were later executed by firing squad). The deaths of the despised couple ended a quarter-century of oppression and misery for most Romanians, and opened new opportunities, including for travel.

※

As a travel writer for almost fifty years I've pushed myself to do out-there things: racing in a Formula One car at 150 mph (See: Monaco), taking to the air in everything from balloons to gliders to blimps, even hanging out in jungles with angry tribes (See: Honduras).

But I didn't expect anything unusual cruising on the Danube.

I was on assignment, and brought along my friend, Merle. Our boat stopped at a Romanian river town on a cloudy spring day, and we decided to stroll into the historic center. On this late Sunday afternoon few people were out, and we wandered toward a row of leafing trees with fragrant blossoms, passing an old church, where we stopped to watch a wedding ceremony.

Beggars pestered us, but we wore no valuables or purses, and were dressed in jeans and tees. We looked them in the eye and they must have figured we were not worth the trouble to pickpocket.

We walked on, peering behind us to make sure the kids were not following, and after a few minutes, fields appeared, and we realized that we were at the edge of the town. Nobody was around. The air was warm and still.

Suddenly we heard sharp barking, and in a few seconds saw a pack of perhaps a dozen dogs in the distance running toward us. There were no trees nearby to climb, no building to run into. I remembered advice I had heard about dealing with bears. The correct thing may be to stand still, but the instinct is to flee. But what about wild dogs?

Merle and I decided to head back into town at a quick walker's pace as the barking got closer behind us. There were no safe places as we retraced our steps, as the noise at our backs got louder.

Suddenly a beat-up car stopped and a young man in a grimy shirt leaned out, gestured, and asked in Romanian if we wanted to get in. Merle wanted to do this, to get away from the dogs.

I didn't. I was fearful of wild canines, but even more, of getting into a vehicle with a suspicious-looking man. Headline: "Clueless Americans Running from Rabid Dogs Raped and Butchered by Crazed Transylvanian."

So, which is worse: the pack of dogs heading our way, or getting into a car with an unknown man, in a town I can't spell, in the middle of Romania?

As the barking got louder, I had an idea. I gestured to the man that I was about to jump on the hood of his vehicle, and I immediately did. Merle, somewhat bewildered, followed. The man looked perplexed at two strange women sprawled in front of his windshield, but thankfully did not move the car.

The emaciated dogs passed right by, perhaps with some other prey in mind, like a rabbit or a bird, or another hapless tourist. Perhaps we had over-imagined things, as privileged American women are prone to. But I don't think so.

We scrambled off the hood and headed toward town quickly, the dogs well past us. The man looked annoyed, lingering behind, then caught up and drove slowly next to us as we walked with eyes averted. A new problem?

After a few minutes, he finally shook his head and sped ahead, leaving us alone in the dust, safe for the moment. We rushed back to the safety of our river boat.

Aside from staying with a group from the beginning, and not walking out of town, what would you have done?

RUSSIA

People Who Need People

Soon after Perestroika, the reformation within the Communist Party of the Soviet Union during the 1980s and 1990s, and Glasnost "open" policy reform, off I went to review hotels in Russia. American tourism was about to arrive, and travelers were understandably wary of the accommodations.

Remnants of the Soviet past remained. On a cruise from Saint Petersburg to Moscow, a steeple poked up in the Volga River, a chilling reminder of how Stalin rerouted the water wherever he wanted, villages be damned.

At one stop, an old lady met the boat and invited me to her cottage behind a cabbage patch. She did this so that her daughter could practice English with me, and I was delighted to accept. The cozy place was decorated with paintings of cats and dogs, and looked like a dwelling from a Russian folk tale. She poured tea from a tarnished silver samovar, and insisted I take some homemade sugar cookies back to the boat.

Along the river, men were patching roofs and rehabbing village churches. On a short stop I entered one with smoky interiors and frescoed

walls, and as a men's chorus sang deep, throbbing harmonies, became so mesmerized I almost missed the boat, which has happened several times in my travels. *(See: Norway.)*

The Russian riverboat was pretty basic, with tiny cabins and earth-tone food. The highlight was the cultural program, and the best of the lecturers was Ludmilla, a cherry-lipped, platinum-blonde Russian. Many evenings we would talk late, sharing stories about being divorced, raising two children as single moms, and our similar hopes and dreams.

Ludmilla was put-together, but soon a few of the passengers noticed that she was wearing the same two outfits throughout the two-week cruise, with a few different scarves. We realized that it wasn't about the packing. She had no other clothes.

Some of us decided that we would each leave her at least one really good item of our clothing or accessories, but we didn't want to embarrass her. We collected earrings, necklaces, blouses, and I gave her my cardigan sweater. As we departed, we all hugged and handed her the suitcase filled with goodies. She was touched and teary when we told her what was inside, and we contented ourselves by imagining her pleasure when she opened it.

A couple of years later I heard that one of the passengers was so impressed with Ludmilla's skills that they found her a position at a Washington, D.C., museum. I wouldn't be surprised if Ludmilla had married a powerful lobbyist, and now wore Louie bags and Jimmy Choos. In any case, the moment at the end of that river cruise remains a heartwarming memory.

Except for a few, Russian hotels seemed really seedy when I inspected them, with dusty velvet drapes, musty smells and dark halls where a dim light bulb would be triggered as you walked along. I suspect most rooms were bugged in more ways than one.

At one ornate old place I went up to the front desk and explained that I was reviewing hotels for a guidebook, and would like to see a room.

The receptionist stared at me for quite a while, and then sighed in heavily accented English, "Why would anyone stay *here*?"

Her comment became my entire review.

※

Russia was slowly emerging from the Soviet era. Life was cool for former officials-turned-oligarchs, who were gaming the system, and devastating for people including teachers and scientists, who had lost the security of the Communist system. Many were selling clothes under overpasses, and with mixed emotions I bought my son an army hat from a soldier who had been stationed in East Germany.

I had arranged to meet Boris, a former Soviet scientist who lived in Moscow, through a Russian friend of his who was now my neighbor in the New York suburbs. Boris's life, like that of so many people I've met through my travels, was a tragedy of wrong place, wrong time. He was a baby during the siege of Leningrad, when his father was killed. A Jew growing up in a Communist country where anti-Semitism was official and sanctions were stringent. And now, middle-aged and out of work, an overeducated remnant of post-Sputnick education, living on his meager post-Soviet safety net.

My Russian neighbor suggested I pack a box of toiletries, basic tools and grooming aids to give him, and when I met Boris, I stealthily passed the box to him as if it were contraband. He mumbled a thank-you, but I know he was crushed at having to receive it.

We talked of life's ways, and how to deal with trouble, and Soviet art versus Western art, and with great aplomb, he asked me to be his guest for cabbage soup and blinis at a local hang-

out. I didn't want him to pay but he insisted, and I understood that he needed and wanted to. That evening he joined me for dinner, which he now enjoyed without shame.

Our mutual Russian scientist and friend had escaped Russia and lived in luxury in America, while Boris was stuck. I hope that at least at the end of his life he caught a break. He was not only a brilliant man but a proud and good one.

"There but for the grace of God…." I have said so many times throughout my travels, and in Russia I met exceptional people who made me realize once again how true that is.

Saint Kitts and Nevis

Non-Maidens and Maiden Voyages

This off-the-beaten-path dual-island nation in the Caribbean is one of the smallest sovereign states in the Western Hemisphere, from population to land size. Since the state-owned sugar company closed in 2005, tourism has been the major industry, with sandy beaches, a bustling capital city of Basseterre and a volcanic mountain to tempt visitors. You can still visit and stay in the remnants of the plantations.

Back in the 1980s I was booked at a small inn in Saint Kitts where each room opened to a private plunge pool. The fey owner had been an editor at a major shelter magazine, and I dined with him the first night amid hand-painted plates and cut crystal. Flickering candlelight cast palm-frond shadows on red walls, and the scene could have been featured on his magazine's glossy cover.

Perfect, except that he was wearing a caftan and velvet slippers and I was in the jeans and scuffed sneakers I had worn on the plane. My lost luggage arrived too late for the dinner, but he had the charm to praise my "laid-back look." And I had the nerve to say, "Thank you, love your look, too."

＊

Alexander Hamilton has become one of our most popular Founding Fathers. Beyond the draw of Nevis's sparsely populated beaches, lush forests and generally laid-back vibe, visitors now come to walk in Hamilton's boyhood footsteps.

Before he was born, his mother had fled an abusive marriage to an older man and moved to Saint Kitts, under British rule at the time, where she met Scottish trader James Hamilton. Alexander arrived in 1755 (or 1757—he himself was unsure) on Nevis. The rest, as they say, is history—or a blockbuster musical.

The landmark Trott House, known as "Hamilton House," reconstructed in 1983, is on land owned by the patriot's mother on Charlestown's Main Street.

All this reminds me of when I met historian Ron Chernow a few years before he wrote the biography of Alexander Hamilton. At the time he was researching a book on the Rockefellers, and I was living near their estate in Pocantico Hills,

New York, which held the archives. I was renting my house to make some extra money *(See: Anguilla)*, and he came close to renting half of it. It didn't work out, but we had a lovely talk about history. Not a word about Hamilton. He may not have even known then what was in store.

＊

On my one trip to Nevis I participated in a hard-hat ceremony, cutting a ribbon on the Four Seasons Hotel golf course, along with a bunch of other writers.

I've been the first guest to stay in a room many times, usually on a cruise ship. These launches are usually soft shakedowns with a short float to test out the vessel. They used to be called "maiden voyages" way back in the last (twentieth) century, when there were probably still a few maidens.

On one ship, I was the first non-crew member to set foot on a new vessel while it was still in drydock in Germany. We were cruising the Rhine from the shipyard to Amsterdam on a shakedown cruise. There are almost always glitches that need tweaking: lights that need tightening, doors that squeak. On this media tour, only one of us complained of something missing in the stateroom. But it was a big miss: a toilet.

Bad enough. And the person who was missing the toilet was the cruise company's CEO. You can be sure that a toilet was swiftly found and installed.

＊

After years of planning and building and furbishing and testing, there's usually much fanfare when a cruise ship is inaugurated. Speakers of various faiths bless the ship and the spectators; execs from the cruise line mingle with passengers; and the designer and head builder boast of their part of the experience.

At the ceremony's climax, the ship's esteemed godmother, chosen for her good deeds, good looks, great legs, great pedigree, fame, or the just fact that she is still alive and kicking, usually hurls a huge bottle of dubious sparkling wine to crash against the bow, sometimes abetted by a pulley system that ensures that the bubbly spews in a symbolic fountain.

At one launch I sat in the balcony section, and right after the ceremony, a Cirque du Soleil wannabe troupe flew so close over my head that I could see the holes in the trapeze artists' tights. A once-in-a-lifetime experience, I hope.

As the ship moves, passengers settle into their never-before-slept-in beds, or head for the deck to watch the leave-taking. The ship then blasts her bass horns, a mournful, tear-inducing sound, like a great mythic animal bellowing her strength. And with a sendoff of waving crowds, and even streamers and music—a scene that may be repeated at every port on this first trip—she wends her way forward to begin life on the waters of the world.

Saint Lucia

Waterfall and Lost Luggage

The Pitons, two iconic mountains, dominate the Saint Lucian landscape throughout much of the Caribbean island. We lingered at a lighthouse overlooking the south side of the island, toured the sulfur springs and therapeutic mud baths by the volcano, strolled in the flower-filled botanical gardens by a waterfall, and visited the charming town of Soufrire.

I like spotting unique birds, and the island has a half-dozen endemic species. The most colorful is the jacquot, a parrot with green wings, blue face, red breast and yellow tail tip. You can't miss it—not just because of the colors, but because its cackle sounds more like a honk, like a model who squelches her beauty when she opens her mouth.

※

In Saint Lucia we stayed at a resort called Serenity, with our own private plunge pool and its own little waterfall. It reminded me of another special room—without serenity—in the South Pacific paradise of Moorea.

Overwater huts throughout the world are deservedly popular. You don't have a pool, but the whole turquoise ocean is around and under you. Many of these lodgings have cutouts in the floor where you can watch the fish beneath your feet as you brush your teeth, or even when you're on the toilet (beats reading). These bungalows are famed wherever there is quiet, swimmable water, such as the Seychelles, the Maldives and the South Pacific islands.

Bill grabbed our black suitcase when we arrived at the Tahiti airport on the way to our overwater bungalow in Moorea. All was perfect except when we got off the ferry, ready to relax, we realized the suitcase *wasn't ours*.

We spent the first night and next full day hunting, tracking and finally ferrying back to Tahiti to return the suitcase to an understandably ornery couple who had no idea what had happened when they didn't find their luggage. They probably spent *their* first day in paradise even more stressed than we were.

We eventually tracked down our own luggage, too, and only had one day to relax. Lesson learned. We now put yellow straps around our luggage so we can identify it immediately.

SAN MARINO

The Paparazzo's Secret Trove

After attending the Umbria Jazz Festival in and around Perugia, Italy, a few writers and photographers were invited by one of the directors of the festival to Rimini, director Federico Fellini's town on the Adriatic coast. *(See: Venezuela.)*

We stayed overnight in the home of a famed paparazzo, and I rode on the back of his son's motorcycle to pick up bread, fruit and cheese for breakfast—a bit like being in *La Dolce Vita*, whizzing along, observing the kinds of outsize characters Fellini loved to feature in his films.

That night our host took out a locked briefcase of raunchy photos that he couldn't or wouldn't sell. One was of a famous married opera singer with a bunch of pretty men, and he also brought forth a folder of women celebrities exiting limos in exposed positions. In this age of the dick-pic,

his photos would have been considered not all that shocking, but this was in the 1990s.

Before returning to Perugia, we detoured just northeast of the Apennine Mountains to the Republic of San Marino, also known as the Most *Serene* Republic of San Marino, a fancy-schmancy name for a place with fewer inhabitants than the University of Florida. Despite being the world's fifth-smallest country, it is the sole survivor of Italy's once powerful city-state network of Genoa and Venice, and remains the world's oldest surviving sovereign state, and the oldest republic (since A.D. 301).

The little country's name was familiar to me since childhood, when stamp collecting was a popular hobby. I liked a nerdy boy named Herman, who was especially proud to possess a stamp from San Marino.

Our group visited the Serene Republic's main castle up on a hill and we bought some traditional candies, which we ate on the way back to Italy, talking about the paparazzo and his stash of photos.

I forgot to buy a stamp, but I did think about Herman, and I think he'd be pleased that I made it to San Marino.

SINGAPORE

Solo and Sick

Singapore brings to mind times that I was a sick traveler. In Vienna in the 1960s I had some kind of flu, and no appetite, and my husband brought me a chocolate Sacher torte that I couldn't eat, and I was delighted by his thoughtfulness.

In Belize and Guatemala, I returned home early; and in Vietnam extended my stay. *(See: Belize, Cambodia.)* In all three cases, it was the correct call.

On cruises I have picked up versions of the norovirus, and dealt with food poisoning. *(See: Chile.)* Flying around and getting overtired, I've caught countless colds. In Taiwan a guide was sneezing and coughing on the first day, and I was sick the rest of the trip. I now carry, beyond wipes and sanitizers, face masks. I also will not ride with someone who seems contagious unless I have no choice.

✳

In Morocco, traveling with a women's group, the whole dozen of us walked in lockstep to a pharmacist in a village who didn't have enough stomach-soothing medicine for all. The woman who couldn't hold it in got the first dose, in an informal triage.

Traveling with women is special: bonding, late night talks, zany situations.

A favorite anecdote, which happened in Iceland, may have had wine involved. A women's group on a tour bus was traveling through a canyon, but word got out that someone was missing. The search was called off hours later when it became clear that the missing woman had been accounted for. She had changed coats, had not recognized the description, and had been searching for…herself.

✳

In Singapore, back in 1984, I was sick alone. I traveled there on my own on my way back from China. I stayed two nights so that I would have one full day at least to experience the city/state/country that at the time was known for a benevolent dictator rumored to be such a micro-manager that he would fine or even jail people for chewing gum or jaywalking.

And sure enough, arriving at the squeaky-clean, get-you-through-customs-in-17-seconds Singapore Changi Airport, a friendly sign said, basically, "Bring Drugs Here and You Will Die."

Okay. So I crossed at the light, and threw away my gum—imagining life in prison if I blew a bubble. Drugs? Not even a baby aspirin.

The only problem was that while I was worrying about following the rules, I caught some sort of virus. On a morning bus tour, when I felt nauseous, I did what I needed to do. At a long light I got out of my seat and the bus, walked quickly to the nearest waste can, and threw up. I then proceeded to wipe my mouth with my ever-ready tissue (you do carry tissue, right?) and returned to the bus, looking straight ahead without a comment.

In the afternoon of my one day in Singapore, my stomach now thoroughly emptied, I decided that rather than hunker down in my room and watch old movies, I'd find a bench in a park and sit there and watch the Singapore world go by.

I observed kids playing and dogs walking, and felt the sun and breathed in the oxygen from the sea breezes, and as the day waned, I returned to a bath and some room service soup and crackers, and the next day I flew out of the super-duper airport. I had seen enough of Singapore.

And I may have been sick, but I did not get arrested.

SLOVENIA

Seeking Beauty, Finding Dragons

My friend Bob was my first romantic interest after I had become a widow a couple of years before, in 2001. He invited me on an odyssey to his favorite areas of Italy, including Venice and nearby Padua and Mantua. Portofino and Cinque Terra on the Ligurian Coast. The Lake District north of Milan, and the Amalfi Coast, south of Naples.

Can you imagine a more beautiful journey?

We had seen an old movie called *Bonjour Trieste*, so we also couldn't resist visiting the city that translates as "sorrow" on Italy's northeastern coast. But it was indeed a sorry choice, more industrial than romantic.

"Let's cut our stay here," Bob said after the first night. "Slovenia's nearby."

Last-minute add-ons can be risky, but we quickly researched and found we didn't need a visa, although for some reason at the Italian border we were turned away for not having one. But we were determined, checked again, and sure enough, entered Slovenia this time at the Austrian border.

And that was not a sorry decision.

Slovenia has been settled since prehistoric times, and was part of Yugoslavia until its independence in 1991. Mountainous and heavily forested, with a tiny Mediterranean coastline, it contains thousands of miles of rivers, streams, lakes and waterfalls, and almost a hundred thermal and mineral water springs.

Kranjska Gora, with its towering mountains and reflective waters, reminded me of Switzerland. Farmers bring produce to market in wooden carts, and we wandered off-road, enjoying the grazing cows and horses, fields of wildflowers and cozy, alpine farms.

At Bled, in the foothills of the Alps, we pedaled a boat on a glacial lake and admired the much-photographed church on a little island in the lake's center. Later at the cliffside medieval Bled Castle, we enjoyed a red-gold sunset.

We made the most of our time and our car. Near Piran, on a narrow Adriatic peninsula filled with medieval buildings, we bird-watched and strolled the trails along the Secovlje salt flats. We rode a traditional wooden Pletna boat to the island of Otak to visit the tenth-century church of St. Catherine.

And since Bob was a Hemingway fan, we toured the museum in Kobarid, known for the 1917 Battle of Caporetto, the Italian retreat written about in *A Farewell to Arms*.

The true magic of this unexpected little trip was an hour's ride away from Slovenia's pretty capital and largest city, Ljubljana. We descended into the huge, prehistoric Postojna Cave system. Only a small portion had been explored until 1818, and then a lamplighter uncovered twelve miles of caverns while preparing for a visit from an Austrian emperor.

We rode a train for three miles along an old railroad system within the multicolored caverns, and then walked a mile along a trail. And what impressed us most weren't the massive halls or giant stalagmites.

Nope. The most special discovery was a translucent amphibian less than a foot long, and found nowhere else: the olm. First discovered in the seventeenth century, this salamander eats worms, snails and other invertebrates, and, like a little dragon, engages in mock ferocious combat.

Olms are blind, and move around the dark caves by reading electrical fields. They can survive up to ten years without eating, regenerate limbs lost in battle and live over a hundred years. Maybe they *are* mythical dragons.

Later, at Prejama Castle, high on a cliff, we sipped hot tea and reflected on the pleasures we had just shared by changing plans and adding Slovenia to our Italian trip.

"Salamanders and humans," I quipped. "To each its own. I just know I don't want to go ten hours without eating, let alone ten years."

"Can you imagine living a hundred years in a cave without seeing?" Bob asked.

Bob was terminally ill, and we knew this would be his last trip. I could understand why he wanted to leave a city named Trieste, and why he had planned such a remarkably beautiful journey.

To this day, when I hear or read about Slovenia, I still think of its lakes and mountains and historic towns. But most of all, the little dragons that live a hundred years in a dark cave. What a strange, amazing world we live in, and how important it is to appreciate it.

SOUTH AFRICA

Haunting Smile

I traveled from Durban on the Indian Ocean inland to Johannesburg and of course to Cape Town, and experienced game preserves, the Cape of Good Hope and the mountain-framed wine country west of the city.

Most of all I wanted to pay respects to South Africa's first democratically elected president, Nelson Mandela, who, during the apartheid government, spent eighteen of his twenty-seven years in prison on Robben Island, a few miles off Cape Town.

Robben Island is actually the peak of a mountain in Table Bay and a migratory stop for about 130 bird species, including colonies of African penguins. We didn't see many birds—or tortoises, springbok, eland, southern right whales, or Cape fur seals ("robben" is derived from the Dutch word for seal)—but we weren't there for creatures.

In the seventeenth and eighteenth centuries, the Dutch sent political prisoners to Robben Island from the Dutch East Indies. When the Brits took over in the Cape, they too used the island to imprison resisters, and in the second half of the nineteenth century, lepers were forced to live there. During the Second World War, the island was used as a military base, and artillery batteries and fortifications remain.

Few prisoners escaped Robben Island. The first was a convict named Jan Rykman in 1690, who swam through Table Bay's treacherous rocks, icy water and sharks.

But Nelson Mandela served his time. And we were there to honor him.

Nelson Mandela toiled every day, digging up rock in a lime quarry so bright and dusty that he was stricken with "snow blindness." Much of that rock paved the road we were driving on.

When I envision South Africa, I do not see a lion or Table Mountain. I think of courage and fortitude in the face of brutality in a prison cell. And now, added to that, a former prisoner's smile.

South Korea

Turning Back

Bill and I waited in line to catch a ferry from the Nelson Mandela Gateway at the V&A Waterfront, awaiting a tour that would last about three-and-a-half hours. We disembarked at Murray's Bay Harbor, and buses transported us to sites including the leper graveyard, army and navy bunkers and the maximum-security prison.

Many guides on Robben Island are themselves former prisoners, and speak openly about their lives inside one of the world's most notorious gulags. Ours described severe beatings, hunger and solitary confinement. He arrived at the end of Mandela's confinement, and talked of how Mandela influenced other prisoners to not take revenge. Sure enough, our guide smiled much of the time.

The visit ended powerfully at Mandela's cell, a 7-by-9-foot room where a bulb burns day and night overhead. As Mandela recalled in *Long Walk to Freedom*, "I could walk the length of my cell in three paces. When I lay down, I could feel the wall with my feet, and my head grazed the concrete at the other side."

The late-fall weather meant crisp air and blue skies in Seoul, as my husband and I sampled ancient neighborhoods clinging to hills, and soaring glass skyscrapers, Korean barbecue and fried chicken joints, and ancient temple sites. We hung out at futuristic Dongdaemun Design Plaza, a convention hall with curving architecture and a rooftop park, walked around Gyeongbokgung Palace and Jogyesa Temple, and experienced a traditional meal and show at Korea House.

On our last day in South Korea we drove north to Pyeongchang, where the 2018 Winter Olympic games were to be held, to interview executives and check the progress. I hoped to meet the Olympic mascot, a white tiger named Soohorang.

Halfway up the highway, snow started falling, thick and wet. When the wipers got clogged and the tires spun on the slick expressway, I got nervous. You could hardly see out the windows.

But the driver insisted on getting me to the destination, hell or high blizzard.

It reminded me of a time in the 1960s when I was driving our MGB, from San Antonio down the Pan American Highway. It was getting dark, we were in the mountains, and it started to rain. My wipers weren't working and there was only a

narrow shoulder overlooking a steep drop to the valley below. I was panicked, but managed to stop the car and wait it out.

The weather in South Korea was worse ahead, so we told the driver to stop and return and find us a place to wait before returning to Seoul. I could interview the execs on Facetime and see

videos of the site. Sometimes you don't achieve your goals. Clouds might cover a faraway mountain vista you had hoped to see all your life, or the Northern Lights might decide not to show. Something will happen to spoil your plans, and you won't be able or have the time to fix it.

Disappointments happen in travels *(See: Mexico)* as in life. I still remember an invitation to fly private to Paris, then on to Saint Petersburg, Russia, for the anniversary celebration of a great French cognac. The singer Erykah Badu was among the handful of lucky ducks invited on this trip. But I had a family event, and passed.

Put things in perspective and move along. The Winter Olympics went on just fine without my interview, even though I won't meet another white tiger.

✳

The Korean Demilitarized Zone (DMZ), thirty miles north of Seoul, is the most armed border on earth, a strip of land splitting the Korean peninsula in half, creating a buffer zone between North and South. The peace treaty after the Korean War in 1953 was never signed, and the ceasefire between North and South Korea still holds almost seventy years on, at least technically.

In the DMZ buffer, 160 miles long, and about two-and-a-half miles wide, barbed-wire lines fences, tank traps and active minefields abound, and soldiers stand guard at outposts, staring into forbidden lands housing long-ago family and friends. So why would I want to go there?

Ever since I was a child I've been fascinated by the concept of the DMZ. Was it a line, like in a football field, where if you crossed it you were in the other territory? Was it a space with trees and flowers?

In a bus, with a DMZ guide, we visited a land that looked very much like the rest of South Korea, and included a park, a bridge, a train station and a museum, where I bought a refrigerator magnet that said DMZ. (A bragging rights winner!)

In 1974, South Korea discovered four tunnels crossing the DMZ that had been dug by North Koreans, who claimed that they were for coal mining but were probably planned as a military invasion route.

We entered the third tunnel, and if you're claustrophobic or have an aversion to getting caught in a tunnel in the DMZ (all of us?) you might pass on this one.

Our last stop was to an observatory where, through binoculars, we could look across the DMZ into North Korea. No photos were allowed, and I wondered if I could possibly contain myself, so I decided to turn off my smartphone. (I was aware of the American student Otto Warmbier, who was imprisoned, tortured and eventually murdered for the crime of stealing a poster in North Korea.)

On the way to the observatory our bus suddenly stopped, and a sullen-looking man in a uniform came aboard and whispered to our guide. The bus abruptly turned around and raced back to the front area, where we could get our cars to go back to South Korea. There was no explanation, just the repeated phrase, "You will have to leave now."

We found out when we returned to Seoul that North Korea had launched its first missile in years, into the South China Sea, as a warning to

South Korea. Both governments were on alert. The ceasefire remains tenuous after all these years.

I may have missed the observatory, but at least we weren't rounded up while we were in the tunnel and told to wait there. And I proudly display the DMZ magnet, the star of my refrigerator door.

SPAIN

Art, Castles—and Bourdain

I first traveled to Spain in the 1970s—to Madrid, Seville, Cordoba and Granada. In the Prado museum in Madrid, the actor Edward G. Robinson was appreciating a painting by El Greco. He was one of the first movie stars I had ever seen in person. Robinson played gangsters in B movies, and here I watched him standing in front of a work of fine art, smiling beatifically. I learned about illusion and reality more from that brief encounter watching him than from the art.

✳

While we were living in England, we ferried across the Bay of Biscay to visit Spain and Portugal. It was a rough overnight, and my sons, the nanny and I were sick. I remember my husband cheerily eating a hot fudge ice cream sundae while we were all moaning and barfing.

Nanny was most useful as a formidable backseat barrier between the boys, who were two and four, and squirmy, as we drove throughout the Iberian Peninsula. We started in Bilbao, in the Basque region, before there was a Guggenheim Museum there.

We stayed in inexpensive government *paradors*, lovely hotels that had only recently opened in restored castles and historic buildings. Today they are privately run luxury hotels, hard to book and pricey.

I can still hear my toddler son—who later in his life ran with the bulls in Pamplona *(See: Czech Republic)* and is now the editor of a major magazine—complaining bitterly as we would pull in each night to a magnificent lodging, often with turrets and moats.

"Nooo, Mommy, no! I want a good place, with swings. I won't stay in another castle!"

✳

Which reminds me of a very different establishment far from Spain, and far from a castle.

I was driving through Poland with a friend, checking out hotels for a trade publication. We were tired from traipsing around and had forgotten to make a reservation for the night. The only lodgings we could find in a last-minute search in the dark were a couple of basic rented rooms in Gdansk.

My room was worn, but I immediately fell asleep in the creaky bed. I was soon awakened by a knock and a man's voice. I would not open the door and he yelled something for quite a while that I assume was nasty.

Taken aback, I decided to spend the night in my friend's room. The next morning we found out that we were staying above a whorehouse.

✳

I returned to Northern Spain forty-five years after my first visit, to San Sebastian, because I viewed a segment on Anthony Bourdain's travel series in which women fishmongers teased him about his masculinity; he was so playful, soulful, and warmly attractive. I sought out the *pinxto* bars in the old town that he had featured, walking among establishments that proudly served small, fine specialties, maybe only cheese, or ham or fish. Bartenders pour *Sagardoa*, the region's signature cider, from a height of two feet or more above the glass. (I tried, and splashed my pants and best shoes.)

I had read Tony's books and watched his shows and wanted to live my experiences as deeply as he did, and because of that I stretched myself to travel better and more adventurously than I might have otherwise.

He was never just a foodie or a tourist. Food may have been what started his travels, but more

and more he opened his own mind, and ours, to the people and places where he ate. He defined what a real traveler is, not just because he visited places where most of us had not yet been and probably would never venture to, but because he was open and authentic—the way we hoped we could be when maybe we got where we longed to travel.

But he left us too soon, and reminds us that success does not always mean contentment and that we should be good to ourselves and alert to our problems and moods, and to those of others.

"If I am an advocate for anything, it is to move," he said. "As far as you can, as much as you can. Across the ocean, or simply across the river. Walk in someone else's shoes, or at least eat their food. It's a plus for everybody."

SWEDEN

Pretty City, White or Rye?

Sweden is not just a successfully governed modern monarchy, but a looker, with gently rolling green countryside; tidy red-brick, cupola-topped buildings; and long pink twilights on white summer nights.

Sprawling on fourteen islands, the capital of Stockholm is home to the Nobel Prize, the pop group ABBA, a mosaic-studded city hall, and the superbly preserved seventeenth-century Vasa ship. And Gamla Stan, with cobblestone streets and thirteenth-century buildings.

So many lovely towns around the world to remember, but my roster of prettiest cities would also include Paris, Prague, Budapest (especially Pest), Barcelona, San Sebastian, San Francisco, Saint Petersburg (in Russia, not the one near Tam-

pa), Vienna, Krakow, Porto, Amsterdam, Bruges and San Miguel de Allende.

And then there are the cities with the grandest vistas, like Hong Kong, Rio, Sydney and Queenstown, New Zealand—a stunning site in the Remarkables (an appropriate name for this mountain range). I was flown there by helicopter to the very site over a fjord where *The Bachelor* had proposed a week before (except to the wrong woman—he would later change his mind and marry the runner-up).

I like to close my eyes, put my feet up, and think of these places as a kind of meditation. I don't even have to say "ohhhhhmmmm."

On a summer night many years ago, when I was traveling with my husband and two small sons through Scandinavia, we pulled into a campground outside Stockholm.

The next morning our Volkswagen camper's expandable top was popped, and my two little boys were still snoring lightly. Hubby was already puttering behind the boxy van, and I was outside getting things ready for breakfast. I was literally a happy camper.

Suddenly, out of nowhere, a thin young man wearing sunglasses and a baseball cap came into my vision. He stood there and said quietly, "Give me your bread."

At first I thought, I wonder if he wants white or rye? We had just bought some hot dog buns. But then I realized, as my stomach dropped to my toes, that the man didn't mean bread. He meant money.

He was mugging me in pretty, friendly, law-abiding Stockholm.

It was absurd in a way, like the scene in Woody Allen's first movie, *Take the Money and Run*, which had come out a few years before, when Allen hands the bank teller a botched note that reads, "I have a gub." The tellers can't read the note and get into a heated argument over what "gub" means, with the robber trying to assure them that it was "gun," not "gub."

This man suddenly in front of me didn't have either a gun or a gub. But he had a knife.

I was young, knew nothing about handling a situation like this in a place like this, all leafy and supposedly peaceful, and I just stood there, confused.

And again the man said, this time louder and with a darker sound, "Give me your bread."

I figured he must have watched too many American movies, using the slang "bread," like "dough" in an earlier era. I was still hoping that maybe, just maybe, it was a joke.

But the knife in his hands wasn't.

I stood there hapless, not knowing that my husband would come around in a few seconds, all six-feet-five of him, and that the guy with the knife would scurry like a rat into the woods, with no "bread" in his hand.

And I certainly had no idea, as my husband held my shaking body, that twenty years later I would be mugged in Barcelona and dragged along the street while the man I was with wrestled the mugger to the ground and then held my shaking body. *(See: Andorra.)*

Or that I would be a victim of a smash-and-grab robbery a couple of years after that, with a lead pipe shattering the windshield of my car when I stopped at a light at an I-95 underpass, alone in Miami after a cruise. And nobody was in my life to hold me then, and I drove with broken glass all around me until I reached a friend's house in tears.

I couldn't know those things, or the ups and downs of my life to come. But I sure did realize right then and there in the camping area in Sweden that life wasn't as benign as I thought it had been a few minutes before. Even in such a pretty place.

SWITZERLAND

Blind Leading the Blind

Food is not just about taste, we know. But how much it depends on visual stimuli was a surprise to me. And so were other revelations I can't forget.

A few years ago I was at a conference in Zurich, and heard about a restaurant called *Blinde Kuh* (Blind Cow). It was almost impossible to get a reservation there, but my friend Belle and I prevailed.

We took a streetcar from our hotel to a residential part of the city as dusk was falling. For a while we couldn't find the place. We got a bit panicky, as our reservation was hard-fought and someone else was bound to take it if we didn't get there on time.

Finally, on a side street we found a small building with a cow on the sign. We announced ourselves, deposited our belongings in a locker in the reception area, and waited.

Our server, Heidi, came to fetch us. She wore an apron. She smiled and led us through a doorway and then through heavy drapes to another doorway and into a room of pitch-black darkness. There weren't even lighted exit signs. Our eyes never got used to the darkness because there was no light at all. If you would worry about a fire, this place wouldn't be for you.

Heidi carefully sat us down on benches at a long, communal table, and Belle and I reached out our hands, facing each other. I could hear others nearby. We didn't want her to leave us.

Oh, and Heidi was blind. All the servers were. I guess this job was a chance for blind people to find employment that they couldn't otherwise have. The blind leading the temporarily blind.

Courses were served one at a time. We ate, our hands tentatively reaching to awkwardly bring food to our mouths. Heidi would come by and help us find the fork or spoon. We groped for the glass. We held onto the plate. We measured with a fork to judge how much food was left.

Soup, roasted potatoes and meat. Veal? Chicken? Bread, and butter, which we spread messily. Some pudding for dessert. Vanilla? I can't remember. It tasted like vanilla but it might have been chocolate. Maybe it wasn't pudding, but it seemed to be. None of the food tasted very good.

I forgot what we drank, but I remember I was afraid to drink alcohol.

We heard others talking in foreign languages, but I heard no other English words fly into the darkness besides ours. There was laughter at many tables and a birthday celebration going on.

Belle and I felt connected in the darkness, toes touching on purpose, just to be sure we were there. She was a quiet, conservative woman who hadn't opened up much to me in the past. But through the course of the meal she talked about her family, her husband, her stock portfolio, her mother, fears, feelings, doubts.

When the meal was over, Heidi led us outside to the lockers slowly, our eyes adjusting to the light. She smiled as we said goodbye and she walked to another couple who was coming in.

I realized that the darkness of that room was the condition she endured all of the time. I never realized the depth of blindness as much as I did at that moment.

Belle and I left and took a cab back to the hotel. We were both quiet.

"I said a lot in there," she said.

"Yes, but now we're outside. No worry." We were in the light again. We never talked again of what she told me, and how the darkness bonded us.

I often think of that dinner. How the food lost its taste. How Belle confided in me. But what I remember most of all, by far, is Heidi leading us into a darkness from which she can never leave.

TANZANIA

Migration, Destruction, Renewal

Observing animals in the wild helps us appreciate earth's creatures and contributes to their welfare. And if you are able to bring young people on safari, they can learn for themselves the magnificence of nature—the brutality as well as the nurturing.

Safaris come in a variety of ways. *On wheels:* classic game drive in open and closed vehicles, bumpy; you move fast and are often joined by other vehicles when you spot something. *Walking:* with a guide packing a rifle with one bullet, because that's all the time you probably have if something comes rushing toward you. You'll notice the ground: droppings, plants, paw prints, bugs, tiny critters and hidden natural phenomena you'd never notice on a traditional game drive.

Then there's the *river* safari. Hippo- and elephant-centric—where the big boys play—and lots of crocs, too. And, *nighttime:* eyes in the bush reflect in flashlights like ghosts. Porcupines, hyenas, mongooses, genets, civets, aardvarks and most big carnivores are nocturnal. You might spot a leopard on the hunt or something really rare, like a pangolin, the scaly, prehistoric-looking critter whose only defense mechanism is curling up into a ball. And, of course, there's the clear, starry sky.

Besides the pure joy of observing wild, glorious nature, a safari is a reminder to slow down, to open your senses. And to be still, and patient.

If you choose only one safari in your lifetime, I strongly suggest it be the wildebeest migration in Kenya and Tanzania across the plains of the Serengeti to the grasslands of Masai Mara, in East Africa. Millions of wildebeest and hangers-on up and down the food chain. Zebras, lions, elephants, antelope and more sprint across the plains, trudge like refugees in lines stretching miles, and rush across the Mara River to food and breeding grounds, despite the crocodiles that await the stumbling and the weak.

And the sounds! At night the roar/moan of thousands of unseen beasts emanating from the darkness, constant as crickets on a summer night but a lot louder and hornier. Truly awesome.

※

Which reminds me of one of the most joyous sounds I have ever heard, near Arusha, in Tanzania. A bunch of mischievous bachelor elephants had just stolen corn from a local farmer—as they often do, I'm told. They were running and trumpeting their

success and full stomachs though a canopy of baobab trees, triumphant trunks held high.

※

In rural Tanzania, where roads suddenly become rutted paths, locals use landmarks as directional clues. Sure enough, as we passed through a tiny village, a butcher's display of a goat's innards hung on a tree.

The driver abruptly turned, and I heard what our guide had told him. "Go left at the liver."

※

Because of excessive fishing and farming, and indirect activity, like fossil fuels that accelerate climate change, scientists warn that up to a million species of plants and animals are headed for extinction if we don't act now.

That's every individual creature in a species—*times one million.* Not just one rhino, but every single one of that animal's kind, as well as

every one of 999,999 other species. Not just poster animals like polar bears, tigers and elephants; the lesser-known natural world is disappearing.

Seeing creatures in their habitats humbles you and helps you realize that we are only one of many species on this earth. Even coral reefs are colonies of living organisms, as I had indelibly witnessed on a submarine tour in Bonaire in the Caribbean, when a reef erupted in a cloud of sperm, an event that happens only once or twice a year, I'm told.

A true celebration of life, and a bittersweet memory when I now so often find dead coral—eerie white sea skeletons caused from warming waters and human carelessness.

When a marine biologist traveled to a remote string of islands in the Indian Ocean to see how much plastic waste had washed up on the beaches, part of what she found was almost half-a-million toothbrushes and almost a million shoes, largely flip-flops.

They just floated in—and no one was picking them up. Can you imagine how much is bobbing around the ocean? We need to do better.

✻

Off the Tanzanian island of Zanzibar, snorkeling from a dhow with a curved sail, I was delighted that the water was clear and the vivid coral was not bleached or destroyed as it is in so many waters of the world. Iridescent schools of fish and clouds of blush-pink jellyfish swerved among red, yellow and blue coral. The water crackled electric, with squeaky sounds of the sea.

I appreciated my afternoon snorkel, and it wasn't until I was sitting back in the boat and discovered itchy red welts that I realized I had been stung all over my body by the delicate jellyfish that had danced around me. The experience was so beautiful I didn't even notice.

✻

In Tanzania in 2003, a couple of years after my husband Chaim had died, I made two meaningful purchases. He had always wanted to buy me a piece of tanzanite, the blue-violet gem that comes only from Tanzania. And there I was in the country. I had little time, so I went to the most reputable jeweler in Dar es Salaam, and bought a round tanzanite stone that I still wear around my neck. I feel he is a part of me when I wear it.

The other purchase was a surprise. We were taken to a shop that had all kinds of trinkets and touristic art pieces. I wandered around the area and saw a charming hand-painted sign in a clinic. Illustrated sections showed good hygiene, AIDS protection and such. It was folk art.

"Very nice sign," I said.

"We have these in clinics all over the country," the receptionist said. "This clinic has several. We make them into stories because many cannot read."

"Is it possible to buy one?" I asked. "If not, I could donate some money to the clinic."

The deal was made. The second purchase of the day. The tanzanite gem and the poster could not be more different. And they both could not be more special.

✻

On that same trip our Masai guide discussed with us how the cow is the symbol of prosperity in his tribe. "We eat the meat, we drink the blood, and show off our herd."

The number of cattle a Masai man possesses is so important to tribesmen, the guide confided, that stealing cattle is his birthright.

We met the guide's grandfather, an elder who had never traveled far from his small Masai village.

"Where are all the other white people?" the elder asked his grandson.

"They're afraid to fly. A man named Bin Laden bombed their country."

"How many cattle does this man Bin Laden have?"

"None."

"None? He is not an important man. The white people will return."

And so they have, and will, as long as the animals prosper and the sea stays clean.

THAILAND

Tone Deaf

I was working in Thailand in 1989, as executive producer of an interactive video production, using an early version of DVD. The U.S, Army had hired the company I worked for to create a language-training course for army personnel and diplomats stationed in Thailand.

I wrote a script of fifty-two sessions, each following a week in the life of "Ed," and we made it into a mini-movie to use on an interactive TV screen, to train Americans how to speak Thai.

Thailand has never been colonized, and retains ancient customs that I learned about from the Thai crew as soon as I arrived. One was that it's disrespectful to point your toes at someone, or touch them, especially on the head. I thought these rules would be impossible to follow, but I soon found myself walking to people sideways, with my hands in my pockets.

I enjoyed many beautiful moments in Thailand. At Loi Krathong, a night festival of the harvest season, music is played on ancient instruments, and offerings of banana leaves topped by candles float throughout the country's waterways, as if the stars had fallen into the waters.

I love viewing and, if possible, participating in festivals throughout the world. *(See: Malta.)* There's no better way to enjoy the essence of a country's culture and tradition.

At the Palio in Siena, Italy, an ancient horse race of flags and ritual, you can sip a glass of Tuscan Red and watch muscled steeds encircle the Campo, the main piazza, as they have for centuries.

I have attended less exalted, but no less fun, festivities. At the Duct Tape Festival outside of Cleveland, I chomped on corn dogs and shopped for artwork, baskets, even clothes made of the sticky, all-purpose tape. Even parade floats were made of, as locals call it, "duck tape." I do believe that, like the wheel, it is one of humanity's great inventions.

You need to check ahead, and often reserve for popular festivals. Many times I've traveled to a site at the wrong time, just missing an event. And sometimes I hit one by chance. *(See: India.)*

I did get to perhaps the best holiday light show in the world at Medellin, Colombia, but just missed the glorious Flower Festival there. I also missed the World Beard and Mustache Championship in Nevada by a hair (ugh).

One festival I am most fascinated with, and still hope to attend even as an observer in a raincoat, is La Tomatina, the world's biggest food fight. Now held around the world, it started in 1945, on the last Wednesday of August, in Buñol, Spain.

Shopkeepers cover their storefronts in plastic, and for about an hour, twenty thousand participants, who have paid a fee for the privilege, get to throw ripe tomatoes at each other. Who hasn't dreamed of being covered in tomatoes? And if they ever add ripe avocados to the mix, it will become guacamole.

Fire trucks hose down the streets right after, and red, sticky participants jump in a pool to wash. The citric acid in the tomatoes makes the town and people clean, so I guess the festival has a sensible purpose, after all.

✳

Anyway, I enjoyed living in Thailand, but what I will remember even more than the festivals is one awkward moment in a car.

Thai is a multi-toned language, and my vocabulary was limited to "hello," "please" and "thank you." I did, however learn one other word—*kwai*—which means water buffalo. I could remember the word because it sounded like the title of a movie I loved, *The Bridge on the River Kwai*—even though the bridge was in Burma.

And I was proud to use the word often, as there were so many water buffalo in the Thai countryside. "Oh, look, there's another kwai!" "Look at that big kwai over there." Kwai, kwai, kwai.

The video production I was working on hired a fixer, a gentle Thai man who worked for the government and who helped us get permits, scout locations and translate. He came along with me most of the time.

Several days of shooting in rural areas gave me the opportunity to use my Thai word whenever possible: "I like kwais so much." "I wish I had a kwai of my own!" And so on.

One afternoon we were driving along and I kept up my patter: "Kwais are so useful." "Kwais are so huge." "Every Thai in rice paddies seems to have a kwai."

Suddenly the quiet Thai fixer, who was sitting in the front seat of the car, turned to me with a strange look on his face.

"Dear lady," he said in a small voice, "I have a favor to ask." He spoke so softly I could hardly hear him.

"I know that you like using the word kwai," he said slowly and deliberately, eyes averted. "But you are pronouncing it all wrong. You aren't saying water buffalo."

He paused.

"You are saying PRICK! Water buffalo is pronounced *kwhaai*."

Thai has twelve tones, and each one obviously matters. So, when you travel in Thailand, do watch your tones, or when you speak Thai you'll sound like a kwai.

TUNISIA

Deserted in the Desert

Both times I traveled to Tunisia I felt the pressure of being left in the lurch. On the first trip, in the mid 1990s, I was with an increasingly abusive man. I had been with him for about a year, and while we were flying around on this trip I had asked him, as a joke, about other women he had been with, and he listed them. Let's just say even if he were a centipede he'd need more digits to count them all.

My independent nature set him off. He wouldn't talk. He wouldn't come down to dinner. He got off on stirring me up and making me squirm, and he was doing it full force, perhaps spurred on by the hot Saharan winds, the *chehili*, that supposedly can drive people wild.

Our guide drove us to coastal towns with blue doors, and to vast Roman ruins and palm-fringed oases. We explored the village where the original *Star Wars* bar scene was filmed, and, as he was acting like a nasty alien, I wanted to drop my companion off and keep going.

When I came down to dinner on the last night, the guide was caring, and when my guy finally came down, he chastised him for me. There was silence, and I decided if the abusive man left early I would happily travel solo for the rest of the trip. And that's just what happened.

When I returned to the States, I escaped with a girlfriend to an inn in New Hampshire, and, just as I had hoped, when I returned he was already in another relationship.

※

Twenty years later, I was traveling in Tunisia with my current husband, a loving man who makes me feel safe. Our group visited mosques and souks and galleries and wandered through desert towns. It was a delightful day, with a long lunch, lots of bargaining and free time to wander in a marketplace.

But in the midst of the fun, we heard a blast like a wounded monster. We regrouped as fast as possible and raced to the ship. People lined the railings wanting to move on, but the ship had to wait for us because we were a ship-sponsored tour. If I had been late on a local tour, the ship would have left, and we would have had to carry on solo, driving or flying to the next port. Keep that in mind when you're cruising.

Thinking about it, although Tunisia is a beautiful and historic destination, what I remember most about both my visits is dealing with the unexpected idea that I might be left behind. In both cases things worked out, as they usually do when you travel. And when the situation is over, your troubles make good little stories.

TURKEY

Penny and Ali Bauble

Researching hotels for a month throughout Turkey, I invited a friend to join me for part of the time. Penny had a twinkly personality and liked to make knock-knock jokes using countries as we drove along.

"Knock-knock."

"Who's there?"

"Tunis!"

"Tunis who?"

"Tunis company, three's a crowd!"

"Knock-knock."

"Who's there?"

"Iran!"

"Iran who?"

"Iran over here to tell you this!"

"Knock-knock."

"Who's there?"

"Jamaica!"

"Jamaica who?"

"Jamaica lotta money last year?"

This level of wit went on for over a month. (And you think travel writing is an easy way to live!)

Penny was an exceptional bargainer, offering half of any price, even in a shop, and always able to at least get a discount. And if the bargain was excellent, she would buy two or three of the same items, "to give as gifts."

She also enjoyed her makeup, waking up with lipstick and lashes on, ready to go.

One afternoon in Istanbul, three girls surrounded us by the Blue Mosque, and one grabbed something from Penny's purse and ran away. She seemed resigned.

I looked in her purse and assured her, "It's not so bad. They didn't grab your wallet! It's here in the pocket."

"Oh, no!" she said. "They took my makeup bag! My Chanel lipsticks are gone!" And then she got really upset.

✳

Penny also enjoyed spas, especially the magnificent one at Pamukkale. We splashed in a cascade of limestone pools, then were led to a *hammam* by a hirsute lady who poured waves of warm rose water over us from a silver pitcher as we lay naked on adjoining marble slabs.

Penny was well-off, so I figured we would have no trouble sharing and keeping records of costs. But I had no idea she would be quite so exacting. She listed everything we spent. If a candy bar was 49 cents, she wouldn't round it up to 50 cents. Her notes were scribbled with minutiae, and figuring out the exchange rate from euros to dollars: peanut butter bar, 93 cents; comb, 55 cents; water, 52 cents.

Oh, and she wasn't named Penny. That tag was given to her by our driver, who listened endlessly to her discussion of tab-splitting. When she got out of the car, he'd mutter under his breath, "Goodbye, Miss Pennies."

✳

In 1971, before I knew Sharia from Sunni or Bosphorus from Bodrum, I spent a few days with my first husband in Istanbul. *(See: Israel.)*

We visited mosques, of course, and in the Grand Bazaar drank liters of tea, cup by cup, and sat on low chairs with merchants as they unrolled dusty, hand-loomed Turkish rugs at our feet and cajoled us to buy.

Out in the sunshine, rugless and with full bladders, we met a thin, friendly man named Ali, who asked if we would be willing to talk with him a bit, as he was an English teacher at an Istanbul school, and he sought to learn American idioms.

In those days, before suspicions and fear clouded open-minded street connections, we said, "of course." Ali accompanied us as we walked around the marketplace, and we used as many idioms of the time as we could think of. "Super-duper." "Have a ball." "Best of the bunch." "Okey-dokey." "Cool as a cucumber." We sounded like a cliché machine.

As we said goodbye Ali asked if we would honor him and his family by having dinner at their home, a short walk away. We hesitated, but he was warmly insistent, and so we agreed.

Ali had no phone at home so he couldn't alert his wife, but he stopped at a butcher's stall to buy some meat and at other stalls to buy tomatoes, greens and sweets. And he wouldn't allow us pay for anything.

His small apartment was up several flights of stairs. When we opened the door, his father was praying on a rug in the main room. Ali's two boys ran to hug him, and, although surprised to see us, his wife was gracious and cooked a tasty dinner with what he brought, treating us as special guests.

For a few minutes after dinner we sat on a couch talking with Ali using as many idioms as we could think of. He asked about life in the United States and said that although he probably would never get there, he would use his new English phrases whenever possible.

He was proud of his family and glad that we came to his home, and we left feeling good about the world. But when I returned to the hotel and took off my coat, I realized that the thin gold bracelet that I had been wearing was not on my wrist.

My heart sank. We had been duped.

Upset at our stupidity, we were getting ready to go to bed when we got a call from the front desk. A man wanted to see us.

We threw some clothes on and went downstairs, not sure of what to expect.

And there was Ali, holding a box.

"Your bracelet fell in the pillows," he said. "My son found it."

I realized that, as sometimes happened, I must not have locked the clasp. And Ali had traveled at this late hour to bring the bracelet back to us.

I was overwhelmed with relief and joy that our hopes were not dashed about the goodness of this man.

I wish I had kept Ali's full name and address. I wonder what has become of him and his sons in this increasingly suspicious world, and if he would still have been as interested in learning English and about America today. And would we have been as willing to go to his home?

I think I know the answer.

UKRAINE

Near-Death Experience?

I was on a riverboat in 2010 somewhere between the Ukrainian towns of Nikopol and Nova Kakhovka on an interesting cruise on the Dnieper River, into the Black Sea. Besides the capital of Kyiv, we were visiting the opera in Odessa, submarines in Sebastopol, and Tolstoy's house and Stalin's retreat in Yalta.

As we walked through one museum, we noticed a group given special attention and escorted to the head of the line.

"Chernobyl people," said the docent. "They've suffered all kinds of medical problems." They must have been children when the nuclear reactor exploded in 1986.

Our restored boat was clean and acceptable, providing basic wood-paneled cabins not much larger than walk-in-closets, and tiny bathrooms with sink, toilet, and a hose for a shower.

"I only have a washcloth; could I please have a towel?" I asked the cabin attendant. "That *is* the towel," she answered, and walked away.

The weary young staff were trained in the post-Soviet era, and muttered, "What would you like to eat?" and "Have a nice day," with gritted teeth and plastered-on smiles, as if they were bad actors in a play about a zombie river cruise.

Although most of the people I've come across in my travels have been kind, there have been exceptions. In a marketplace in the Atlas Mountains of Morocco I made a face seeing a calf's head with flies buzzing around it. The butcher saw me and came running and yelling. And he was swinging a bloody knife.

In one of my favorite Paris bistros, a server placed a plate of flaming Crêpes Suzette in front of my son, who took out his smartphone to take a photo.

She raised her hand and swiped him across the face, causing his phone and his glasses to fly across the room.

"*I* am not a flambé," she announced, and stomped away.

Nothing was broken, but we reported her assault to the manager, who said he would fire her. I will never go back to find out.

Anyway, one morning as I awakened on the Ukrainian riverboat, I felt dizzy and attributed it to vertigo, which I sometimes get when I'm on the water for a while. My thyroid gland had been removed years before, but I'm fine as long as I take synthetic thyroid hormone once a day. Without those pills I guess I would eventually fade out and expire like a hologram, and so I'm especially careful about bringing pills on a trip.

As I readied for breakfast, I went to my pill container to take my morning dosage of Synthroid and noticed that there were only two pills left, with a couple of weeks to go. How could that be? I had gotten a refill of thirty pills before we started our trip in Italy ten days before.

And then I looked more closely and realized that the container said "Xanax," not "Synthroid." Which would mean I had been taking an anxiety reliever for the past ten days, not the lifesaving drug that I needed—which may have explained my easy-going manner!

But how come I wasn't comatose?

My husband and I rushed to the bottom deck to speak to the boat's doctor, a heavyset Ukrainian with long red fingernails and beet-colored hair. She spoke no English, but through an interpreter from the front desk (whose hair was the color of the butter that spurts out of Chicken Kyiv), I was told with a grave look that she had no thyroid pills. The good news was that there might be a Ukrainian version of Synthroid at the next stop, the industrial town of Zaporozhye.

"*Might* be? *Zaporozhye?*" The doctor scribbled something on a piece of paper, and I flopped back into bed suddenly feeling as faint as tuberculosis-ridden Camille in *La Bohème*.

My husband was beside himself about my dire straits, and I had to calm him down like in that classic old episode of *I Love Lucy,* when Lucy is about to go to the hospital to have little Ricky, and big Ricky is a total wreck.

I was scared, and started to imagine the consequences. What if they don't have the drug and I had to be helicoptered to Odessa? Do they have a helicopter or would I have to be bused? Maybe there wasn't a bus. Maybe a Cossack from the horse show we had seen yesterday would have to gallop over the miles on his mount to save me. (Maybe that would be fun.)

And I was befuddled. How could I have descended into those monks' caves in Kyiv the other day without so much as an extra breath? How come I hadn't been lolling around, like a Ukrainian Easter egg?

And then, through the haze of my anxiety, I vaguely remembered something. Three days before, in Rome, we had to check our luggage rather than carry it on, and at the last minute I removed my Synthroid and put it in my purse in case my luggage was lost, just to be sure I had it with me no matter what.

When we arrived at the riverboat in Kyiv, I assembled my things in our cabin and placed my pills on the bathroom counter, as usual. But I forgot that the Synthroid I had carried on the plane was in a zippered pocket in my travel purse. Eureka! I got out of my former deathbed, rushed to my purse, unzipped the pocket and—sure enough—there were my pills!

I did not have to be rescued by a Cossack.

True, I had not taken the lifesaving meds for three days, and that's probably why I felt dizzy that morning, but I indeed would live to see the end of the cruise. I immediately swallowed a pill and enjoyed a late breakfast served by the grimacing, faux-friendly servers as we glided along the calm waters of the Black Sea to our next stop.

But my poor husband, Bill, had a terrible headache all day and I had to bring him his dinner in bed, in the tiny cabin. And give him one of the Xanax.

United Arab Emirates

Over the Top

I landed at the Dubai airport in the 1980s, on a stopover from India to the United States. Flying over the region, all you could see was desert, and a small town. Major oil had been discovered there only a few years before.

Now modern cities of enormous scale have soared to the skies in the Middle East, interspersed with the remnants of an impoverished nomadic past.

The United Arab Emirates was founded by a semiliterate nomad, and is now run by Mohammed bin Zayed (MBZ), perhaps the richest man in the world, controlling sovereign wealth funds worth over a trillion dollars.

Although it has fewer citizens than Rhode Island, the UAE contains seven states: Abu Dhabi, Dubai, Sharjah, Ajman, Ras Al-Khaimah, Fujairah and Umm-Al-Quwaim. Five of them are probably relevant only if you live there or are into obscure trivia, but the two familiar states offer every possible cultural diversion and activity, from dune-bashing to indoor snow-skiing, to dining on an open-air platform high above the desert.

A solo woman can feel safe. A third of the UAE's cabinet ministers are female. Unlike Saudi Arabia, the United Arab Emirates contains Christian churches and Hindu and Sikh temples. (The country is estimated to have nine million residents, but fewer than a million citizens; the rest are foreign workers.) The prince last year created a Ministry of Tolerance and has hosted the Special Olympics and Pope Francis.

Abu Dhabi

The capital of the United Arab Emirates sits on an island in the Persian (Arabian) Gulf, focused on oil exports and commerce, and, lately, art, architecture and, of course, an ultra-lavish way of life.

Tracing its rich history back to around 3000 B.C., Abu Dhabi maintains a more distinctly Arabian ambiance than glitzy Dubai. Travelers can take to the dunes by sandboarding or riding camels at sunset—and stay at a luxury resort in the heart of the desert.

A construction craze has hidden the former coastline behind man-made islands. One is intended to become a financial district similar to Wall Street. Another includes a campus of New York University, a planned extension of the Guggenheim Museum, and the Louvre Abu Dhabi, with over six hundred pieces of artwork, including the most expensive painting in the world, Leonardo da Vinci's "Salvador Mundi."

I first traveled there on a day trip off a cruise ship, and headed for the nearby oasis at Al Ain, a cluster of green springs and date palms in the middle of a bustling town. I also hung out at a camel market where interactions were intense, as the camel is important not only for transportation and work, but for racing, meat and milk.

The falcon is treasured in myth and emotion, trained as a hunting bird and cherished by families who can afford its upkeep. At a falcon hospital waiting room, dozens of hooded birds perched on benches, awaiting medical treatments or filings of their talons or beaks. I did giggle, as it reminded me of my local emergency room on a Saturday night combined with a mani-pedi salon.

Beneath white marble domes, the vast Sheikh Zayed Grand Mosque features an immense Persian carpet, crystal chandeliers and capacity for 41,000 worshippers. The mosque became an obsession for me, as I missed it on the first trip. So I returned to Abu Dhabi and we stayed in a hotel right across from the mosque. I viewed it when I got up, when I dined, and when I looked out my window. And then I spent an afternoon, covered from head to toe, walking among its miles of inlaid marble. And like the Taj Mahal *(See: India)*, it exceeds expectations.

Dubai

This city-state offers the ultimate, from the world's largest marina to the world's longest urban zipline. And the superlatives include hotels.

The Burj Al Arab from afar looks as if it's about to sail into the Arabian Sea on a windy day, and touts itself as a "seven-star hotel," the most luxurious in the world.

I was invited to stay there on a fact-finding mission about five years ago. (This is a good time to remind you that often I've had to sleep in less-than-desirable places. *(See: Spain.)* And I warn you not to read further if you're turned off by excess—although perhaps you will consider it amusing.

We could have chosen to helicopter to the hotel's rooftop landing pad, but Bill and I decided to keep it simple and were greeted at the vast Dubai airport and escorted by the hotel rep to a private lounge. We were offered lemonade and pistachio sweets, and then brought to a white vintage Rolls, where a uniformed driver awaited me with an armful of white roses.

We were offered a choice of music for the half-hour drive to the hotel through morning rush hour (we chose Middle Eastern), while the driver enlightened us about the city.

The building is set around an atrium, with buttresses and soaring spaces, an interior perhaps even more interesting than the sail-shape exterior. I'd call it high-end Arabian-themed Las Vegas, if that can be called a style, and works in Dubai, where more is never enough.

Our butler greeted us at the reception desk on our open floor, and led us to a standard two-story suite. He asked if we wanted our clothes unpacked or ironed, but I realized that would be a "no way," as I was pretty sure my clothes would not meet the standards normally set here. Most of my labels said "Chico's."

The butler then explained the room's technicalities, a procedure that at most hotels takes five minutes or so, but not here. For example, when opening a door, you normally look through a peephole and then choose whether to let someone in. At the Burj, when the doorbell rings, you answer the *phone*, listen to an announcement of the visitor by a monitor in the hall, and then turn on the TV to see an image of who is at the door, just to be sure.

I had trouble remembering how to let my husband into the room, and one time when I napped, he ran around in the hall until he could find someone to identify him.

Our basic one-bedroom suite was only 2,000 square feet, puny considering that the hotel's largest suite is over 8,000 square feet. We made do with an entryway/study, a winding staircase worthy of Tara, and a downstairs living room, kitchen/dining area and powder room. Upstairs we had a bedroom, dressing room and a bathroom bigger than some New York City apartments, clad in marble and tile, with a mosaic-mural focus wall.

The shampoo and similar products came in pint sizes. (Thankfully each guest gets a large tote bag with the hotel logo, so it was convenient for hauling the goods out of there, as I only used a tiny portion on the trip.)

If you have a mobility issue, that winding staircase to the bedroom may be a problem; unless, of course, butler service includes carrying you up and down the stairs. Or, you could stay in the Royal Suite, which has an elevator, for about $20,000 a night.

Furnishings are a mix of Middle Eastern and contemporary, in bold colors with scads of gold plate, and the canopied bed has a mirror above and a pop-up TV in front, so there's little time for boredom no matter whom you're with. Views of Dubai, the desert and the man-made Palm Island in the Arabian Sea are suitably dramatic when you open the automatic curtains. Fresh roses beyond my original armful were strewn around the suite.

The outdoor pool area, and beach fringing the Arabian Sea on the man-made island, are not the hotel's strong points, but there's a better beach

a walk over a foot-bridge. The spa is dramatic and gorgeous, with all amenities, and Dubai views stretching beyond the indoor pool.

A standard suite rate includes breakfast, which tips your stay over to a bargain, right? Al Mahara, "The Oyster Shell," is surrounded by floor-to-ceiling aquariums, and you can come for a drink or a super-expensive meal at one of eight venues from lobby level to skyline, Asian to contemporary.

Or you can pay a fee just to enter the hotel and gawk.

The price may be sky-high, but so are bragging rights. And if you've read this far, I commend you. With all the world's problems, this excess is truly a form of masochistic escape.

UNITED KINGDOM

Bits and Pieces

I lived in England in the 1970s, so I have many grand memories of Great Britain and of many trips there before and since. Here's a variety of short takes, mostly light-hearted, with the sense of absurdity Brits just love.

Wales

As I write this, the world's fastest zipline, the longest in Europe at a mile, is almost five hundred feet above the largest slate of quarry in the world, in North Wales. But back in the 1970s, the pace was slower and there were no such things.

My friend Emily lived down the street from me when I lived in London *(See: Holy See)*, and one week I traveled with her to visit her family in Wales. She took me and her sister on a steam-operated, narrow-gauge railway built in 1865 to haul slate from the quarries near Abergynolwyn. The line had fallen into disrepair, and would have been absorbed by the woods if not for the Talyllyn Railway Preservation Society.

The train chugged along the seven-mile-long trip through the peaceful Fathew Valley at less than nine miles an hour. On this short, unhurried journey in the middle of nowhere, I noticed that Emily had a posh English accent, but her sister sounded like a Welsh country girl.

I asked Emily how come she didn't have a Welsh accent.

"Very simple," she said. "I bought myself an English one."

Border collies are the smartest breed, I do believe, smarter even than my late poodle, Apricot. At a Welsh farm, the dogs rounded up an ornery flock of sheep to impress a bunch of us tourists.

After the demonstration, we were seated on wooden benches facing a small stage, as a dozen or so sheep bolted one by one into tiered enclosures into a line-up. A narrator who sounded like Tom Jones boomed about each one's horns, wool, and genetics.

The animals stared forward, sheepishly, of course. We stared back, stifling giggles. This went on and on, for maybe an hour. I thought of the play *Waiting for Godot*, an existential statement about life that I saw when I was a teen, at its world premiere at the Coconut Grove Playhouse in Miami. Bert Lahr, the man who played the cowardly lion in *The Wizard of Oz*, starred, and Dade County thought it was a kids' show and invited students to come to the premiere. It was the first adult drama for many of us, and since nothing much happens in the play, it might have been the last.

Anyway, in honor of that play I've dubbed the Welsh farm show "Waiting for Sheep." And if there were music, I'd call it "Lambilton."

⁕

I had read Welsh travel writer James Morris's books about Oxford, Venice and Spain when I was young. The prose was redolent with sensuality and adventure, and I remember thinking: *How could anyone be lucky enough to write about places around the world for a living?*

At the Society of American Travel Writers conference in Cardiff in 2000, I was thrilled to meet the great author, who couldn't have been more gracious, and whose biggest journey didn't involve travel after all: James Morris had become Jan Morris. And she was the first transgender person I was aware of, although I'm pretty sure not the first I had met.

More important to me, she was the first travel writer who made me think that I could change my life and write about what I love.

Scotland

Flying in a piloted seaplane, compared to, say, a G4, is like carpooling in a VW after racing a Maybach flat-out on the autobahn. But the bonus is taking off from the water, skimming along on pontoons and lifting from liquid blue to sky blue, and for a few seconds feeling a part of both sea and air.

Sitting up front gave me the illusion of co-piloting, but I preferred watching the panorama unfold below: mountains to the west, and rivers contrasting with green hillsides. Eighteen lochs lie in the National Park alone, as well as some of Scotland's finest Munros, mountains that rise over three thousand feet.

We flew over rock outcrops jutting from the ocean. Clear water lapped the coast, and clouds trailed over the landmark hills called the Sleeping Warrior. Our flight ended over Loch Lomond, with views of the Trossachs and Arrochar, and glens, gardens, stately homes and castles, above corners of Scotland rarely seen.

Getting around another interesting way, I rode sidecar in a yellow tricycle in Edinburgh, a wind-in-your face way to see the imposing castle and the Royal Mile, and to hug some scenic Scottish byroads.

Geared up in goggles, a helmet and oversuit with headphones for music and driver commentary, we tooled around Edinburgh and its nearby hills—a thrill ride leaving the driver responsible for staying on the left and following road signs. I could just enjoy the wind! The chauffeur/laddie even set tea and biscuits on the sidecar when we stopped at an overlook.

※

Memories are often bittersweet. My husband Chaim was an excellent tennis player and I surprised him with a press pass to Wimbledon, where we sat in the box right behind the players and could hear them mutter as well as grunt.

We later drove up to Scotland and ferried from the mainland to the wild beauty of the Isle of Skye, and dined at an isolated lodge where it was whispered that Barbra Streisand and her soon-to-be husband James Brolin had just courted, far from paparazzi. We felt the mood.

Chaim and I were staying at a B&B property owned by the laird and lady of the Macdonald clan. Like many titled Brits, they rented rooms and gave tours, I guess to pay off taxes and upkeep and retain their family estates. The laird wore a green plaid tartan and his wife ran a cooking school and served pancakes and strawberries for breakfast.

Chaim had a headache, so we skipped a planned hike and instead remained in what was formerly their son's room, fooling around among toy trains on the shelves.

This trip was the last we would take together. I remember the sea crashing onto craggy cliffs, and wooded hillsides where golden eagles soared. But mostly I think of those toy trains, and how we laughed about them.

※

My niece married a Scottish lad on his family sheep farm near the Firth of Forth (or is it the Fourth of Firth?), and the ecumenical service contained a delightful fusion of "in the name of Jesus" and "Mazel tov." The groom's father, in his kilt, had no idea he'd be lifted in a chair high above guests at the reception. I now better understand the meaning of "family jewels."

Northern Ireland

A 1998 agreement between Republicans and Loyalists had brought an end to what had been called the Troubles. Tourism was taking off.

The rain was heavy when we slogged around the Giant's Causeway, the massive blocks of stone that create thousands of interlocking basalt columns from an ancient volcanic fissure eruption.

Soaked and exhausted, we looked forward to Irish coffee in a nearby pub. Sitting in the warmth, we drank more than one and got a bit silly.

A woman with a scarf over her hair, tied at the neck, was drinking alone at a table. I giggled to my companion, "That lady looks like that hunky actor Liam Neeson, with a scarf around his head." We giggled, imagining the big actor in drag, and sipped more Irish coffee.

Turns out it *was* Liam Neeson's mother.

England

On my first trip to England, in 1965, we headed straight for Fortnum & Mason in London for a proper high tea. We had only one afternoon to experience cucumber and watercress sandwiches; scones, strawberry jam and clotted cream; and Earl Grey tea with milk.

No tables were available unless we were willing to share, so we sat next to a white-haired couple who were also having tea. The round table was no bigger than a truck tire, and as my husband was almost six-and-a-half-feet tall, we were bumping elbows and touching knees while making polite conversation. Awkward enough, except that the elderly man next to us slowly nodded off, his head falling gently onto his plate of crustless tea sandwiches.

The funniest part was that as he gently snored, his wife kept making small talk and wiping her mouth with a linen napkin as if he were not right there, planted in the meal.

※

I've slept in beds from a hammock in a farm shed to a super-king in a presidential suite overlooking a private indoor pool in a Milan penthouse (for research purposes only).

But the most historic bed was Queen Elizabeth's (the red-haired original one, not the one who carries a purse). As a girl, Liz the First had been locked up in this inn for some historical reason to keep her from becoming queen. A window retained a message she had scratched into a pane with her ring—something to the effect of "Let me out of here!" in Elizabethan style, although it wasn't yet called that when she etched it, of course.

Others on the press trip were staying in normal rooms in the inn, but I had won the room lottery to stay in the Queen's queen, canopied, with carved oak posts. And I was feeling truly royal vibes as I was about to retire for the evening until the innkeeper said, "You know who else has slept in that bed?"

Hmm, I thought. Mary, Queen of Scots? Charles the First? George III?

"Robin Williams."

The idea of Queen Elizabeth I, the late, great comedian Robin Williams and I sharing the same bed—even at different times—was too much, even for me. The dreams alone had me tossing and turning most of the night. There was a threesome of me under the covers in my usual oversized tee, the young future Queen of England from yore in a prim gown, and a hairy-armed court jester with a cap on his head.

And my most frequent thought as I tried to sleep: When had they last changed the mattress?

Too much of a good thing. And while "two's company, three's a crowd" may apply here only in terms of haunting, I was exhausted the whole next day from sleeping with the images of those famed bedmates, and would have been better off in a standard double by myself in a non-historic bedroom with no famous ghosts.

And last, one of my very favorite travel memories:

I had spent a morning visiting the historic cathedral in Warwick, and an afternoon watching an endless game of cricket that went on until sundown. I still don't understand the game even after having it explained countless times. I've concluded it's basically an excuse to sit in the fresh air and drink beer.

That evening I arrived at an ancient inn, and after I checked in at the antique desk, I heard a whooping sound, then a shout. A tall, dark-haired chap, chin-challenged, smiled a toothy grin and came toward me.

"F**k you, turd face! ... Can I help you miss?"

I wasn't sure I was hearing right.

"You have a nice rack there, Miss. Let me take that bag for you."

He grabbed my suitcase and walked me down the hall, then opened the door to my guestroom and shouted at the top of his lungs, "I want your pussy!"

I eventually surmised that this hard-working, potty-mouthed man had a bad case of Tourette's Syndrome, and couldn't help himself. In between the hollering and obscenities, he was polite and soft-spoken.

Awkwardly I asked him about the affliction to let him know I understood. He explained that he couldn't get another job, but that the owner of the inn was his cousin, willing to hire him. He had gratefully worked there for years, and emphasized that he never took the early-morning or late-night shifts so that he wouldn't disturb sleeping guests.

According to him, most visitors were understanding about his problem, and chalked the whole thing up to English eccentricity. Plus, like me, they talked about the quirky experience when they arrived home, and the owner figured that it certainly didn't hurt business. In fact, people from all over probably came to see—and hear—the potty-mouthed bellman.

After he pointed out the attributes of my room in both practical and pornographic terms, I tipped him heavily, as most folks probably did, as much for the entertainment as for the labor.

"Thank you kindly, Miss," he smiled as he carefully closed the door. "Up your ass!"

UNITED STATES

Looking Up, Into the Light and Dark

Antelope Canyon in Arizona is among the most exquisite and rare creations on earth, plunging over a hundred feet to the desert floor from its open rim. Water and wind have scoured it into shapes and colors beyond imagination. Hollows stacked on hollows climb to many stories: a magical, mystical cathedral of rock.

The light in this slot canyon is best for a short time at midday, when the sun pours in and the sandstone striations become almost incandescent. But the day of my visit my alarm didn't go off and

I overslept. My annoyed fellow travelers were impatiently waiting in the van.

The driver sped us past ravines, towering saguaro cactus and dry scrub along this sparsely beautiful Navajo land. We skipped the requisite stop for turquoise trinkets and woven rugs, as photographers were still worried that we might miss the noon light.

We arrived at the town of Page and jeeped with our Navajo guide to an unassuming formation in the desert. He explained that the beauty of this slot canyon lies deceptively *within* the rock. Over time, water from a nearby creek cracked through the sandstone, and as it swirled in, hollows appeared and softer material washed away.

Flash floods may pour in before there's time to escape, and hikers have drowned at Antelope. But this day was sunny, and we had traveled far for these precious moments within the canyon. The only danger was missing that midday light.

We anxiously squeezed through an opening, single file. I gasped and aimed my point-and-shoot camera to capture the surreal world around me.

Sunlight poured from above like a waterfall, refracting sand in the air and setting the walls aglow. Looking up, warm yellow and orange deepened to red to purple, to deep gray, to black in the shadows. Waves, curls, arches, folds, curtains and whorls dazzled me as I maneuvered in a space where lines bent, up seemed down, and inside seemed out. Not an inch was less than magnificent.

Yes, indeed. We had captured the light.

※

Which states have I not yet visited? The Dakotas, Oklahoma, Iowa, Kansas. I hope to get to them all. Which favorite places do I remember, looking back over seventy-five years? I think of magnificent canyons, ravishing coasts, majestic

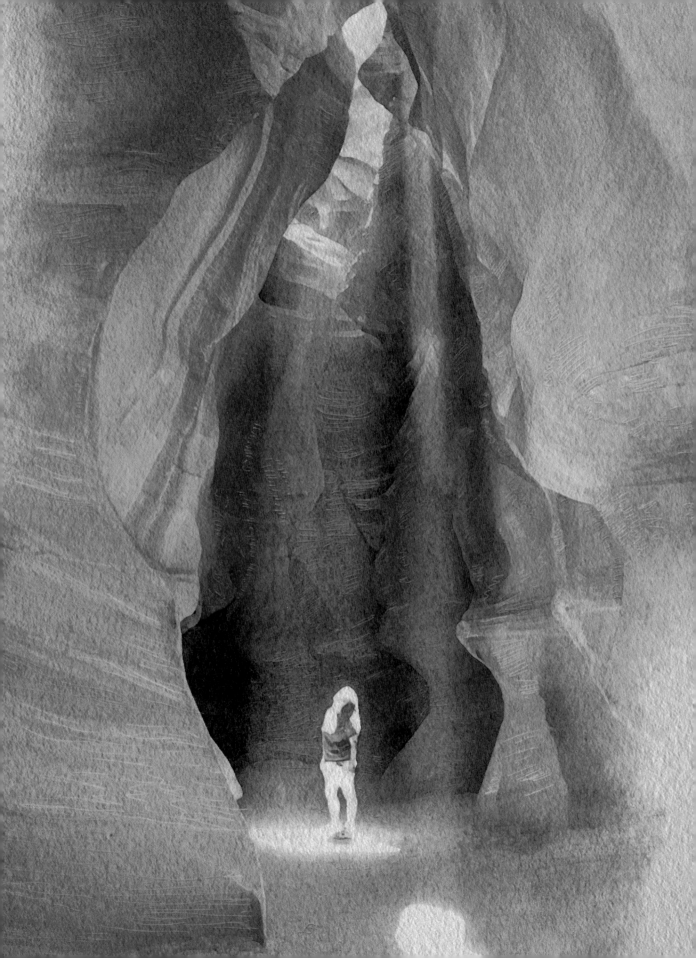

mountain ranges, fertile plains, dynamic cities and charming small towns.

I've followed The Crooked Road, a music trail along the Blue Ridge in Virginia and Tennessee. And Vermont byways in autumn. I've watched the setting sun turn the grassy river of the Everglades pink and orange, and climbed the towering sand dunes along Lake Michigan. I've driven the Cailfornia coast along Route 1, and the Mississippi cotton fields. So many, many exceptional places in my homeland, over a long life of travel.

But I recall most of all a trip to watch an event that didn't happen in the United States. It was in the skies above.

✳

I've appreciated celestial events including the green and purple curtains of the Northern Lights in Alaska and the smudge of comet Hale-Bopp through a telescope on a ship near the equator. I've witnessed lunar eclipses in Miami and Perseid meteor showers in northern California, oohed at double rainbows over the South Pacific and wished on falling stars all over the world.

But I had never experienced a total eclipse of the sun, considered perhaps the greatest sky watch of all. So for a big birthday, my dear husband gave me a once-in-a-lifetime gift: We flew from Miami to Nashville, the biggest city where we could experience, on August 21, 2017, the first total solar eclipse visible from anywhere in the mainland United States in almost forty years.

On average there are almost four-hundred years between total solar eclipses for a given location, and the last one visible from Nashville happened on July 29, 1478. I (just) missed that. So of course the planned celebration in Music City was major, as it was coast-to-coast in cities, towns and rural America within the seventy-mile path of totality.

The day before, we walked through the leafy Vanderbilt campus and nearby Music Row, and took a hop-on/hop-off tour trolley to visit the capitol, the Parthenon and other Nashville sites. In the evening we attended a special pre-eclipse show at The Grand Old Opry, featuring Little Big Town, Darius Rucker and ever-sassy Wynonna.

This trip wasn't about country stars, but our closest star. We were staying two nights in Nashville to experience less than two minutes of darkness—an event so hyped, I was secretly afraid I would be disappointed.

On the morning of the eclipse, we Ubered to a hotel near the airport, where we could view the event on the grounds outside and then be able to shuttle quickly to our flight home, avoiding traffic. A few dozen fellow viewers were ready to view the sun through specially darkened binoculars and telescopes, pinhole cameras and, of course, protective glasses.

As the moon began its inexorable alignment in front of the sun, we waited, darkened glasses in place, cameras in hand, heads up. At 11:58 and for almost three hours after, the sun peaked in and out of clouds, teasing us terribly as the moon moved steadily in the sun's path.

A sudden low sunset wrapped around us, 360 degrees, something I had not expected.

And starting at 1:27 p.m., our protective glasses came off for the long-awaited, much-coveted two minutes of totality, as the sun skirted out of the clouds into clear sky. And we stared at our strange-looking star.

And it was gorgeous.

As we gazed at our blacked-out sun, eyes wide open, light turned violet, insects hummed, shadows became exaggerated—as if in moonlight, only sharper—and the hot, humid midday air became gently cool.

I most remember:

- *anticipation:* Like a child waiting for Santa Claus, there was a communal innocence. We could be unabashedly excited.

- *the diamond-ring effect:* The sun's gases—the corona, the aura of plasma that surrounds the sun—created a clearly glowing ring surrounding a black void. (The corona is there all along, usually lost in the glare.)

- *bonding:* Sharing with people we didn't know as if we were friends was sweet. I did not know their politics, nor did I care. Together, in the purple darkness, we were moved to smiles, shouts and even tears.

- *reflection within:* The sudden loss of light and change in atmosphere emphasized the power of nature and our individual insignificance. We are all small, together, under that life-giving sun.

Totality is something everybody should plan to experience at least once, and the next one coming up in the States is in 2024. Less (light) is *(so much)* more.

URUGUAY

Cannibals and Zombies

I hung around the harbor of Punta del Este, a resort city of wide beaches, fancy houses and low-rise luxury condos. Sea wolves—the name locals call their sea lions—begged for fish, swam and sunbathed on the rocks.

Later I viewed paintings at a quirky white house in Punta Ballena called Casa Pueblo, a one-of-a-kind seafront property of whitewashed cement that looks like something architect Antoni Gaudi would have created if he had lived on Mykonos.

The compound is a hotel and museum, designed to resemble the mud nests of the region's native hornero birds, by the artist/muralist owner, Carlos Paez Vilaro, an elderly but still handsome man when I met him painting in his gallery, alongside his cat.

Vilaro was a ladies' man and a friend of Brigitte Bardot and Picasso. He was among a search-and-rescue team looking for Uruguayan Air Force flight 571, carrying nineteen members of a rugby team, along with family, supporters and friends.

The chartered flight originated in Montevideo heading for Santiago, Chile, and crashed on a glacier in the remote Andes in 1972. Of the forty-five people on board, twenty-five survived the crash. Facing starvation, the survivors reluctantly made a pact to sacrifice their flesh if they died, to help the others live, and then resorted to cannibalism. After over two months on the glacier, sixteen people were rescued. Vilaro's son was one of them.

※

Our ship, the Azamara Journey, on its way back to Bueno Aires from a cruise to Antarctica *(See: Argentina)*, docked way earlier than planned in Punta del Este, because in the early morning the ship's popular comedian, Mike, had suffered a major heart attack. and was taken off ship to a local hospital.

I pondered the meaning of life at a café table over a typical Uruguayan salad of nuts, apples and cream, thinking of Mike. Comfort food must have helped us forget the sad event of the morning, and that night I dined with another solo woman, who practically inhaled two orders of foie gras, two orders of Brazilian stone crabs, and a crème brûlée as large as a frisbee.

It was Academy Awards night, and the cabaret was set up with numerous screens, unlimited popcorn, champagne and a huge ice-carved Oscar—the ship's version of a *Vanity Fair* party, diverting us from worry.

For an in-house video we walked a red carpet and the cruise director played announcer. She giggled when I bragged "I'm wearing Tar-jay."

Later I won a prize for correctly guessing the most Oscar winners.

The ship moved on to Montevideo, and the most impressive thing about this small, riverfront capital city was its open-mindedness. Many ethnic groups have found refuge here, and a Holocaust memorial was a surprise by the beach.

Captain Leif, in a red shirt, lunched with crew members at a marketplace filled with bars,

open fires, ceilings fans and meat, meat, meat. The captain celebrated having steered our ship past 65 degrees south latitude in Antarctica only a few days before—a record accomplishment.

Our ship then traveled back to Buenos Aires, after eighteen days. At our last gala dinner onboard, the maître d' again sought interesting companions for me to sit with. With open seating, each night I'd met new people.

But what's this? Standing next to me waiting to get into the dining room was Mike, the comedian who'd been evacuated with a major heart attack two days before! Maybe it was the IV fluids he took in, but he looked better than ever. And he was still wearing his hospital bracelet.

"Mike! We were so worried," I said. "What are you doing here?"

"I told them I'm outta there. I'm not dying in Uruguay."

And when we got to Buenos Aires and we all disembarked, Mike returned to a major hospital, where I assume he continued his remarkable recovery, and did not die in Argentina either.

Venezuela

Man With A Plan, and an Unfortunate Mustache

As I write this, Venezuela is going through terrible times, but I have happy memories. In the 1990s I met a New York correspondent for an Italian paper on a press trip to Venezuela. Marcello was born in Turin, Italy. He had black hair swept to one side, a small mustache, and looked, unfortunately, like the German dictator.

At one point, near Angel Falls, the highest cascade in the world, our group changed into bathing suits and swam through tea-colored water in a narrow canyon faced with green rock. Marcello followed, wearing a suit and tie, sitting under an umbrella on a raft, with two locals paddling him along.

The other writers cracked jokes about weird Marcello. But I liked him. He was droll. And he was a foodie. We sat together at dinner and he would comment with quirky observations: "That salad looks so tired it's falling asleep." "The food is meager... good thing."

Marcello had the biggest appetite of anyone I have ever met. If any food was left on my plate, even half-chewed meat, he would lean over and eat it. But he wasn't fat, which made me wonder if maybe he had a cocaine habit, or a tapeworm.

People avoided Marcello throughout our week in Venezuela, and we soon became an odd couple, sharing meals and comments. He was one of those people who didn't fit in but had lots of nice qualities.

On the plane flying from Caracas back to New York, Marcello surprised me when he whispered: "Lea, would you like to spend a week at the Umbria Jazz Festival? I'm one of the directors. Most of the journalists I'm inviting will be music writers, but I'd like you to come. And you can bring a friend."

"Yes!" I said, not even knowing when the week was.

People who overheard the conversation came over and were suddenly complimenting Marcello's attire. Someone offered him a candy bar.

Marcello just winked at me.

And a few months later, in July 1993, a lucky friend and I spent the most amazing week in and around Perugia, Assisi and Orvieto, hanging out with Wynton Marsalis, B.B. King, The Manhattan Transfer and dozens of other great talents. *(See: San Marino.)*

And the most amazing thing of all was that Marcello was now hanging around beautiful Italian women in the same suit and tie he wore in Venezuela, and still pilfering food. But now, in his element, he seemed cool to just about everybody. Even with that mustache.

VIETNAM

A Diary

Awash with neon, Ho Chi Minh City (locals still call it Saigon) was hot and humid on the evening I arrived, in 2006. *(See: Cambodia.)* Women rode astride motorbikes, some in traditional Vietnamese *ao dai*, the colorful two-piece outfit with the top extending to the ankles, a long slit down one side, and long white pants. Some wore elbow-length gloves and face masks for protection from the elements.

Locals told stories of when TV network bureaus headquartered at the ornate nineteenth-century Opera House during the war. They remembered that enemy Viet Cong rocket teams aimed their weapons on downtown Saigon from the light of the neon sailing ship atop the Caravelle Hotel—until Saigon authorities finally realized—*turn it off.*

Just north of Saigon, many residents of Phan Thiet are Cham, an ethnic Muslim minority whose kingdom reached its pinnacle in the seventeenth century, and whose ruins still tower over the beach road.

Nearby Mui Ne is known for *nuoc mam*, pungent fish sauce that tastes better than it smells. Here in the 1968 Tet Offensive, Viet Cong attacked the American military base, but today the long beachfront is lined with low-rise resorts. Fully-clothed moms (most Vietnamese abhor a tan) splashed with children as fathers built sand castles, and tiny round fishing boats sailed against the sunset.

Winds have carved massive red dunes, a mini-Sahara, across the road from the beach. Friendly kids offered tires to sled down the steep sand slopes for a couple of bucks. I balked, and then took my chances. Fun!

※

Da Lat was created as a French colonial hill town early in the last century, and hundreds of grand villas still line the boulevards. At the Sofitel Palace terrace I was served a course I still remember for its delicate description on the menu: "Stuffed baby squash and pumpkin flower with crab nectar," plated in a "confetti of edible flora." That same dish would be served the following week to President George W. Bush.

Less pleasant but just as memorable was when I petted one of the few dogs I saw in Vietnam, in an enclosure outside a yard. But then, aghast, I realized the unlucky canine probably wasn't a pet. And later, I rode atop a lonely elephant in a park. Sad animal day.

※

Elegant Hanoi has been a center of war over thousands of years, but crossing the street is the main danger now, and I was instructed to just look ahead and keep going, despite the swirling cars, cyclos and motorbikes veering around me. Word is that Robert De Niro got hit while crossing— maybe he got confused and said, "Are you lookin' at me?"

In a local art form, puppeteers stand waist-deep in water behind a screen, manipulating puppets with poles, pulleys and strings, enacting skits of myths and magic. Percussionists accent the action with occasional smoke and fireworks. It reminded me of Cirque du Soleil's "O" starring Howdy Doody, the goofy marionette star from my childhood.

※

In nearby Ha Long Bay, I cruised among hundreds of odd-shaped limestone islands on a replica of a three-level 1920s paddle steamer. I visited a floating fishing village, and later pulled off my bathing suit and swam alone and naked into a limestone cave.

It reminded me of an earlier time in upstate New York when I was a young-married reporting on a touchy-feely retreat for a magazine article. I was shocked when I returned from the bathroom to see all six-feet, five inches of my nude husband, spiking a volleyball. I ran inside and stayed in my clothes.

But skinny-dipping years later in the bay, I was happy. And alone.

※

From 1802 to 1945 Hue was Vietnam's capital on the banks of the Perfume River, and it remains the country's cultural, religious and educational heart. Thirteen emperors resided in the

Imperial City complex, plus mandarins, princesses and scholars.

Bridges and moats connect a regal and tragic present and past. Three thousand were killed in Hue during the Tet Offensive, when the city was the center of conflict for twenty-four days. But it retains the aura of royal times.

Hoi An, the ancient trading port on the Thu Bon River, escaped destruction in recent wars and is now a World Heritage Site. There's a covered bridge, an old quarter, and pagodas and museums filled with antiquities. Near the sprawling market, vendors wore cone-shaped Vietnamese hats and carried baskets balanced on long poles over their shoulders. Men lingered on street corners beside their motorbikes, ready for customers needing a short ride.

The area is best known for exceptional handmade silk and wool clothing, and scores of stores advertise one-day tailoring. Tailors take your measurements, offer you tea, and ship if time is short. I was custom-fitted into a lavender silk suit that no longer fits me but hangs in my closet. It makes me smile.

ZIMBABWE

White Falls, Gold River, Red Teeth

The Zambezi River teems with catfish, crocodiles and hippos, and creates a border between Zimbabwe and Zambia. It drops over 350 feet—twice the height of Niagara—at the massive precipice the world knows as Victoria Falls.

Bill and I purchased visas to visit both countries and also nearby Chobe National Park in Botswana. On this trip I got pretty confused about just where I was, which sometimes happens when I'm jet-lagged, even when there's only one destination.

We walked to the middle of the bridge connecting Zambia and Zimbabwe to watch bungee jumpers plunge just above the river. I could see both sides of the massive Falls, and that was enough for me. I figured out pretty fast that I didn't really need to view the water close-up and upside-down while hanging by a thread.

Another adventure I skipped was at Devil's Pool, a rocky basin at the very edge of the Falls on the Zambian side. You boat to a small island in the Zambezi River, then swim to a large rock before leaping into the hollow, with cascading torrents just beyond along the rocky ledge of the Falls.

Gutsy (stoned?) folks splash (and of course, take selfies) *this* close to the deadly waterfall drop. The ultimate infinity pool, yes, but I was content watching the scene and then cooling off back at the hotel pool with a swimming noodle.

On our last night we took a Zambezi sunset cruise, zig-zagging between the two countries to pick up passengers. Zambia's riverbanks are densely packed with green bush, while Zimbabwe's plains run down to the water, palm trees stretching to the sky. Both are beautiful.

The lowering sun turned the river golden, and the mist from the Falls looked like low-hanging clouds in the distance. And as we got closer to the Falls we could hear, louder and louder, why natives call this natural wonder "The Smoke that Thunders."

Another water-related Zimbabwe adventure was riding in an open jeep on a half-day safari, and near the end getting caught in a thunderstorm. Wet giraffes loped near us, water shaking off them as they ran in the downpour, and we all got drenched under the big, slate-colored African sky. Some tourists complained. I found it memorable.

Our hotel was historic and grand, but our assigned room was small and had no view. An upgrade is often given at the discretion of the front desk, and they size you up and figure if they're able or want to please you. How you present yourself matters.

I must have been on point because we were upgraded to a gargantuan suite, with a balcony overlooking the white mists of Victoria Falls. In fact, the president of Zimbabwe had recently slept in the canopied bed where we would be snoring that night. We practically jumped up and down for our good fortune and chutzpah, and ordered room service just to soak in the luxury.

One small glitch, as there so often is: An infection in my mouth wasn't clearing up, and we asked the hotel to contact a doctor. He arrived at our lavish room in under an hour, dressed in a suit and probably thinking we were moguls or hedge-funders.

He prescribed some antibiotics and the hotel bought them and brought them up within minutes. I grabbed a dark-glass bottle as instructed and gargled a few times with the solution.

The strange smell was familiar from my childhood—but it was too late.

Bill looked at me as if I had bitten off the head of a snake, and I saw in the mirror that my teeth were as red as blood. I looked closer at the bottle and read "iodine." I remembered using iodine for cuts as a child, brushing it on with something that looked like a shoe-polish dispenser.

I brushed and brushed my teeth, gargled and gargled with mouthwash, but the red remained, fading from rust to pink. My teeth were not that white to begin with, but now I looked like a well-fed vampire.

For the rest of the trip I covered my mouth when I laughed, like one of those "before" people on a dental implant commercial. And when I returned home I made an immediate appointment with a cosmetic dentist, who said he hadn't seen stains like that since he was a child. (And those were on his arm.)

My teeth came out of their whitening treatment about the shade they were before—still not bright white, but at least not able to stop traffic.

That stained memory is canceled out by the gorgeous room in which the incident occurred, and by witnessing Victoria Falls, the animals in the storm and the golden river.

Travel offers ups and downs, and over so many years around this unpredictable world, I try to concentrate on the ups, and learn from and, when possible, laugh at the downs.

And most important of all, I keep traveling.

Bio

Lea Lane, an award-winning writer, is a regular contributor to forbes.com and has blogged at sites including Huffpost, Salon, The Daily Beast, CNN and cntraveler. She's written for *The New York Times* and *Miami Herald*, was a columnist for Gannett Newspapers, managing editor of *Travel Smart* newsletter, written over a thousand travel pieces and columns, and contributed to Fodor's guidebooks and Unofficial Guides. She has authored eight other books, including *Solo Traveler*, and *Travel Tales I Couldn't Put in the Guidebooks*.

For a dozen years, Lea was a panelist at The New York Times Travel Show, and she appeared regularly on The Travel Channel. She is a member of the Society of American Travel Writers.

And to fill in a bit more beyond travel writing, Lea grew up in Miami Beach, earned two-and-a-half college degrees, has been a high school and college teacher, and president of her own writing and training company. As the author of *Steps to Better Writing*, she trained hundreds of Fortune 100 and government workers to communicate clearly.

Fun facts: Lea's also been communications director of a tech company, an actress ("Nurse 1" in a low-budget indie), an off-Broadway associate producer, a (produced) musical playwright, and a counselor for foster children. She has appeared on Jeopardy!

She lived in New York for many years and once again resides in South Florida, now along with her husband and cat. Lea's two sons and two granddaughters sometimes travel with her as she explores new places to remember.

Tweet her @lealane
Follow her at instagram.com/travelea
Her travel blog is forbes.com/sites/lealane
Like & follow: facebook.com/placesirememberbylealane
Check out her pages on Amazon and Goodreads.
Visit placesirememberlealane.com
Follow her travel podcast, *Places I Remember.*

THANKS TO MANY

Thank you first to Greg Correll, exceptional artist, for the cover design, illustrations, and editorial advice. Greg is a multi-talented mensch with creative gifts and a brilliant mind.

Dorothy Stein provided steady, meticulous copyediting and proofreading. Judy Bluth, a steadfast friend, offered useful suggestions and edits. Deborah Kaufman advised wisely. Michael Marquez, Katy Djoba, Mario Spindola, Karen Fetter, Bryan Mesas, Zhanna Kulshanova, Connie Anderson, Cathy Keil, and Jennifer Reingold helped in varied ways. I am grateful to all.

Thank you, Joan Walsh, CNN commentator and correspondent at *The Nation*; and Kerry Lauermen, executive editor of news at *Forbes*. Both were supportive editors at Salon, where a few of my essays first appeared.

I was inspired and encouraged by contributors at Open Salon, a talented group of writers and artists. Many of us still interact on other media platforms, projects, and meetings throughout the world.

Thanks to tourism boards, lodgings, restaurants, sites and public relations companies that have informed and assisted me. Also, a shout-out to The Society of American Travel Writers, a terrific resource for networking and professional development.

I note with pleasure the contributions of Cheryl Benton at The Three Tomatoes Book Publishing; former editors including Paul Eisenberg, Robert Fisher, and Oliver Nixon at Fodor's; and Bob Sehlinger at Unofficial Guides. And I appreciate working with Random House and St. Martin's Press, who sharpened my skills in past years.

Also, thanks to April Merenda, President of Gutsy Women Travel, who moderated our dozen years of panel presentations at The New York Times Travel Show.

My travel role models have been my aunt, Hilda Schacht, and my grandmother, Katinka David. Both solo travelers—my grandmother on a ship from Frankfurt, Germany, to New York, at seventeen. They inspired me as I hope I might inspire others to keep discovering new places throughout their lives.

Much love to sons Randall and Cary, and granddaughters Sabrina and Chloe. I have enjoyed traveling with all of you, and hope to continue. To Gail, Fielding, Jim and Caroline, I look forward to travels ahead. And to sibs Stu Bussey and Carol Levy, thank you for making me laugh and sharing outrageous tales ("the meat man") since we were children.

And most definitely a great big smooch and hug to my husband Bill Lewis, a loving, thoughtful companion in travel—and life.

※

And as a kind of postscript, I offer a tribute to animal companions who factor in our lives, whether they stay behind or accompany us.

First, Apricot, my poodle, who traveled with my family to Miami Beach for many years until he was misplaced in the cargo section as we deplaned in New York. He flew alone to Hawaii, survived the confusion, and was returned to us a forever-after reluctant traveler who never flew again.

Sweetie, my Maine Coon cat, mischievously hid in a motel room, causing agita to both of us, and a much-delayed road trip. Suddenly, sadly, she crossed the Rainbow Bridge while I was cruising to Easter Island, unable to be with her. Let this be a formal, loving goodbye.

And shy and loving, Cali, my calico cat, snuggled next to me, or on the keyboard, as I wrote this book. (I had to fix her edits.) She's a definite homebody.

Pets offer unconditional love despite our frequent travels, and I honor all by honoring mine.

ILLUSTRATION NOTES

This was a fun project. Going over Lea's photographs with her, sifting and selecting, cropping and combining images—always with an eye on the stories, the right details, the telling scenes and found moments—was a complete pleasure.

The images are produced with several techniques. Paper sketches, textures, and washes replaced photo elements, and were combined with digital transformations, using a Wacom. Software used includes Photo-Shop, Rebelle, and Painter.

—Greg Correll

Greg Correll is a multi-media artist with a varied career, including illustrator for the New Yorker, CLIO winner/judge, and creative director. As project manager and developer, he designed and delivered the Yale Climate Institute's collaborative tools for scientists. He created and ran, live, the first multimedia stage set for Avery Fisher Hall at Lincoln Center, in 1996.

As a CUNY Writers Institute Fellow for both 2017 and 2020, Greg has worked with Leo Carey of The New Yorker and Jon Galassi of FSG. He writes plays and has been produced off-Broadway. His poetry and essays have been published in anthologies, including wVw, Late Summer Orphans, Into Sanity (preface by Mark Vonnegut), CAPS Poetry 2016 and 2020, and Vanguard Voices.

Made in the USA
Columbia, SC
12 January 2020